Insured To Fail

Why do over 50% of businesses fail to reopen after a disaster, or close within three years of reopening?
Despite being insured!

by

David R. Leng, CPCU, CIC, CBWA, CWCA, CRM

Publisher: White Publishing, Norwell, MA
Editor: Steve White

© 2021 by David R. Leng, Irwin Capital Management
All rights reserved.
No part of this book may be reproduced, scanned, or distributed in any printed or electronic form without the permission of the copyright owner. Requests for permission or further information should be addressed to David R. Leng, Irwin Capital Management, 311 Main St, Irwin, PA 15642

This book contains information concerning insurance and coverages, disaster recovery planning, human resources, and safety. The information is not intended as a substitute for insurance, legal, or financial advice from an appropriately qualified professional and should not be treated as such. If you have any specific questions about any insurance or disaster planning matters, you should consult an appropriately qualified professional.

Information which is copyrighted by and proprietary to Insurance Services Office, Inc. or its affiliates ("ISO Material") is included in this publication. Use of the ISO Material is limited to ISO Participating Insurers and their Authorized Representatives and other licensees. Use by ISO Participating Insurers is limited to use in those jurisdictions for which the insurer has an appropriate participation with ISO. Use of the ISO Material by Authorized Representatives is limited to use solely on behalf of one or more ISO Participating Insurers.

First Edition: July 2021
Printed in the United States of America
ISBN: [9798511139951]

DEDICATION

To Winnie,
thank you for a wonderful
30 years and counting!

Table of Contents

	Foreword by Ken Clifton	i
	Acknowledgments	vii
	Introduction	1
Chapter 1	**WHY** do so Many Businesses Fail?	11
Chapter 2	Be Careful of What You Ask For	33
Chapter 3	Why Isn't My Check Big Enough?	59
Chapter 4	To Rebuild, or Not to Rebuild? That is the Question…	93
Chapter 5	Know what they *Giveth*, but also know what they *Taketh Away!*	111
Chapter 6	Cash Flow Is King!	139
Chapter 7	Retaining Customers is the Key	165
Chapter 8	You Reopened, Now What?	177
Chapter 9	Do Not Run Out of Money!	197
Chapter 10	Tenants Beware	233
Chapter 11	Choose Your Own Chapter Title: If you fail to plan, you are planning to fail! Plans are Nothing: Planning is Everything!	239
Chapter 12	People vs. PDFs	273

Appendixes   **308**

  Appendix A – Answers To Get Before You Hire A Broker   309

About The Author   **311**

What They Are Saying About David   **313**

About The Books –
  Stop Being Frustrated & Overcharged   315
  The Laws of Insurance Attraction   316
  Turning Premiums Into Profits   317

Reader Bonus!   **318**

FOREWORD

Early 2014 was a memorable period for me. Unfortunately, it was for all the wrong reasons.

During that time, I was truly in a bad state of mind, having lost my son in February. I had previously planned a golf trip to Florida with my brother, and I was not going to go, but my brother suggested I should go to relax a bit. So, I went on April 2nd.

We played golf on April 3rd. Just when you think you have hit bottom and things will start to get better, life pulls out a shovel and digs the hole even deeper. At 7 am April 4th, my phone started ringing. The alarm company was calling to tell me my business back in Pittsburgh, CCF Industries, which I started in 1995, was on fire.

I rushed to the airport, jumped on the first flight I could, getting me back to Pittsburgh just after 2 pm. The building was gone, and I was looking at ashes. An errant spark ignited the metal filters in the buildings' air filtration system, igniting the dust in the ducts of the dust collection system. It took less than 10 minutes from the time the spark occurred for the raging fire to spin out of control, and the roofline started to collapse.

I was suddenly living every business owner's worst nightmare; the destruction of my business, over 30 of my employees out of work, and failing to meet the demands of countless customers.

I am writing this forward almost seven years to the day of this horrific event. I now realize how close I came to not surviving and enjoying the thriving business I have today. My survival was 100% dependent upon just one thing. If that one thing had not happened, my 20 years spent laboring and building my business would have been over.

That one thing? Meeting David Leng!

About a year before the fire, David came to talk about our insurance programs. At the time, I was set in my ways. I preferred to stay with my current insurance agent, who we, and those in my industry, considered as "the industry expert."

Even when I did consider other agents to quote, no one could touch what I had. But what even started this conversation with David was that he did not mirror or sound like all the other agents. He asked questions no one else had asked before. He clearly wanted to understand me, my business, how we operated, everything.

He focused on trying to help find better ways to improve my business. He took me through scenarios, such as what would happen if I encountered a situation that might put me out of business, just like the devastation that occurred.

Looking back now, it was as if David was predicting the future. He essentially walked us through and protected us for what – *did* happen – *before* it happened. Even more importantly, by digging into other parts of our business, such as our employee safety and injuries, David was able to help us shrink our workers' compensation premium. This allowed us to afford the coverage changes he recommended, which we clearly needed.

What always impresses me about David is his accessibility. This weekend was no exception. Even though he was meeting with a client in Upstate New York along the Canadian border when the fire happened, he cut his trip short and was here the next morning, helping me sort out what it would take to get back on my feet. We talked in detail about what it would take to rebuild and what was covered. David understood the stress I was clearly under, and he did everything in his power to lessen it. And I can unequivocally state that without David Leng, I would not be in business today.

Just think, if I had stayed with my previous agent, I would have to dig into my pocket to try to find nearly $1.3 million to rebuild and well over $2 million to protect my cash flow. Amounts I just did not have. My old program provided "building," "contents," and "business income" coverage "the industry expert" recommended. In looking back at the "before David coverage," the shortage that was staring me in the face was way beyond simply increasing "building," "contents," or "business income" limits. There were holes in the types and structure of the coverages I needed. David added these coverages no other agent ever mentioned, including ones missed by my former "industry expert."

With these monstrous holes in my coverage, I could not have afforded to rebuild. I would not have been able to keep all my employees and most of my customers. I would not have been able to stay open after rebuilding. I would not have survived. Period.

But I did.

Owning a business for over 25 years, I have known a number of business leaders, including a former client who faced a disaster and ultimately had to shut their doors permanently. This is why I feel too many business leaders may not fully realize when a catastrophe occurs how much they could possibly be *under-insured*, nor *under-prepared* for what it actually will take for them to rebuild, reopen and endure the long, difficult road they must travel after reopening.

Clearly, do not assume how your insurance program is designed and how your recovery plan is laid out will be good enough to survive when facing your own disaster. Be aware of what it will take and verify you are prepared for it, and insured for it, now!

This is why David's book is essential for every business owner to read. What David says in these pages can make the difference when your business suffers a catastrophe, the difference between restarting and continuing to endure and grow, or not being able to restart, or even having to give up after trying to make it work.

David makes you realize "having insurance" is not the automatic solution when you must rebuild, and there are factors that seem destined to derail the best-laid plans. But David has that unique ability to minimize those factors based on one simple goal; getting you back up and running as quickly as possible, plus knowing the additional issues facing you once you reopen your doors. Most importantly, his knowledge and understanding of the "fine print" in the various available insurance coverages allowed him to craft our insurance programs and plans, making it possible for us to thrive today.

We buy insurance because we want to be made whole again

when we suffer a disaster; we want to be back in business. I would think most businesses do so for the same reason.

In looking back, I would not wish the devastation I went through on my worst enemy. However, it became clear that how I bought my insurance before David was not the best way to buy insurance. In hindsight, following that old way seems to reinforce renewing my insurance with my old agent year after year, typically with minimal changes, if any at all, despite my continually growing business; that way is an inefficient process that rewarded an ineffective agent. You may not like insurance and probably do not like paying premiums. Just imagine paying premiums for years or decades, and when you need your insurance the most, your heart sinks when you discover you did not buy enough, nor did not buy the right coverages.

Trust me; *after* your disaster is *not* the time you want to find out you have a problem.

After my fire, many business leaders reached out to me to see how I was doing and discuss what I went through and what I learned. During those conversations, one thing struck me as scary. What was genuinely concerning was that it appeared that almost every business I spoke to purchase their insurance the same way I used to.

I cannot stress enough that it took going through the process of David and his team analyzing my business to clearly see that there was a better way to buy and manage our insurance program. Their assessment process we went through was unlike anything I have experienced before, and when talking to other business leaders, the extent of their analysis is something others cannot seem to grasp until they too experienced it themselves fully.

Think about it, without a deep analysis that creates a clear understanding of a business, the goals, and what issues are being faced, how could anyone truly advise a business leader? How could they understand your business well enough to help you be appropriately insured to survive a disaster? And help you plan for that disaster? The assessment findings and action plans David showed us, even before we committed to working with him and his team, made it clear that they understood our business. He knew what it would take for us to be properly insured and had a plan to get us through the rebuilding, reopening, and business recovery phases needed after a disaster. It also showed us that David and his team were solely focused on helping us and not themselves.

I feel fortunate to have met David and have him be part of the team that helps me guide my business. I just cannot say enough about David personally and professionally. He is always in our corner, advising us as to what we should be considering, and he has always controlled and even reduced our insurance costs over time, but not at the sacrifice of our program's coverage. I believe that is because he always has *our* best interests at heart.

With this book, David Leng puts it all on the page, so you know where you stand *before* anything happens. And that alone makes this book a must-have for every business owner.

Ken Clifton
President, CCF Industries

Forward by Ken Clifton – CCF Industries

ACKNOWLEDGMENTS

I want to thank the following associations and organizations and their members for introducing me to the 86 businesses that suffered a disaster and unfortunately failed to reopen or closed within three years. They also introduced me to almost three dozen business leaders that barely survived as the effort required them to pour hundreds of thousands to millions of dollars into their business to do so:

> Wood Products Manufacturers Association
> Manufacturers and Business Association
> Hardwood Manufacturers Association
> Alliance of Automotive Service Providers
> SMC Business Councils
>
> And several Advisor members of the
> Institute of Work Comp Professionals

I would also like to thank my friend Christopher Boggs, CPCU, ARM, ALCM, LPCS, AAI, APA, CWCA, CRIS, AINS, Executive Director Risk Management, and Education IIABA, and fellow Technical Affairs Committee member. He has been a tremendous sounding board over the years when solving complex risks and the insurance coverage issues that they bring about.

Insured to Fail

INTRODUCTION

You are driving down the road and see a boarded-up, burned-out business. Your first reaction is almost always, *"WOW! What happened?"*

Then you drive past the same location over and over, month after month, and see that nothing is changing. At some point, you start asking yourself, *"Why are they not reopening?"*

Or maybe one day, you were happy to notice that the business reopened. Then, months or a year or more, you are driving down that road again and are shocked to see the "Going Out of Business Sale" banner hanging out in front of it. Inevitably, you are back to, *"WOW! What happened?"*

Driving almost 30,000 miles a year to work with clients, I, too, have seen these roadside scenarios play out too many times. However, there is one difference when I see one of these businesses closed as compared to most people; being a degreed and credentialed risk manager, now trapped in the "insurance world," where designing, managing, and procuring insurance programs on behalf of business leaders for 30+ years, I wonder *"Who insured their business?"*, *"What did their insurance program look like?"* and the biggest one, *"What was the business's plan for reopening?"*

In other words, what went wrong *before* and *after* the disaster?

Decades ago, this roadside scenario played out for a particular business that had me wondering to a point where I reached to see if they could use some assistance. I approached for several reasons: one, my family ate dinner there one to two times a month; two, he was a local business active in my community, especially with the schools; and three, I knew the business had insurance. Being friends with his insurance agent for most of my life made it easy to know the restaurant was insured and even who his insurance company was.

Unfortunately, after digging into the restaurant owner's insurance program and talking to his agent, accountant, and insurance company, the insurance company had paid *every penny* they should have. But yet, the business reopened and shut down after being open for just 11 months.

So, *WOW! What happened?*

One of our family's favorite restaurants became another number in a terrifying statistic. According to the Institute for Business & Home Safety[1] and other insurance industry sources like FEMA, approximately 25% of businesses that suffer a catastrophe do not reopen. An additional 25%+ see their doors close within three years after, even though they are insured! These statistics do not even contemplate disasters like Hurricane Katrina.

So, would you bet your entire business on a flip of a coin? No rational business owners would do so, but as you can now see, statistics show otherwise...

When you see such a failure rate, it makes you pause and wonder, *WHY*:

- A – Did they have the wrong "get-back-in-business plan," a Disaster Recovery plan to rebuild, reopen, and regain customers; or
- B – Did they have the wrong insurance program design?

A few years ago, this scenario played out again. While at a client's facility performing a periodic Risk Analysis with the owner and navigating through his 70+ employee machine shop, he walked over to introduce his new general manager. When the GM turned around, he said, *"Hey, how have you been, David?"* Taken aback for a moment, I had to pause a second to recall the name that went with the familiar face. It turns out it was John, who used to own a machine shop that burned to the ground four years prior, and I had called on John's business about three years before his fire. It appeared that John too became one of those affected by that scary

---

[1] www.ibhs.org

statistic when he was forced to sell the business sixteen months after his grand reopening.

Everyone could see the anguish in John's face as he told the story over an hour-and-a-half lunch that day. John had built a 47-employee operation from scratch over 32 years, put his three children through college, had two of them working there, and planned on perpetuating the business to the next generation in about another ten years or so. John poured in his life savings and even sold their vacation home on Hilton Head Island for more cash to try to save his business for his family. Now, all of that was gone, and everyone had to find new jobs. The only thing John had left was the new building he rented to his machine shop's new owner, who did not want to keep John, or his children, employed there.

That meeting was the compelling motivation for this book. The goal is to help business owners avoid losing their life's work and their family's livelihood, not to mention leaving all those employees without jobs. Especially when failing to survive could have been avoided.

Fast forward almost nine months from that reunion with John, an event shook the world and affected businesses like nothing else anyone has seen before. COVID-19 hit the world.

Because of this pandemic, business leaders began to address the realities of challenges with insurance coverage when COVID surprised them. Almost every business leader stared at their insurance policy when their insurance policies did not respond to their "Business Income" needs and asked, *"Wow! What happened?"* Liability policies did not respond to lawsuits filed against them for the accusations of spreading COVID-19 to a customer. All of this left business leaders asking, *"What else is not covered?"*

FEMA states roughly 40% of businesses never reopen their doors following a disaster, and another 25% fail within one year. The US Small Business Administration states over 90% of companies fail within two years of being struck by a disaster.

Introduction

According to FEMA, there were 103,600 non-residential structural fires in 2018[2]. If 60% of fires are considered catastrophic, meaning the business is closed for more than 30 days, and 25% did not reopen, then in 2018, 15,540 businesses were lost. Because of those lost businesses, throughout 2019, 2020, and 2021, statistics will play out that there would be another 15,540 to 35,544 businesses fail. That is a total of 31,080 to 55,944 that no longer exist due to a 2018 fire... According to the National Fire Protection Association, that number grew to over 120,000 non-residential structural fires in 2019, which caused 36,000 businesses not to reopen and another 36,000 to 41,000 that will later fail by 2022.[3]

When you shift away from a business destroyed by fire, and you start to think about all of the cyber breaches with cyber-crime, cyber extortion and ransomware, and so forth. Plus, the data breaches and ransom demand to giant corporations like HBO, Target, and Home Depot garner widespread media attention, but this leads to the false assumption that only large companies face this growing digital problem. According to CNBC, a 2016 study found that 43% of all cyber-attacks targeted small businesses[4]. Even more alarming is that a staggering 60% of small businesses hit with a cyber-attack or data breach go out of business within six months, according to the National Cyber Security Alliance. The average cyber-attack costs a small business $200,000, according to Hiscox Insurance Company.

Do you believe that you do not need to worry about it? A breach caused the 2013 Target Black Friday Credit Card Breach, and it started at a 30+ employee HVAC contractor outside of Pittsburgh, PA[5]. Reports state that a key logger virus enabled hackers to access Target when the contractor used their User ID and Password to upload a work order.

---

[2] www.usfa.fema.gov/downloads/pdf/statistics
[3] https://www.nfpa.org//-/media/Files/News-and-Research/Fire-statistics-and-reports/US-Fire-Problem/osFireLoss.pdf
[4] https://www.cnbc.com/2019/10/13/cyberattacks-cost-small-companies-200k-putting-many-out-of-business.html
[5] https://bestblackfriday.com/blog/could-target-have-prevented-the-black-friday-data-breach/

What about the "Nuclear Jury Verdicts" handed out at such a rate that now everyone is feeling the impact on their wallets and bottom line as auto and excess insurance premiums are surging. More importantly, these Nuclear Verdicts are typically multi-million-dollar jury awards directed against an employer meant to punish them for the wrongdoing. You may recall the lady who sued McDonald's after burning her leg with coffee and receiving a $2,900,000 jury award.[6] But then imagine facing a $22,000,000 award for a lady injured by a delivery truck when she was in a crosswalk[7].

Then you have the surge in lawsuits directed at employers from their employees. Employment Practices claims top the list of management liability lawsuits in both frequency and severity. According to the U.S Equal Employment Opportunity Commission (EEOC) Charge Statistics, the EEOC received and reviewed 72,675 employment discrimination charges in 2019[8], which breaks down to approximately 278 employment-related charges per business day. Retaliation claims led the pack at 53.8% of all allegations.

With today's flattening world, there are many stories about a surge in uncovered employee injuries. Every state's workers' compensation laws are different, and then you must add federal workers 'compensation laws on top of those. Do business leaders need to understand what needs to happen when you have an employee traveling out of state? Out of the country? Or working remotely?

What if your product happens to find its way out of the country and someone sues you? What happens when they file that lawsuit against you in that country?

There are far more risks that a business faces to survive than you may realize... Many cannot be traditionally insured, and you have to customize your insurance program design to address them.

---

[6] https://segarlaw.com/blog/myths-and-facts-of-the-mcdonalds-hot-coffee-case
[7] www.oasisfinancial.com/10-of-the-largest-personal-injury-verdicts-settlements-in-history/
[8] https://www.eeoc.gov/newsroom/eeoc-releases-fiscal-year-2019-enforcement-and-litigation-data

Introduction

Over the years, many business leaders have commented that *"we have an umbrella policy that covers us for everything."* For example, some business leaders believe that if they have a $5,000,000 umbrella policy, that "everything is good"; they thought that the umbrella policy would step in to provide them with coverage over every policy that they purchased, plus some that they did not buy. Nothing could be further from the truth. In reality, an umbrella is a liability policy that covers some bodily injury and property damage liability claims. It does not cover you for any damage to your property. It does not cover you for a lawsuit claiming Breach of Contract. It does not cover you for someone's "Economic Loss" lawsuit directed at you.

Therefore, it is not about what you think you have. It is about knowing and understanding your coverage in detail:

- Which of your insurance policies applies to your specific issue?
    - Example: Building/Property, General Liability, Auto, Cyber, Directors & Officers, Employment Practices, International Liability, etc.
- Does that policy contain coverage that specifically may apply to the issue you face?
    - Example: What specifically caused the damage? What was the specific allegation in the lawsuit?
- Does the coverage you have address the specific issue? Or, are there any coverage limitations or "exclusions" that would lead you not to have any coverage for the problem or not enough coverage?
    - Example: Is the specific piece of property defined as *covered property* or *property not covered* within the property policy? Is the lawsuit allegation worded in such a way that it may be excluded?
- Are you covered for where the issue occurred?
    - What is the coverage territory?
- Assuming you have coverage, do you have enough limits to pay for the issue?

- And most importantly, do you have an effective plan you can implement that will help improve your odds of survival?

This book is not intended to be a scare tactic to get you to buy every type of coverage and buy more of it. It is intended to help you understand how insurance works, how it responds, and what your responsibility is *before* and *after* a catastrophe to improve the odds that your business will survive and succeed.

It is also to help highlight that, unfortunately, business leaders today are facing a crisis that they are not aware of, one where too many insurance agents have misled them to believe that:
- Insurance policies are "comprehensive" or "All-Risk."
- Insurance policies are ALL the same.
- A Business Leader can focus on the general coverage headings items like "Building," "Contents," "Liability," and feel confident that they are appropriately covered when comparing quotes, and the limits are the same.
- Since everything is the same, take the lowest premium.

Think about these tidbits:
- How can a 300+ page, small type policy be adequately summarized into a 10-15 page, or even 50-page "proposal"?
- What process did the insurance agent go through to understand your operations to determine what coverage your business should have? Or are they guessing?

To drive the point home, let us go a little further. A few years ago, teaching a continuing education class to a room of 263 insurance agents, I asked the agents to play a game. They were to raise their hands and leave them up if they were still in the game throughout the series of questions. These were the questions:
- How many of you have a business as a client? – everyone raised their hand.
- How many of you had a business that had a disaster? – a little over ½ the room leave their hand up.
- How many had a disaster that required the business to be closed for more than a week? – about 30-40 hands.

- How many had a business that was closed for more than a month, and by closed, it meant that they were not operating at all or operating from a temporary location? – 11 hands still up.
- How many had a business that was closed for more than 6 months? – 4 hands.
- How many had a business where the building was completely destroyed and needed to be rebuilt from the ground up? – 3 hands.
- How many had a business that was closed for more than 9 months? – same 3 hands.
- How many rebuilt their buildings? – 2 hands.
- How many had their business reopened? – 2 hands.
- And is that business still in business? – **just 1 hand left.**

Although far from an actual in-depth study, a sample none the less: 4% (11) of the agents had clients that suffered a significant loss, 1.5% (4) suffered a severe loss, 1.1% (3) a total catastrophe, 0.7% (2) had buildings rebuilt, and businesses reopen, but only 0.4% (1) had a successful outcome.

Here is the question you need to ask yourself – Did the agent have a client that experienced a catastrophe? If an agent has not experienced what challenges a business will have to face in the process of trying to operate temporarily elsewhere and rebuild a new building, then how confident are you that an agent can adequately guide you? Can they assist you in determining what your insurance program needs to look like, identify what you need to do before the catastrophe occurs, and then guide you after you reopen so that you can survive?

This book will review how all seven clients that had their businesses wiped out by a disaster are open and still in business today and highlight some of the pitfalls that business leaders have faced that led to their failures. These pitfalls are often overlooked or misunderstood. Now, not trying to blow smoke up somewhere and state that all destroyed businesses I worked with went perfectly in their reconstruction and post-opening; that would not be the case. I vividly remember the words Jack Kirsopp, the owner of Kirsopp Auto Body, my second total fire, when he said to me one day, *"David, there are days I want to deck you and days I want to hug you!"* You will learn why in this book.

It is essential to understand that their insurance programs were close enough to get the job done. However, it is more important to know that they would not have survived without dramatically improving their program designs from what they had before working with us.

You will see that their reopening plans were at least sufficient for them to not only reopen but, once again, more importantly, enabled them to stay open. In the end, each of these seven has been a learning experience as each was different, and earlier ones, in essence, helped benefit the later ones.

There will also be stories of other interviewed businesses but were not as fortunate and either could not reopen or closed after reopening. Stories where things outside the business owner's control caused such delays or issues that made reopening or surviving long term impossible.

More importantly, the book will map out what you need to do *before* and *after* the disaster to increase the odds of survival and help you build a blueprint toward building your insurance program so it will respond the way you believe it should.

This book will focus on the effects of a *Disaster* upon Your Stuff, Your Employees and even address some 3rd Party Liability issues that a disaster will cause you to face. It will provide an overview of what you will need to know to prepare before a disaster and what you should do after one occurs. Unfortunately, there is no way to condense everything about insurance, risk management, or disaster planning into a single book. We cannot address all your potential liability issues either. This book aims to provide you with enough knowledge to begin to lay the groundwork to build a better insurance program and help you better choose the professional or professionals to work with doing so.

Introduction

WHY Do So Many Businesses Fail?

No rational business owner would bet his entire business on a flip of a coin. However, as you read in the introduction, the statistics show otherwise.

We have all seen TV reports showing clips of businesses that have suffered a disaster. Inevitably, there will also be an interview with the business owner talking about the devastation this event had on his business and his employees. And even though you have heard the business owner say, *"We will rebuild!"* you continue to drive past the charred or decimated remnants of that same building, month after month, year after year, and yet, they did not rebuild nor reopen.

The question that needs answering is **WHY?** Once everyone understands **WHY** what actions are necessary to avoid such a tragic outcome.

After interviewing 86 business leaders from failed businesses, we compiled a multitude of various causes that led to an incredible over 50% of businesses going out of business, even though they were insured:

- A – The business did not have a "get-back-in-business plan," such as a *Disaster Recovery Plan* to rebuild, reopen, and regain customers; or
- B – The business had the wrong insurance program design.

Digging deeper, ***WHY*** did A and/or B happen? Let us dissect ***WHY***.

It may come down to ***tangible*** versus ***intangible***:
- It is easy to *SEE* that you have a building to protect, and therefore you buy coverage to protect or "cover" your building – *tangible*.
- You can *SEE* that you have things such as equipment, inventory, and computers to protect – *tangible*.
- From what you *SEE*, you will probably make an educated guess as to how much insurance coverage limits you may need to buy to "cover" your property and your "stuff" – *tangible*.
- You can *SEE* your physical insurance policy sitting on your shelf or your computer screen but understanding what is *covered* versus *not covered* by your insurance policies – *intangible*.
- How will your policy respond? – *intangible*.
- What will it take to rebuild your facility, including changes that need to be made to construct the new building? – *intangible*.
- What will you need to do to purchase your equipment, machinery, contents, and inventory – *intangible*.
- How long will it take for you to rebuild your facility and obtain your equipment, machinery, contents, and inventory– *intangible*.
- What will you need to do to keep customers while rebuilding or acquire customers after reopening – *intangible*.
- How long it will take to financially return to where you were before the disaster – *intangible*.
- How much money will you need to keep paying the bills while you are either closed, or your business is open but yet significantly hampered? Not only do you have bills to pay, but you also have employees, loans, and taxes. Plus, you need to bring home money to support your family–

intangible.
- What process you need to go through to determine if your insurance program design will respond for you – *intangible.*
- How do you determine which insurance advisor to use to help you with all of this? – *intangible.*

Based on experience and the interviews with business leaders who did not survive a disaster and some that did, *INTANGIBLE* causes employers to lose their business due to a catastrophic event.

But you are probably saying to yourself right now, "I have insurance coverage!" You saw the statistics...

The coin is flipping through the air...

Some of the reasons business leaders have trouble planning for a disaster and designing their insurance program have to do with how people make decisions when addressing risks. Noble Prize-winning psychologists Amos Tversky and Daniel Kahneman[9] created a scenario to demonstrate how framing questions impact people's decisions and highlight their risk tolerance. The scenario below has been changed only as to the event's cause compared to what originally was proposed.

There were two breakout groups. The same event scenarios were given to each:

➢ Imagine that a ship carrying 600 people has started to take on water and is now in the process of sinking.

Group 1 - received the following solutions to the scenarios to choose from:

➢ If **Solution A** is adopted, 200 people will be saved.
➢ If **Solution B** is adopted, there is a one-third probability that 600 people will be saved and a two-thirds probability that no people will be saved.

---

[9] A. Tversky, D. Kahneman, Science 211, 1981 p453±458

Which of these options, A or B, would you choose?

Group 2 - received the following solutions to the scenarios to choose from:
- If **Solution C** is adopted, 400 people will die.
- If **Solution D** is adopted, there is a one-third probability that nobody will die and a two-thirds probability that 600 people will die.

Which of these options, C or D, would you choose?

In Group 1, 72% of the respondents expressed a preference for Solution A ± the risk-averse alternative.

In Group 2, Only 22% of these respondents opted for Solution C, even though it is the same risk-averse alternative as Solution A, while Solution D is the same risk-seeking alternative as Solution B.

Framing risks impacts decision-making when comparing available options and also highlights someone's tolerance for risk. If you are more apt to take a risk, you are more likely to roll the dice, so to speak, on the side that something catastrophic might not happen to you, or that if it does, it will not be as bad as what could happen.

There was a need to dig in even deeper into **WHY** business leaders have trouble with the intangible and decisions on addressing risk. From 2013 through 2015, researching and interviewing business leaders, compiling stories, and creating the outline for this book, a list of why business leaders had trouble surviving was collected. In interview after interview, business leaders stated one or more reasons **WHY** they struggled with implementing a *Disaster Recovery Plan* or making necessary *Insurance Program Design* changes to better position themselves to survive a disaster. Although no one issue was solely responsible for any of the business failures, it took the cumulative impact of several of them to lead to the heartbreaking outcome for each of the businesses. Stories were

listened to, and root causes were analyzed. Each of the reasons provided was categorized into one of the following:
- Business owners, by their nature, are risk-takers. Therefore, they are reluctant to believe that a significant or catastrophic event will affect them.
- Many business owners started their company from scratch; thus, they believe they can do so again while forgetting that they have families and lifestyles that would be significantly and negatively affected.
- Most insurance agents do not fully understand what efforts and capital it will take for a business to survive while being closed, reopen, and then rebuild or regain their clientele following a disaster. Therefore, these agents cannot help in educating business leaders as to what to expect.
- Most insurance agents do not understand how to calculate **How Much** business income coverage a business will need. Therefore, they cannot explain it to a business owner to calculate the amount themselves.
- Business leaders often believe that they will be back in business faster than it will take them to do so.
- Business leaders struggle to perceive how much extra expense they would incur when attempting to keep the doors open and retain as many customers as possible.
- Business leaders did not realize the significance of the risks that they were facing from something catastrophic occurring. This is simply because it never happened to them before, nor to anyone that they know.
- Business leaders think all or most of their clients are loyal and will return as soon as their doors reopen.
- Insurance Terms do not always correspond to Business Terms or how business leaders believe they should, so misinterpretations occur.
- Financial Industry terms that accountants and business owners use are different from "Insurance World" terms. For

example: "cost of goods sold" and "net income" means different things in each world.
- Business leaders are reluctant to share their detailed "financial picture" with insurance agents.
- Business leaders struggle to distinguish between the purchasing of an insurance policy and the value of selecting the right insurance advisor to help build the correct insurance plan design.
- Business leaders and agents do not like to discuss uncomfortable topics, such as the business's death, and more importantly, what the plan is when something happens.
- Business leaders did not fully understand their insurance coverages nor how the insurance companies would respond to their disaster.

After completing the first draft of this book in late 2020, a risk management colleague forwarded a podcast that included Wharton Professor Howard Kunreuther as one of a number of people interviewed by the host. The topic was on the insurance industry and its response to COVID-19 and why insurance policies were not designed to respond to pandemics. The biography section of the podcast referenced that Professors Robert Meyer and Howard Kunreuther, from the Wharton Risk Management and Decision Processes Center, wrote the book *The Ostrich Paradox - Why We Underprepare for Disasters.*

What is fascinating is that both professors dug even further into the *psychology* of **WHY** people struggle with preparing for disasters, which leads to so many businesses not surviving. The psychological reasons also caused business leaders not to have insurance programs properly designed to respond adequately to such disasters.

Professors Meyer and Kunreuther identified **6 Behavioral Risk Biases**[10] that people have that lead to distorted perceptions of risk, and how such misperceptions may manifest in preparedness errors,

---

[10] Robert Meyer and Howard Kunreuther - *The Ostrich Paradox - Why We Underprepare for Disasters* - Wharton School Press, 2017

and possible remedies:
- **Myopia**: *a tendency to plan over short future horizons*
- **Amnesia**: *a tendency to base decisions on most recent experiences*
- **Optimism**: *a tendency to underestimate the likelihood of harm*
- **Inertia**: *a tendency to choose default courses of action*
- **Simplification**: *a tendency to process only limited subsets of information*
- **Herding**: *a tendency to make decisions by social imitation*

The *6 Behavioral Risk Biases* dovetail nicely with the reasons business leaders state **WHY** they struggled with implementing changes to be better positioned to survive a disaster.

- **Myopia**: *a tendency to plan over short future horizons*
    People focus on what is right in front of them, such as: the next customer or contract that they are trying to land; an issue they are having with one or more employees; a staffing shortfall that they need to fill quickly; or a capital expenditure that needs to be funded and implemented. This can lead business leaders not to decide upon taking necessary action now relating to things that are best for the company in the long term because they are not the pressing issues. Therefore, focusing on a long-term project of constructing a Disaster Preparedness Program gets tabled. While taking the time to analyze the actual coverages and limits within their insurance program, the design also gets delayed or rushed through, ultimately leaving the program short regarding responding to a disaster.
    Meyer and Kunreuther used the example of someone spending $10,000 to flood-proof their property to save $2,500 per year on flood insurance premiums. Given this scenario, Meyer and Kunreuther stated that most people would postpone the decision as they did not want to spend

the $10,000 today even though they would recoup the costs in four years, save money, or essentially profit from the investment they made to improve.

In reality, taking the time to formalize your Disaster Preparedness Program can be used as leverage with the insurance company underwriters to reduce your insurance rates. Not only does that free up capital, but it also gives you time to analyze your insurance program and adjust coverages, deductibles, or your waiting period for business income coverage to start. The reduced rates you will receive will then help you afford higher coverage limits that you will need to help survive your disaster.

- *Amnesia: a tendency to base decisions on most recent experiences*

    If something has not happened to you before or for a prolonged time, then there is a tendency to forget those very real risks still exist. For example, many business leaders will drop flood insurance since they have not had a "flood" before, or at the very least, their only experience with a "flood" was minor or a long time ago. Flood insurance is typically frequently canceled when the "bank no longer requires the coverage."

    Therefore, there is a tendency to cancel coverage or a policy to save the premium paid to the insurance company to protect their business for that specific risk. Business leaders also tend not to keep their Disaster Recovery Program up to date for this same reason. Dropping coverage was one of the main reasons some business leaders stated that they were not covered when Hurricane Sandy pulverized the New Jersey coast in 2012. This is also why many business leaders become openly frustrated, as they think to themselves, "I don't know why I pay all these premiums since I never had a loss before."

    Then there is also the common effect an event has on businesses. Following a flood or earthquake in a specific area, the number of property owners that purchase the coverage surges. This was the case when a 6.7 magnitude earthquake hit Northridge, California, in 1994. The event leads to more than 40% of property owners purchasing earthquake coverage. Then, years later, when nothing else happened, people decided to drop the coverage for one reason or another. Today, barely 10% of businesses in California have earthquake coverage[11].

There have been cases where business leaders canceled insurance coverage or allowed the reduced limits when looking at bids since they "did not use" those coverages in the past. Thus, it is vital to make decisions to determine the minimum coverages that you *must have* included in your insurance program, separate from the process of deciding what insurance program to use. Then stick to the minimums you have determined.

- ***Optimism***: *a tendency to underestimate the likelihood of harm*

    The likelihood of a disaster affecting your business is minimal, which is why the underlying fundamentals of insurance work. Insurance is based on the *Law of Large Numbers*, where you have a large number of businesses that pay small amounts of premium, in proportion to their risk, to pay for those few that have something catastrophic impact them. By looking at the more significant numbers, risks become more predictable. Actuaries know that a certain number of businesses will have a catastrophe and approximately how much will have to be paid out. The actuaries just do not know which businesses will be affected.

    This thought process of "it won't happen to us" leads business leaders not to identify, analyze, plan for, and implement an appropriate Disaster Recovery Plan or design

---

[11] https://www.npr.org/2018/10/18/658570642/quake-insurance-california-pushing-people-to-say-yes-to-coverage

their insurance program to respond to such occurrences. This optimism leads to thinking the risks are not as large as they are or that the impact of the risks will be smaller than they will be if they occur. Because of this, there is a tendency to undervalue what their insurance needs are. Some of those interviewed stated that they chose a specific building limit because they did not believe anything that might happen could be worse than the amount of coverage they purchased. For example, "our building is all concrete and steel, so there is nothing that could destroy our entire building," or something similar, is what I heard from many interviewed business leaders.

For another example, if you are in the "100 Year Flood Zone" or Special Flood Hazard Area, the odds are that once every 100 years, you will incur a flood. This leads business leaders to feel that there is a 1% chance that they will be flooded, and therefore this 1% chance is a risk that they are willing to take and thus do not insure themselves for a flood. However, if you put it into the context that over 25 years, that you have a 25% probability that you *will* have a flood, you may change your decision. The question is not a matter of *if* but more of *when*. Not to mention that FEMA states that 20% of floods occur in areas that are not in "flood zones."

This optimism also leads business leaders to believe that they can identify and avoid a cyber-attack that would allow someone into their computer system or install ransomware. Therefore, they do not take steps to train and educate their staff and make sure that they have viable backups. And yet, these events are happening at an increasing rate every day.

- **Inertia**: *a tendency to choose default courses of action*

    Inertia is the "if it is not broken, don't fix it" thought process, however, sometimes the business leaders do not realize it *is* broken, or at least it is not fully functional. The continuation of the *status quo* in preparation for risk or design of disaster restoration plan or an insurance program was one of the problems cited by business leaders that were allowed to linger before their disaster. Therefore, they were not fully prepared nor adequately insured.

But if you think about your business, your business grows and evolves. Insurance companies change how they look at businesses and the coverages that they offer over time. Weather patterns have changed as the world continues to evolve. Therefore, if you do not keep your Disaster Recovery Plan and your Insurance Plan Design up to date, you will be the one left behind when you need them.

In September of 2004, an enormous hurricane was bearing down on New Orleans. With three days warning that the storm was approaching, community leaders hurriedly put plans in place to evacuate people and shelter those in need in the Superdome. You are probably thinking of Hurricane Katrina. It was Hurricane Ivan, and New Orleans got lucky; Ivan turned away to hit another part of the US coastline. Professors Meyer and Kunreuther used this as an example of *Inertia*. Community leaders did a post-mortem and came to several conclusions:

- The levees and pumps were not fully functional due to years of neglect by the Army Corps of Engineers;
- Public transit was not able to handle transporting the over 100,000 people in the city that did not own vehicles; and
- The Superdome was not suited to shelter a large number of people.

Eleven months later, Katrina bore down on New Orleans, where nothing had changed. City leaders followed the plan that they already determined was poor, although they had ample time to improve. But it was simply easier for city leaders to do nothing and focus on other "pressing" issues rather than prepare for a disaster as, in their thinking, "hurricanes do not hit every year."

Sometimes, the bias stems from when the perceived cost (i.e., time, effort, and money) of taking action *now* is believed to be greater than the perceived future benefit. If you think about it, most people will choose to receive $100 today instead of waiting 365 days and receiving $120 at the end of the year. However, an investment advisor would be yelling at the person to take the 20% return on their money!

As a business leader, you need to set aside time to analyze your programs and determine what needs to be changed each year or more frequently. The failure of COVID-19 being "covered" by insurance became why many business leaders changed how they assessed their relationship with their insurance design professional. It was also why businesses relooked at their recovery and response programs.

- **Simplification**: *a tendency to process only limited subsets of information*

Remember the Tversky and Kahneman split group study on making risk decisions example? It was an example of making decisions with limited information.

Simplification may be one of the broader biases in terms of what it comprises. Business leaders, unfortunately, often must work with limited or imperfect information. They must then fill in the information holes with their own knowledge and experience. Some of the limited information comes from insurance agents in the form of their condensed or simplified proposals or their vague recommendations as to what risks to address. Some of it is because business leaders tend to provide limited information to insurance agents. Because of this, agents cannot make solid recommendations but must instead rely on guesswork, also know as *Simplification*.

Besides, even if the business leader has reliable information to base a decision upon, he or she will typically seek to simplify the solution, or in other words, mitigate the impact on their business when implementing changes. This mitigation or simplification could also lead to imperfect outcomes or decisions about what program to implement or which insurance program to accept.

The concept of receiving "apples-to-apples quotes" for insurance is *Simplification* in that the business leader will assume that they are receiving the exact same coverage back. However, as you will learn throughout this book, there is no such thing as "apples-to-apples quotes." The imperfect information will lack clarity about what is *Covered Property* and what is *Property Not Covered*, two completely different issues. There are also the actual Inclusions and Exclusions within the various coverage forms that need to be understood before deciding.

One of the biggest *Simplification* problems for business leaders will be discussed later in this book: the actual insurance policy procurement process itself. It is a process that the insurance industry has taught employers to follow. In essence, because of the bias of *Simplification*, the process has become broken. When making a decision, will you look thoroughly into every detailed facet of the insurance program? Will you just give a cursory review with a focus on some key areas of recent concern? Will it be based on price? Or do you have a detailed checklist as to what specific endorsements and coverages you are looking for to make sure nothing you missed nothing? In the end, did you choose the agent with the lowest price that "copied" what you had but really will not be able to truly advise you and your leadership team moving forward? When it is all said and done, will *Simplification* make your comparisons difficult? And what if *Inertia* sets in and you do not make a critical and beneficial change?

- **Herding**: *a tendency to make decisions by social imitation*

The alarm goes off in your hotel in the middle of the night. You annoyingly put on your shoes, coat (and hopefully pants), and proceed out to the hallway to exit the hotel. You see other people standing in their doorways, looking up and down the hallway. No one else is leaving. After making a few funny, sarcastic remarks to each other, you also head back into your room and wait for the alarm to stop screeching so you can return to sleep. This is an example of *Herding* or following the lead of others. But what if you could not see that there was a fire in the main floor kitchen? Would that decision to delay cause you to be inevitably trapped and die of smoke inhalation?

Although this example may be viewed as a little morbid, it is a realistic example that plays out repeatedly. Some of the decision was due to past situations where the alarms that endlessly rang were basically "the boy who cried wolf," but it does show how people tend to follow the actions of others.

Business leaders tend to network with other business leaders; they share ideas, experiences, and actions that they have taken. A business leader asks a fellow business leader how they addressed a particular risk; let us pretend it was about improving security for remote access to their computer system, such as using Multi-Factor Authentication. The other business leader states that they have not done anything or looked into it. Or maybe the solution was costly or cumbersome. This causes the business leader to have a false sense of security because they will then believe the risk does not need addressing. That would be a critical error with today's cyber threats.

The opposite is true; when a colleague experiences an issue or addressing a risk, the business leader finally also addresses a weakness in their overall programs.

For example, we will look at some closely related businesses where the owners are relatives or close friends. After having multiple conversations surrounding the risks of Employment Practices and Cyber Risks and discussing the need to have solid policies and procedures, training, and insurance coverage, this group did not take action or, at the very least, limited action. Within three months, two events occurred, a harassment lawsuit and cyber extortion and ransomware event. Since then, the entire group of businesses updated their policies and procedures, provided ongoing training to employees, and all purchased the appropriate insurance programs.

There is also the tendency for a business leader to copy an early implementer of response to risk. The problem becomes if that particular program design is inappropriate for their business. When reviewing documents provided by the interviewed business leaders, it was not uncommon to find the names of other businesses within their documents. These were the policies and procedures, employee handbooks, business recovery plans, and even insurance specifications used by those unfortunate businesses when they obtained insurance before they had their disasters.

When attempting to categorize the business leaders' reasons into the *6 Behavioral Risk Biases,* you will see when you look at each of them that there are typically multiple biases that are at the root of their reasons for not taking action:

- Business owners, by their nature, are risk-takers, and therefore are reluctant to believe that a significant or catastrophic event will affect them –
  - *Myopia & Optimism* – These tend to cause business leaders to delay focusing on their recovery plan or insurance program design.
- Many business owners started their company from scratch; thus, they believe they can do so again while forgetting that they have families and lifestyles that would be significantly and negatively affected –
  - *Amnesia* – Many business leaders, when they have been so successful over a more extended period, tend to forget how difficult and how much work and effort they put forth when starting the business.
- Most insurance agents do not fully understand what efforts and capital it will take for a business to survive while being

closed, reopen, and then rebuild or regain their clientele following a disaster. Therefore, these agents cannot help in educating business leaders as to what to expect –
- ***Simplification, Inertia & Herding*** – Business leaders often do not work with all the details they need when deciding. Since their "current" insurance program has "met their needs so far," there is often a lack of effort focused on making any changes. They may not have the personal knowledge of others affected or clear stories of other businesses affected by an issue, and therefore do not adequately prepare.
- Most insurance agents do not understand how to calculate ***How Much*** business income coverage a business will need, and therefore cannot explain it to a business owner so they can calculate the amount themselves –
  - ***Simplification & Inertia*** – Once again, business leaders are not working with all the details they need to decide. Also, insurance agents look for simple, positive-sounding solutions, such as *12 Months Actual Loss Sustained Business Income* coverage, without highlighting potential significant shortfalls of the coverage to business leaders.
- Business leaders often believe that they will be back in business faster than it will take them to do so –
  - ***Amnesia & Optimism*** – business leaders tend to forget all the little details of the preparation that took place before the first shovel hit the ground for the Groundbreaking Ceremony. Most business leaders only remember the construction phase while forgetting how long it actually took to build or how long it will take for production machinery to be ordered, delivered, and installed.
- Business leaders are unable to perceive how much extra expense they would incur when attempting to keep the doors open and retain as many customers as possible –

- ***Simplification and Optimism*** – business leaders know how much they spend on their expenses but can only guess how much those expenses might be when trying to keep the doors open. They also tend to believe that they can purchase the services or products from others for far less than they will have to pay for them and think they will have to buy from competitors for a much shorter timeframe than they will have to.
- Business leaders did not realize the significance of the risks that they were facing from something catastrophic occurring. This is simply because it never happened to them before, nor to anyone that they know –
  - ***Herding*** – It is clear that if a business leader has not experienced something before, they have no frame of reference. Business leaders also tend to network with other business leaders to share ideas, experiences, and actions that they have taken. Therefore, if a fellow business leader does not address a particular risk, the other business leader develops a false sense of security.
- Business leaders think all or most of their clients are loyal and will return as soon as their doors reopen –
  - ***Optimism*** – probably does not need explanation, but business leaders may not understand that their customers have options or are creatures of habit, as we will discuss in more depth later in this book.
- Insurance Terms do not always correspond to Business Terms, nor to how business leaders believe they should, so misinterpreting are things are common–
  - ***Simplification*** – Business leaders will make decisions based on their understanding of terms rather than learning the details of the insurance world.
- Financial Industry terms that accountants and business owners use are different from "Insurance World" terms. For example: "cost of goods sold" and "net income" means different things in each world –

- ***Simplification*** – Once again, business leaders will make decisions based on their understanding of terms rather than learning the details of those terms.
- Many business owners are reluctant to share their "financial picture" with insurance agents as they feel that their information is "private" –
  - ***Simplification*** – This is a tough one. As best as can be determined, business leaders do not view insurance professionals the same as they might their financial advisor. A poor quality financial advisor may cause you to invest in some investments that do not yield enough return. A poor accountant may cause you to pay too much in taxes. However, a poor job done by an insurance agent can cause you to go out of business when your insurance program does not respond when you truly need it.
- Business leaders struggle to distinguish between the purchasing of an insurance policy and the value of selecting the right insurance advisor to help build the correct insurance plan design –
  - ***Simplification & Optimism*** – This one is also difficult. Let us pretend that the "apples-to-apples" insurance policy *actually* existed. If that was the case, with everything being identical, then the insurance company that supplies your insurance policy becomes a commodity, which is how most business leaders view insurance today. However, if genuinely identical policies existed, this would enable you to make a better business decision in that you could focus on choosing *who* would be the best advisor to help you properly design your insurance program. Clearly, an insurance agent's knowledge and expertise are certainly not equal, nor is knowledge and experience a commodity.
- Business leaders and agents do not like to have a conversation about uncomfortable topics, such as the

business's death, and more importantly, what the plan is when something happens –
- ***Optimism & Myopia*** – Business leaders tend to believe that a disaster will not happen to them. Therefore, they would like to focus on more exciting things like winning another client or increasing profitability. Having a business leader focus on their business's demise seems to them like cruel and unusual punishment. Oh, wait a minute, you are reading this book about that very matter. So, clearly, this is the most exciting subject that you could ever have the opportunity to learn more about... you get the picture?
- Business leaders do not fully understand their insurance coverages nor how insurance policies will respond to a disaster –
  - Misunderstanding insurance is the broadest description of the reasons given for failures. It may appear to be a catch-all, but it does highlight one of the leading and most stated root causes for many of the failures. The Behavioral Risk Biases that affect this one:
    - ***Simplification*** in assumptions about how the insurance coverages within a business leader's policy will respond. Therefore, assumptions made about what coverages they purchase or assumptions made about how the insurance company will adjust their disaster claim will ultimately impact their business and its survivability.
    - ***Optimism*** in that business leaders believed their insurance policies would adequately respond to their disaster. Optimism in that business leaders believed the agents or individuals that provided them with advice on what coverages the business leaders ultimately purchased fully understood their business well enough to advise them about the proper coverages they would need.

- ***Herding*** happens because business leaders typically do not have a frame of reference organization that previously suffered a disaster to use as motivation to plan for and insure their business properly.
- ***Amnesia*** because a business leader was satisfied by how the insurance company adjusted *a* small claim leads them to assume they have a good insurance policy for *all* claims. There were examples of the opposite. A small claim was handled poorly by an adjuster, which led the business leader to focus on forcing a change of their insurance agent or company. Unfortunately, when making the change, critical insurance coverage that existed on the prior policy was lost.
- ***Myopia*** comes into play when a business leader perceives the cost of the efforts required to change as greater than the benefits of making the actual changes needed to survive. Changing an insurance agent, an insurance company, or the insurance coverages they have, or even implementing a disaster recovery plan, gets pushed aside. Whether it means taking the time to figure out how much coverage a business needs to protect its cash flow, completing applications for new but necessary coverage, or the effort required to change who they use as their agent advisor. If taking that time to do any of these is viewed as more "painful" than focusing on something else in the business, unfortunately, business leaders tend to focus on something else.
- ***Inertia*** inevitably sets in. The business leader does not take any action or changes as they do not recognize the inherent risks of not changing their insurance program or implementing a recovery plan.

One thing is sure; business leaders buy insurance to have their claims paid. It may not be the $500 claim that goes uncovered that is a concern or the $5,000 claim, although that might be smart for some. It may not even be the $50,000 uncovered claim that is a business-ending issue for a business leader. But when you have to cut your own check for $500,000, or $5,000,000, at some point, it gets your attention, especially if it will put you out of business.

As Benjamin Franklin once said, *"Failing to plan is planning to fail."* The key point of this chapter is that you should focus on breaking the more significant complex concepts and programs into smaller, more manageable decisions and actions. Look past your biases and work to build your Disaster Recovery Program and improve your Insurance Program Design.

Accomplishing these will help you avoid being a statistic and, more importantly, avoid the devastating impact that statistic will have on you, your family, your employees, and your community.

We will continue further in this book to provide a deeper understanding of issues that ultimately doomed the failed businesses and even impacted those who survived. These issues will be discussed in detail, aiding you in properly designing your insurance program and a Business Recovery Plan. The goal is to achieve the success of coming out on the other side of a disaster and thrive, rather than ending up out of business and just another statistic.

Insured to Fail

Chapter 2

Be Careful What You Ask For

Jack Kirsopp, Kirsopp Auto Body

On the morning of November 14th, 1997, while in Erie, Pennsylvania, with my wife and our birthday girl of two years, we visited my sister-in-law, who was still in college (on the seven or eight-year plan, apparently.) While there, I received a phone call from Jack Kirsopp of Kirsopp Auto Body, who told me his building burned to the ground that night. Jack said nothing was left; all the vehicles inside, tools, equipment, everything was gone. Jack's dad had started the business 37 years prior and was utterly destroyed. Jack employed 18 employees, most of whom were with him and his dad for more than 15 years. It was a true family business as the financial side of the business was run by Jack's amazing wife, Gale. It was all gone in just an hour or two. I can still visualize the small desk next to Gale's where their daughter, Lori, who now owns the business, would do her homework after school.

It turns out that during the night, a three-year-old overhead furnace exploded, destroying most of the backside of the building, and a large portion of the metal roof was ripped open in the explosion. The fire brought down the entire roof, which in turn brought down most of the walls. It completely obliterated everything inside, along with everything outside that was within 15 to 25 feet of the building.

Throughout this book, you will learn Jack's story (and others), what happened, and lessons learned.

When speaking over the years at conferences, I have had the fortunate opportunity to engage with thousands of business leaders and learn the daily risks and challenges they face while growing and managing their businesses. The challenges are many, from hiring and retaining good employees while facing growing local, national, or even international competition; to navigating the ever-evolving challenges of obtaining resources and supplies while constantly battling the evolving governmental regulations. Today, business leaders are exhausted from the constant strain of dealing with the frustrations regarding the amount of time they need to focus on the too numerous critical items. Today, business leaders do more with less, something that seemed to have been brought about by the Great Recession, a time when you *had* to do more with less to survive, and no one returned to pre-recession practices.

Therefore, when it comes time to "buy insurance," they have been taught by insurance agents the process of attempting to oversimplify what is complex, which has led to the scary statistics we highlighted in the Introduction.

While presenting to business leaders at conferences and engaging with them outside of the sessions, there is the opportunity to ask them why they buy insurance and how they manage risks. Almost every business leader says that they purchase insurance to pay their claims. To further define their most significant concern (other than their premium), they respond that they hope to have a business after a disaster. But yet, a large majority of leaders only request an "apples-to-apples" insurance quote, or in other words, they request agents to provide a quote for only what they currently have, or at the very least, what they *think* they have. Or what they provided the agent, whether or not the business leader included "everything." Those who use this insurance quote comparison process as the way they choose their insurance agent fell into three groups. Listed below are what the business leaders have told me:

    A. There is significant confusion about the insurance industry and what is and what is not covered, so they want to get quotes for at least what they have.

B. There is a distrust of insurance agents (placing them just above or below a used car salesperson.) They believe agents will propose things that they do not need. Therefore, once again, they want to receive quotes for the coverage they currently have.
C. The last group falls into the slightly broader category of focusing mainly on premium. They may believe their insurance program is correct and want the apples-to-apples quote to help them decide who has the best rates. Or they want an apples-to-apples quote to see who has the best rates, so *if* they make any changes in coverages, they will do so using the best rates.

During my Disaster Preparedness keynote session, I asked a question of the participants. You should ask yourself, *"When would you like to know that your insurance program is not going to respond to your disaster fully: when you are purchasing your policies (a.k.a. NOW), or after a disaster when you really need it?"*

By a show of hands, business leaders overwhelmingly said *NOW, as in before the disaster*. But there always seems to be a few stragglers in the audience with their hands down for *now*.

They were asked to imagine this scenario. Picture in your mind that you have a catastrophic fire and are now rebuilding. You receive a $385,000 invoice, or maybe a $1,385,000 invoice, from the contractor for excavating, grading, and pouring the foundation. You submit your invoice to the insurance company, and they send you a letter that generally states, *"Sorry, your groundwork and foundation are not Covered Property. Therefore, we deny payment for these items."* Now, how do you feel?

WOW! What happened?

When asked again, everyone's hands are in the air as to that they would prefer to know NOW that they have a problem with their insurance program.

As the expression goes, *the devil is in the details*. So, let us dig into those details.

Since 1971, Insurance Services Office (ISO) has been the leading provider of advanced tools, data, and analytics for property and casualty insurers. ISO serves insurance companies, reinsurance companies, agents and brokers, insurance regulators, and risk managers in the property/casualty insurance marketplace. It also serves as the statistical, actuarial, underwriting, and claims information source for the insurance industry. The one thing that impacts every business owner is that ISO creates the insurance standard policy language. Look at the bottom of any coverage form in your insurance, such as your property, auto, or general liability policy. You will see © *Insurance Services Office, Inc.* listed at the bottom of the page or possibly referencing that the policy form contains copyrighted Insurance Services Office language.

There are 586 available endorsements or "riders" that your industry-standard business property, general liability, and auto policies can *add* to alter your coverage. These 586 endorsements do not include the multitude of "exclusions" and uncovered items built into those core policies you rely upon to pay your claims. These endorsement numbers do not include the separate endorsements that insurance companies can create on their own to customize your coverage or exclusion. Clearly, a standard policy does not address everything for everyone. Your policy must and can be customized to fit your business and operations.

Another way to look at it is, insurance policies are written for the *average* business. The problem is – neither you nor anyone else is truly average, which requires specific endorsements to be used to more appropriately insure your risks and exposures.

Time to quickly revisit the "apples-to-apples" quote myth. People generally love to evaluate options in the most organized fashion. After learning how many endorsements there are, business leaders have realized that there is no such thing as "apples-to-apples" comparisons. Especially when you consider nearly 2,500 apples are growing just in the United States and over 7,500 different apples are growing in the world. So, when you requested "apples-to-apples," did you specify the Gala, McIntosh, Red Delicious,

Golden Delicious, Granny Smith, or Honeycrisp? And were the apples in the local grocery store that week.

Once again, when do you want to find out that your insurance program will not be there for you when you need it?

For the remainder of this chapter, as well as over the next three chapters, we will discuss the following topics relating to your "Property Coverage":

- What is Covered Property, and what is Property Not Covered?
- What are the "causes of loss" that provide you coverage?
- How does the insurance company determine how much to pay you?
- What are the most missed or confusing issues with property policies?

One of my favorite television shows comes to mind: *MythBusters*. After reading this book, you will see why the *Myth Busted* sign will appear when it comes to "apples-to-apples" comparisons.

Let us highlight several of the issues you will face with the **ISO CP0010 Building and Personal Property Coverage Form.**[12]

> A. **Coverage** - We will pay for **direct physical loss** of or damage to **Covered Property** at the **premises described in the**

---

[12] © Insurance Services Office, Inc. and its affiliates. Used with permission.

When describing insurance coverage forms in this book, Insurance Services Office, Inc. (ISO) coverage forms are used. These are copyrighted forms and are being used with permission. You should be aware that there are state specific versions, as well as insurance company proprietary forms. Please read your policies carefully and consult an insurance coverage design expert.

> **Declarations** caused by or resulting **from any Covered Cause of Loss**.

It is just one sentence from the coverage form, but it highlights key terms and phrases that you must focus on to make sure you are insured the way you want to be:

- **Direct Physical Loss:** That something happens to the property in question that causes the property to have some damage to it.
- **Covered Property:** That it must happen to specifically defined types of property.
- **Premises described in the Declarations:** That it must happen at a location, building, or property listed specifically in the policy,
- **Covered Cause of Loss:** That it must happen from particular actions/issues/accidents/etc.

Covered Cause of Loss – it is mentioned out of order as there is so much to discuss with just this topic, we will need to examine separately and do so in Chapter 5.

> A. **Coverage** - We will pay for **direct physical loss** of or damage to **Covered Property** at the **premises described in the Declarations** caused by or resulting **from any Covered Cause of Loss**.

Premises Described in the Declaration – If the location and structure are not specifically listed in your policy, there is no coverage. If you have one location, that would be easy to deal with as you can see the one location with the Building and Your Business Personal Property listed on the declaration page, with limits for each of them. But what happens if you have 10 locations, 100 locations, or 1,000 locations? The more locations you have, the more you must pay attention to the schedule of locations and the items listed for coverage on the policy.

Are you are thinking, *"But I have Blanket Coverage for all my locations?"*

Yes, you can have Blanket Coverage, meaning you may have just one shared limit for Buildings and one shared limit for Your Business Personal Property, or even one shared limit combined for both. But that does not mean ALL locations and structures are automatically included; you could forget to add one to the policy. Even blanket policies will have a schedule of locations, structures, and coverages that comprise where and what is making up the Blanket Limit.

I have seen some policies with so many locations that the insurance company does not want to enter them into their computer system. Therefore these policies do not have a schedule. Instead, the insurance company may alter the Declaration Page. Where the schedule of locations would typically be, they may display "Schedule of locations per the Statement of Values on file with the insurance company." Therefore, the claims adjuster would look into the insurance company's files to verify that the Statement of Values included the location, structure, and contents before agreeing to pay a claim that happened at a location.

> A. **Coverage** - We will pay for **direct physical loss** of or damage to **Covered Property** at the **premises described** in the Declarations caused by or resulting **from any Covered Cause of Loss.**

Direct Physical Loss - This was the clause that caused all the trouble for business owners regarding COVID-19 claim declinations. Did the virus cause direct physical loss? Some said, *"I had to clean and disinfect my copier, door handles, light switches, etc. Therefore, the virus caused damage."* However, if you left those same property items alone for five days, the CDC said that the virus would no longer be active. Because of this, those items did not technically need to be cleaned, and therefore there was no damage.

The clause clarifies that if the property is rendered useless or cannot be used for some reason, but it is not damaged, that there is no coverage. There needs to be some *physical damage* to the property for there to be possible coverage.

> A. **Coverage** - We will pay for **direct physical loss** of or damage to **Covered Property** at the **premises described** in the Declarations caused by or resulting **from any Covered Cause of Loss**.

Covered Property – This is where the big problems start; what is considered Covered Property and Property Not Covered will be the focus of the rest of this chapter.

Many agents will tell you that you have Building and "Contents" coverage. Therefore you think you have coverage for both your structure and then the items inside the structure. But sometimes what you think is a Building is actually "Contents," and what you feel is "Contents" is actually Building or Property of Others. You need to know the difference to know how much coverage you have to purchase for each respective category and what you may need when customizing your policy.

> 1. **Covered Property**
> Covered Property, as used in this Coverage Part, means the type of property described in this section, A.1., and limited in A.2. Property Not Covered, if a Limit Of Insurance is shown in the Declarations for that type of property.

As this book goes through what is Covered Property and what is Property Not Covered, assumptions were not made about the reader's level of knowledge regarding insurance. Therefore, the book will detail what everyone should know and reference for clarity when the time comes, should you have questions.

A.1. COVERED PROPERTY CATEGORIES:

BUILDING

Building means the building or structure described on the Declaration page of your policy. If the building is not represented on the declaration page, it is not covered. Do not get caught up in the term "blanket" coverage. If the specific building is not on the schedule of locations and buildings, it is not covered. You may think your "blanket" is fully covering you, but in reality, your feet are sticking out.

Completed Additions & Materials for Construction

Building coverage also includes completed additions, which makes sense since it is part of your building. However, suppose you completed an addition or improvement to your building and did not notify your agent and insurance company as to the increase in value of your structure. In that case, you may have issues with receiving a "full payment" on a future loss. This will be discussed later in the book, but remember the word *Coinsurance* (you should now be hearing the ominous, impending *"duunnn dunnn... duuuunnnn duun..."* theme music of *Jaws* approaching playing in your head).

If not covered by other insurance, your building also includes additions under construction, alterations and repairs to the building or structure; and materials, equipment, supplies, and temporary structures, on or within 100 feet of the described premises, specifically used for making additions, alterations or repairs to the building or structure. However, suppose you OR your contractor has Builder's Risk or Installation Floater coverage. In that case, the addition being constructed and the materials being installed would not be covered by your property policy. This is true even if you or your contractor do not have enough coverage on the other policy.

Fixtures & Equipment

The definition of Building includes fixtures, including outdoor fixtures attached to the structure, and permanently installed

machinery and equipment. However, the term Permanently Installed can be confusing at claim time, as there are two schools of thought:
- One, you dress up in your spandex and cape, become the Man of Steel, pick up your building, turn it on its side and shake it. Everything that moves or falls out is not Building.
- Two, if you can dawn your blue overalls with an orange checkered shirt and yellow hard hat, turn into Bob the Builder, and proceed to disassemble everything and then move it to a new location and reassemble. Anything you can move is not permanently installed and not Building.

Besides the costume you chose, the real decision to which applies may come down to your claim adjuster's interpretation at claim time, which could be too late. However, the latter is the most commonly used description. But the good news is, there are endorsements available that allow such issues to be clarified. However, they are often overlooked.

Certain Personal Property

Building also includes personal property owned by you to maintain or service the building or structure or its premises, including fire-extinguishing equipment, outdoor furniture, floor coverings, and appliances used for refrigerating, ventilating, cooking, dishwashing, or laundering. This is where many restaurants and hospitality operations get themselves in trouble when determining how much coverage to have. Most business leaders tend to include these values in their "contents" limits when they should be within the total Building value limit.

Let us revisit Kirsopp Auto Body. When it came to analyzing their operations, Jack Kirsopp did not just do bodywork for cars. He specialized in really big trucks called Tractors, Semi-Trailers, Box Trucks, all kinds of vehicles where you need a Commercial Driver License to operate. Everything they have in their operation was supersized to accommodate the massive sizes of the big rigs; the two paint spray rooms were 40 and 75 feet long to paint tractors and trailers safely.

Jack had many installed or attached equipment to the structure but could be removed should they decide to move locations: such as spray room lighting and exhaust collection systems, dust collection systems, vehicle lifts, frame straightening platforms, and compressors.

The good news is that ISO has an endorsement, **CP1415 Additional Building Property**, that allows you to specifically describe what items you want to be included in the definition of the building. Another advantage of adding these to the building definition and values is that there is no theft charge built into building rates, so building rates are typically much lower than "contents," thereby creating insurance premium savings.

While doing the Coverage Analysis, I worked with Jack to estimate the value to insure his building. It was necessary to determine how much all this "stuff" would cost to replace, and then add it all up and place those values into the total building value you use. To give you an idea, back in 1997, his prior agent insured the building for $274,000, or $39 a square foot for the 7,000 square foot building (the going rate per square foot at the time was about $55-$65). Jack suspected that the building limit had not changed or had not changed much for years as Jack requested "apples-to-apples" quotes from agents. Each quoting agent would copy the policy and provide the same limit for the Building on the expiring declaration page, so the Building value was from the prior year. The current ("incumbent") agent would leave the same values on the renewal policy as they knew the competition would be using the old values. Therefore, they did not want to be at a "competitive disadvantage." When Jack shopped his insurance several years in a row, the Building value did not change for those years.

After explaining the Coinsurance Clause to Jack, he agreed to help estimate everything permanently installed, which allowed the building to arrive at $847,000. Not a bad guess as the insurance company's contractor estimated the cost to rebuild the structure was $865,000.

Failing to take the time to dig in and estimate the replacement cost value, Jack's old agent at $274,000 would have left him short a staggering $573,000 instead of the minimal amount of $18,000 the $847,000 would have. (Just wait to hear what else was also off in terms of values in later chapters.)

For Jack's new facility, the definition of Building had to be changed to now include the $350,000, 120-foot long, 22-foot-tall spray-bake paint booth that can fit a tractor and trailer inside, as well as the addition of a new exhaust system that can be disassembled and moved.

Oh, by the way, by shifting equipment to be defined as Building, which has a lower rate versus insuring them as "contents," you reduce your premium. In Jack's case, the final total premium difference ended up being minimal, even with all the extra coverage.

YOUR BUSINESS PERSONAL PROPERTY (BPP)

Business Personal Property is commonly incorrectly referred to as "Contents." Therefore, "Contents" will no longer be used when describing such coverage in a Property Policy. We will substitute terms of Your Business Personal Property (BPP) or Personal Property of Others (PPO) in its place. The reason for this distinction is that BPP is YOUR stuff and not the stuff of OTHERS; plus, Personal Property of OTHERS (PPO) has a separate coverage category, which will be discussed later.

BPP includes the following:
- Your furniture and fixtures;
- Machinery and equipment;
- "Stock" (which means merchandise held in storage or for sale, raw materials and in-process or finished goods, including supplies used in their packing or shipping); and
- All other personal property that is **owned by you** and used in your business.

Distance & Location/Storage Constraints

BPP consists of the property located in or on the building or structure described in the Declarations **or in the open (or in a vehicle) within 100 feet** of the **building** or structure or within 100 feet of the premises described in the Declarations, whichever distance is greater. To add to the confusion, an insurance policy defines the Building as the Premises, so it is the distance from the Building's edge and not your property line.

As soon as your property leaves your premise, you typically cease having coverage. The policy does provide $10,000 coverage at limited temporary locations:
- A location you do not own, lease, or operate;
- At a storage location you lease, provided the lease was executed after the beginning of the current policy term; or
- At any fair, trade show, or exhibition.

If you are working or operating at a temporary location, then you would not have coverage either. If your property is more than 100 feet from your building and comprises things like tools and equipment, you should purchase separate coverage for these items. The coverage for specialty coverage for property that leaves the premise is referred to as an Inland Marine policy.

Also, when your property drives away from your premises, it is no longer covered. Therefore, if you have property headed to a customer or job site, you have to address property that is being moved or transported with an endorsement for Property In Transit.

Increase in Value of Property of Others

BPP includes your labor and materials or services furnished or arranged by you on the personal property of others. For example, if you receive materials or parts from a customer and spend time (labor), purchase more parts, and assemble them, you have added value and materials to the customer's property. That increase in value is included in your BPP. The customer's original provided items that you work on would still be PPO even when you have completed your services or modifications.

Tenant Improvements and Betterments

Your use interest as a **tenant in improvements and betterments**. Improvements and betterments are fixtures, alterations, installations, or additions made a part of the building or structure you occupy but do you not own and have acquired or made at your expense but cannot legally remove from the building. Believe it or not, this is a more complicated concept that will be specifically addressed in another chapter.

Leased Personal Property

Leased personal property for which you have a *contractual* responsibility to insure is included in your BPP unless the property is provided for under Personal Property Of Others (PPO). For example, you will typically be contractually responsible to insure your leased copier.

Property in the Open

Property in the open or within a vehicle on your premise is covered.

Another issue with many businesses, such as what Kirsopp encountered, is that they use cargo containers, and not semi-trailers, to store excess materials or inventory. They may also do it as part of their shipping process, where they load shipping containers for future shipment of their finished products. We have seen property damaged, totaling tens to hundreds of thousands of dollars, for goods inside a cargo container about to be picked up and placed on a trailer or barge for shipping. When you also include the many large retail facilities that have a significant excess inventory on-premise, particularly around the Christmas and holiday seasons, you need to pay attention to cargo containers versus semi-trailers.

The issue becomes, a cargo container is not a trailer. Therefore, a cargo container is not an auto, and the items inside a cargo container on-premise are not covered property. Using the similar form of **CP1410 Additional Property Covered** and adding the definition of property that BPP on-premise stored in a cargo container as Covered Property. Otherwise, you would need to schedule each cargo container and the corresponding BPP value inside the container on the policy.

PERSONAL PROPERTY OF OTHERS (PPO)

Personal Property Of Others includes personal property in your care, custody, or control located in or on the building or structure described in the Declarations or in the open (or in a vehicle) within 100 feet of the building or structure or within 100 feet of the premises described in the Declarations, whichever distance is greater.

BPPO coverage is only at your premises. If you perform operations away from your premises, and in the course of performing work have to handle or move PPO, you have to address this. You may need to purchase liability coverage such as Voluntary Property Damage Liability Coverage or specialty property coverage such as an Inland Marine Installation Floater. It will depend upon what you do and what type of PPO you are handling. However, whether at your premises or others, you may need to purchase a separate liability policy or Inland Marine Policy for these items: such as Bailee's Coverage, Warehouse Legal Liability, Wharfingers and Stevedores Liability, etc. You may also need to address the property of others transported via a Motor Truck Cargo Policy. The best thing is to have an in-depth conversation with an insurance expert as to the Personal Property of Others and your operations.

Leased Property

You may have more property of others than you realize. Any leased property you are using, such as a copier, postage meter, production machinery, or computer systems, is technically the property of others. However, if you recall, the definition of what is covered property under BPP includes *leased* personal property for which you have a contractual responsibility to insure unless otherwise provided for under PPO. Therefore, you need to focus on the property of others that you do not lease or if you lease property that your contract does not require you to insure their property. Basically, all other property of others needs to be addressed.

Just so you are aware, any payment for loss of or damage to the personal property of others will only be for the account of the property owner.

Personal Effects

The Building and Personal Property Coverage Form do provide $2,500 of coverage for the personal effects. You may own the Personal Effects, or it can be owned by your officers, partners or members, managers, or employees (but does not include theft of such). It also includes the *personal property of others in your care, custody, or control.* You can increase the limit if you need to, but sometimes a different type of overage is better suited for your situation.

Continuing with the example of Kirsopp Auto Body, many of their mechanics owned the hand tools they used every day. Therefore, substantial amounts of PPO needed to be added to cover their tools, especially since a mechanic's Homeowners policy would typically exclude tools of the trade when they away from their residence.

A.2. PROPERTY NOT COVERED CATEGORIES

The examples of Property Not Covered may amaze you, but this is where all the confusion starts. The ISO Building and Personal Property Coverage form goes on to clarify that Covered Property **does not include**:

Foundations, Excavations, and Backfilling

You cannot build a great building on a weak foundation – Gordon B Hinkley.

This relatively known quote is more spiritual but try to imagine constructing an actual building without a foundation. It would be impossible to have the building last for a long time. But yes, foundations of buildings, structures, or equipment are not covered property.

There are many issues with Property Not Covered that can cause significant problems when a disaster occurs and rebuild your facility. As alluded to earlier in the chapter, the cost of excavations, grading, backfilling, or filling is not covered. Nor are foundations of buildings, structures, machinery, or boilers if their foundations are below the lowest basement floor; or the surface of the ground, if there is no basement. Also, underground pipes, flues, or drains are not covered.

Because of this Property Not Covered restriction of coverage for Jack's building, it was necessary to use the CP1415 Additional Building Property to add the cost of excavations, grading, backfilling, or filling, the foundations of the building, spray booth, and frame straightening platform as well as the underground pipes. Failing to do so would have made Kirsopp Auto Body ineligible to receive the $285,000 needed to backfill and raise the ground and pour caissons (piers) down 10 to 30 feet to rock to support the entire new building structure (more story later). Whereas the final cost for the new structure without the new spray booth was about $1,150,000, you can see that failure to account for the ground and foundation work can cause a business not to afford to rebuild.

For those keeping score at home, the total shortage Jack's prior agent would have left him to deal with is at $858,000, and there is more to come.

To explain this issue further, recently, a business built a 150,000 square foot manufacturing facility in a Regional Industrial Development Park. You are probably familiar with the concept of a privately funded, non-profit serving a metropolitan area focusing on a regional approach to economic development primarily through managing and rehabilitating former large manufacturing sites (in this case, a former steel manufacturing plant) into a land development for area research and business parks. Because of this, the entire site was already prepped and graded flat for a building with utility service hook-ups ready to go.

Within the $12,605,766, the bid to build the new facility was $2,165,539 for the foundation and groundwork. That is roughly 17% of costs that would be Property Not Covered and would have to be paid for should the building ever have to be rebuilt. In reviewing construction estimates, foundations and ground costs have been in the 20% to 25% range over the years. Just imagine a tornado destroys your building. You are starting to rebuild when you find out you are financially 20% (or more) in the hole regarding your insurance policy paying the total costs to rebuild your building.

Retaining Walls

Retaining walls that are not part of a building are not covered, and it is common for vehicles to cause significant damage to them. Following the collapse of a retaining wall, we have seen tens to hundreds of thousands of dollars rebuilding the wall and repairing the ground behind the wall, including the parking lots and access roadways that the walls supported. Therefore, you should consider whether or not you feel they should be added to the definition of Building.

Land and Crops

Also not covered is the land itself, water, growing crops, or lawns (other than lawns which are part of a vegetated roof). If you grow a product, buy crop insurance.

Property in Odd Places

Whether or not they are within 100 feet of your building, personal property while airborne or waterborne, bulkheads, pilings, piers, wharves or docks, are not covered. Businesses such as marinas with docks for boats or businesses with piers to load and unload barges can use the same form to define coverage for the docks and piers. That way, you would be covered should river traffic, a runaway barge, or ice flows damage property.

Other Coverage

The form also states if the damaged property is covered under another coverage form of this or any other policy where it is more specifically described is not covered. However, the policy can be excess coverage of the amount due (whether you can collect on it or not) from that other insurance.

Money & Securities

Accounts, bills, currency, food stamps, or other evidence of debt, money, notes, or securities are not Covered Property. Therefore, you will need to purchase separate crime coverage. However, lottery tickets held for sale are not securities and are covered under BPP.

This is also an area where many businesses look for Accounts Receivable coverage to pay for the difference between what they did collect and what they should have collected after a covered cause of loss destroyed their records.

Outdoor structures or property

There is a whole slew of items that are not considered covered property: fences, radio or television antennas (including satellite dishes) and their lead-in wiring, masts or towers, trees, shrubs or plants (other than trees, shrubs or plants which are "stock" or are part of a vegetated roof).

However, the coverage form does provide $1,000 coverage. Still, no more than $250 for any one tree, shrub, or plant, and they only provide coverage for damage caused by fire, lightning, explosion, riot or civil commotion, or aircraft.

Some of the items that would fall into this category of not covered property are signs that are not attached to your building and parking lot lights. As happened to one business, imaging having a tornado take out 141 of your parking lot light posts that cost almost $1,500 apiece in addition to a $183,000 sign for a shopping center that displays the most prominent tenants and even has LED screens for changing displays. How would you feel only receiving $1,000 instead of $394,500?

Animals

Animals, unless owned by others and boarded by you, or if owned by you, only as "stock" while inside of buildings, are not covered. So, if you are caring for others' pets or are in the business of selling animals or pets, animals can be included in your BPP or PPO coverage.

Autos

Anything that is auto is not covered, other than auto parts. This also excludes automobiles held for sale. Autos are not just licensed road vehicles; autos are anything with wheels and a motor. Bicycles are not autos; however, electric bicycles can fall into a gray area: are they self-powered or power assist? Does the state that they are sold in require them to be registered? This is also where ATVs, UTVs, and quads become not covered, as most states require them to be registered for use. Therefore, you would want to use the CP1410 Additional Property Covered to clarify that your property policy covers them. Otherwise, you will need to address coverage with an Inland Marine coverage form for mobile equipment or Dealer Equipment coverage programs, and you may even have to turn to your Automobile Insurance Policy if they have to be licensed. So, please discuss your situation with an insurance expert.

Surfaces you walk or drive on

Not covered are bridges, roadways, walks, patios, or other paved surfaces. Any businesses that need a bridge to access their entire property or a portion of the property should be concerned. These can collapse due to the weight of a vehicle or be washed away in a flood.

A local business had an enclosed elevated walkway so that employees can walk to the building from the rather long and large lot without fear of being hit by a vehicle or soaked by rain (or pelted with snow). More importantly, that parking lot was on the other side of a highway. The elevated walkway was built with a multi-million-dollar state grant to have the manufacturer move into the facility. An oversized, over-height truck damaged it while trying to go under it, and the trucking company did not have enough liability coverage to pay to replace it. The manufacturer could not receive a new grant and faced having to pay $3,140,000 to repair the bridge over the highway.

Over the past 30-plus years, I have seen dozens of businesses that have had a vehicle catch fire in their parking lot. Such fires can cause the pavement to melt and blister or the concrete to crack to a point where one event caused over $180,000 of damage to a parking lot as the fire spread to four vehicles.

With Kirsopp, they used the CP1415 Additional Building Property form to include the paved front parking lot and added the cost of paving into the building value. The $120,000 estimate cost of paving added only $33 per year to his premium. Yes, most of the parking lot was damaged to gain access to the utilities and foundation. The shortage scoreboard is at $924,000.

Illegal Stuff

Sort of self-explanatory, but contraband or property in the course of illegal transportation or trade is not covered. However, please keep in mind that some products may be legal in a state, such as medical marijuana, but only where a state decriminalized it. In other states, it could still be technically illegal, and marijuana would not be covered. So, this restriction of coverage needs looked at on a case by case (or state by state) basis.

Computer Data

The physical computer can be considered Covered Property. However, the electronic data and programs on the hard drive, thumb drive, or the cloud are not. The hard drive is covered, but the 1's and 0's that represent that data on it are not. There is a limited give-back of $2,500 of coverage for data destroyed by a covered cause of loss, but this does not apply if you are programming or selling software. Long story short, if you are looking to protect your data and have insurance coverage for cyber claims, there are better coverage forms and programs are available from specialty insurance programs other than the ISO coverage form. Especially look towards a robust Cyber Insurance Program.

Valuable Papers

Paper itself is covered property, but much like data is to computers, what is on the paper is not Covered Property. Many businesses need to purchase coverage to replace or restore the information on valuable documents and records, including those that exist as electronic data. Valuable papers and records include but are not limited to proprietary information, books of account, deeds, manuscripts, abstracts, drawings, and card index systems. The ISO form includes limited coverage of $2,500, but you should review and determine your needs once again.

However, with today's imaging capabilities, large copier/printers, and cheap computer data storage of pennies per Gigabyte, the coverage is becoming less important. You should still discuss if your operations need such coverage.

Motorized Things that Fly, Float, or Move on Wheels, Treads or Tracks

Vehicles or self-propelled machines (including aircraft or watercraft) licensed for use on public roads, or are operated principally away from the described premises, are not covered. Simply put, if you put a registration plate on it or license it, it is not covered.

This exclusion does not apply to vehicles or self-propelled machines, or autos you own that you manufacture, process, or warehouse. However, autos held for sale are excluded, even if you store them in a "warehouse." If you make it and sell it to others, which sell your product to the end consumer, it is your inventory.

Other items that the property policy can still cover, but you should verify for your particular situation are:
- Vehicles or self-propelled machines, other than autos, you hold for sale;
- Rowboats or canoes out of the water at the described premises; or
- Trailers, but only to the extent provided for in the Coverage Extension for Non-owned Detached Trailers.

Crops

Grain, hay, straw, or other crops located outside of your building are not covered property. In other words, if growing in the field, not covered. But if harvested and brought inside to process for delivery, covered.

WORDS OF CAUTION

As you can now clearly see, and will even learn more in later chapters, Building does not mean what you think it does when it comes to insurance coverage. Unfortunately, insurance agents have taught business leaders over the years to ask for "apples-to-apples" quotes or focus on the core coverages (Building, BPP, or PPO) and then look over the XYZ Insurance Company Property Enhancement Endorsement. The problem is that insurance companies cannot possibly list every meaning and alteration in their Enhancement Endorsement Summary Schedule. A few insurance companies alter the core Building & Personal Property Coverage form itself to add their own limits and additional coverages.

For example, a few insurance companies include within the definition of covered building property the building and equipment foundations, grading, and backfilling in their core policy. These alterations are not listed on an Enhancement Endorsement. And then there are insurance companies that list foundations as "Covered" on their enhancement endorsement summary, but when you read the coverage form itself, it pertains to foundations production equipment only. This is why you should be careful when you share your current policy declaration pages with an agent to quote. We have seen essential coverages become lost, and this highlights why you need to read your policy's language as Enhancement Endorsement descriptions can sometimes be misleading.

The Devil is in the Details...

You also know the mock meaning of the word *assume*, so please do not assume anything. You should request copies of the policy and endorsements to read yourself. If you do not read them, you must make sure that the agent you are using is doing so and prove to you that they did.

Remember, an insurance contract is between you and the insurance company. The insurance company will only pay what it is legally obligated to pay. It is the insurance program design that is critical. The issue is that insurance companies do not design the specific policy coverages that your business buys to protect itself. Insurance companies take the specifications from someone who has made recommendations about what coverages and limits you want. Then that person requests the insurance company to issue a quote or a policy to meet those specifications.

You may also want to know that an insurance agent is not a party to that insurance policy contract.

TAKEAWAYS/LESSONS LEARNED

As you now can see from the definitions, what is Covered Property and what is Property Not Covered. There are a lot of things that you have to consider and address to make sure your insurance program respond the way you want it to:
- Take a walk around your property. Take a lot of pictures of the items you see throughout your property and look inside and outside. You should also make notes as to what is underground. Remember, digital "film" is cheap, and then, later on, those same photos will help you in settlement of your loss as it is proof of what you have.
- Then assess each of your locations: what structures? Installed equipment inside & outside? Outdoor property? Property outside? Storage sheds & containers? What items do you see that are not physically part of the building's structure (signs, towers, processing equipment, air handling systems)?
- What property do you have in the open or stored in trailers, cargo containers, sheds, bins, etc.?
- Determine what leaves the property.
- Look for the property you do not own: Is it leased or rented? And if so, read your contract. Or is it customer goods?
- Ask if anyone is holding any of your property at another location. Or if you are storing any property at temporary locations. Determine if you own or lease any of those sites and how long you have done so.
- Create a Master List of all the items you identified and uncovered.
    - Split into the categories Building, BPP, and BPPO
- Determine if you want them covered or not:

- - Note for each if they need to be added to your policy using CP1415 Additional Covered Building or CP1410 Additional Property Covered.
  - Determine if you need Personal Property of Others or other coverage endorsements or even separate coverage policies to address.
  - Determine if you need coverage for any unique items or structures.
- If you do not want something covered that is typically included, then use CP1420 Additional Property Not Covered to remove it from the coverage list. Not doing so could affect how much the insurance company pays out on a claim due to the Coinsurance Clause (see Chapter 3)

Insured to Fail

Chapter 3

Why Isn't My Claim Check Big Enough?

The devil is in the details.

Although we used this idiom before, it is the perfect idiom. It refers to a catch or mysterious element **hidden in the details**, meaning that something might seem simple at first glance but will take more time and effort to complete than expected. With insurance policy language, it is not what is listed as "covered"; it is the "hidden" exclusions and limitations that are the "devil" or the problems with paying your claims.

In the very first week after Jack Kirsopp's fire, the insurance company had provided Jack a check for $100,000 towards his building and another $75,000 towards BPP and his business income loss to help pay bills and make payroll. Then, at about two weeks, the adjuster and I sat down to go through adjusting his claim and rebuilding. The insurance company had approached a contractor and received an estimated $865,000 cost to rebuild Jack's old building, based on square footage, type of material, and the floor plans from the Borough Code Enforcement files. The worksheet presented to Jack showed the policy limit as $847,000 and the Replacement Cost Estimate as $865,00. It also indicated that the insurance company reduced the $865,000 amount by 40% for "Depreciation" and handed Jack a check for $416,500 for his building.

Jack looked quite confused for a moment and then started to

become agitated quickly and shouted, *"What do you mean all I am getting is $400,000? I have almost $850,000 of coverage!"* I asked Jack to be patient and stressed that he would be receiving more money. What was needed was to allow the adjuster to fully explain the entire adjustment process, ensuring that Jack received every dollar owed him.

You do not have to do the math. Reducing the $865,000 Estimated Replacement Cost by 40% is $519,000. The insurance company then reduced it by $100,000, the amount they already provided Jack, and removed his $2,500 deductible.

After a few minutes, Jack understood that the insurance company first "settles" the claim on the Actual Cash Value of the property. If Jack rebuilt, the insurance company would reimburse him for the actual cost of rebuilding and replacing his BPP up to his policy limits. The insurance company also went through all the additional items they were going to pay for because we had customized his policy.

Going through these meetings does cause one to be nervous about how things would play out. However, there were significant coverage changes made to Jack's program to help improve his ability to rebuild and reopen. Having the advantage of being through a large fire before and because my father and grandfather, who started our family insurance agency, pass down lessons learned to me, I went into this meeting somewhat more prepared than most insurance agents would have.

Remember Jack's comment: *"David, there are days I want to deck you and days I want to hug you!"* Jack was probably in hug mode until the adjuster started to discuss how they would "settle" the business income claim, which perhaps sent Jack into "deck" mode. We will discuss this in more detail in Chapter 6 (Business Income issues).

Despite explaining the insurance adjustment process when a client reports their claim, even for small "routine" claims, Jack's response was similar to almost every other business leader's reaction the first time they go through this adjustment process for a large claim. When they receive that first check or the first communication from the insurance company about the amount of a payment they are about to receive, they are usually stunned. It is always because the first "settlement" check is much smaller than they expected.

Their response is quite understandable as a business leader's complete focus should be on growing and running their company and getting the repairs done quickly, or in the case of a large claim or disaster, getting back in business as quickly as possible. With that laser focus on minimizing the impact of the loss on their business until they see the math (aka the check and adjuster worksheet), the conversation does not fully sink in.

Once a business leader sees the math, they begin to understand the adjustment process even more. We will review that in this chapter as well. For the most part, all my clients that had their catastrophe went through this process. At first, they were in shock at what laid ahead of them. But as they saw the notes and the math laid out by the adjuster and the reopening game plan, they understood that they did have a light at the end of the proverbial long, dark tunnel. They saw that they could see an exit on the other side of this catastrophe.

However, this first review of their adjustment process, with their math laid bare in front of them, is when so many interviewed business leaders realized that they had an insurance program design problem. As you just saw from the list of Property Not Covered, at this first review, besides the shock of the smaller than expected Actual Cash Value check, this is when a business leader finds out what is and what is not covered. They learn what the insurance company expects to pay and how they will pay them for the claim after providing documentation and receipts to the insurance company.

Unfortunately, this meeting is also when the majority of the businesses that did not survive their catastrophe first realized their insurance program design failed them and can not financially afford to rebuild and reopen. Besides your policy limit for Building or Business Personal Property possibly being incorrect in the amount you need to replace or rebuild, this may be when you find out that 15-25% of the constructing cost of your new building is not covered. And you may learn what other Property Not Covered items the insurance company will not be paying. In the end, you may realize that you cannot afford to rebuild.

Sadly, this meeting was also when the remaining businesses that failed, those who reopened and eventually closed, missed some of the details that inevitably left them unsuccessful. Some may press on thinking that they can still quickly rebuild and reopening, and have customers waiting for them. Based on the statistics, many *Optimistically* begin working towards rebuilding and reopening without a clear game plan and understanding of all the issues and costs that the business will face in this rebuilding process. They will not discover some of the unknown challenges that will affect their outcome until later on, and often too late. Unfortunately, during many business leaders' attempts to recover, they reach a point that ultimately leads to the sad conclusion that they have to pull the proverbial plug. The lack of a clear plan to reopen and the lack of funds seals their fate.

However, when they reach that breaking point, many business leaders believed they could run out and get a loan and borrow all the money needed to fill the funding gap as they *had* a thriving business before the disaster. Especially since the Small Business Administration loans are too small to bridge the funding gap fully. The gap they are looking to fill in is the amount of money between the insurance proceeds they received and what they need to rebuild, purchase equipment and startup inventory, and reopen and pay for the initial payrolls until the money consistently and sufficiently flows in. Unfortunately, due to the disaster, you may no longer have business assets as collateral. Thus you may face the possibility that you will have to use personal assets as collateral or as actual cash, to pull this off. Banks will be reluctant to loan a lot of money, particularly when reviewing your insurance program response to your situation.

This was the case of John, the former machine shop owner that is now GM of a client of ours. We will discuss John more in Chapter

6. But as a preview, the bank saw the lack of proper and sufficient business income coverage after reopening and was concerned about the future cash flow of John's business and his ability to repay. Therefore they denied his loan request after he banked with them for decades.

Once again, each of the successful client's programs was not 100% perfect, and lessons learned will be discussed along the way. Two of the successful survivors did borrow money to cover the shortage in the costs of rebuilding. What helped was their actual insurance program design was able to demonstrate to the bank that the business had its cash flow protected into the future enough to survive and reopen successfully. And because of the insurance program design, the bank had confidence in the prospects of being repaid.

After reading the previous chapter, you understand why many who failed to survive had significant confusion over what is Covered Property and Property Not Covered, and what is Building, Business Personal Property, or Personal Property of Others. But these were not the only areas of confusion. As you read on, the other policy conditions below, the rest of this chapter, and the following six chapters will help you understand the other areas of their confusion and why you need to pay attention to the details and the design of your insurance program.

VALUATIONS

Valuation – This is the basis upon which the insurance company determines the ultimate cost of what was damaged and what they will payout for a covered loss. The most common valuations of a loss are Actual Cash Value, Replacement Cost, and Functional. We will also discuss Agreed Value. And they are probably not what you think they are.

ACTUAL CASH VALUE VALUATION

The default of any property policy is to pay Actual Cash Value (ACV). Most people's experience with an ACV settlement is when their personal auto was "totaled." The insurance company said that the cost of repairing your vehicle is greater than the value of the car, so they cut you a check for the "market value" or "Blue Book value" of the vehicle. In other words, what they can find is the used price of the car that is the same make, model, features, and similar mileage.

But there is no Blue Book for property. You may find used property online, such as used mobile equipment and machinery, but sometimes that equipment needs to be repaired before it is usable.

So how does the **CP0010 Building and Personal Property Coverage Form** insurance policy define ACV? The problem is, it does not.

> We will determine the value of Covered Property in the event of loss or damage as follows:
> a. At actual cash value as of the time of loss or damage, except as provided below...

Actual Cash Value is commonly referred to by insurance industry personnel as *Replacement Cost Less Depreciation* as the ISO policy conditions go on later to describe replacement cost as:

> Replacement Cost (without deduction for depreciation) replaces Actual Cash Value in the Valuation Loss Condition of this Coverage Form.

But ACV is not clearly defined, and neither is depreciation. Some states have defined ACV laws, but most do not. Sometimes insurance companies apply Accounting Depreciation practices to the calculation. Other times, the insurance company pours over the documentation about how well a building or piece of equipment was maintained to determine how much its life expectancy had passed or how much it had deteriorated when selecting the final ACV settlement amount.

It seems that the final ACV valuation is a negotiation when the latter approach is used for the final valuation used for your loss. One takeaway from this is that you need to maintain and protect your purchase and maintenance records if you want to maximize your ACV valuation. Otherwise, the insurance company may assume that the "wear and tear" and depreciation are more significant than you think.

As you can see from the meeting Jack when the insurance company handed Jack the smaller than expected check, insurance companies will settle the claim on an ACV basis first. They will pay you the total ACV amount as soon as it is determined. This is all you will receive unless you have designed your insurance program with one of the other valuations: Replacement Cost, Agreed Value, or Functional Replacement Cost. We will explain each of these in detail here as well.

The policy does provide some additional terms for valuation at the time of the claim. First of all, if the Limit of Insurance for Building satisfies the Additional Condition, Coinsurance (described later) and the cost to repair or replace the damaged building property is $2,500 or less. In this instance, the insurance company will pay the cost of repairs or replacement. In other words, the damage amount is so small that the insurance company does not want to take the time (or cost as time is money) of calculating ACV or depreciation.

However, the property insurance policy says that insurance companies will settle certain types of property on an ACV basis even with these small claims. These are the types of items settled at ACV, even when attached to the building: awnings or floor coverings; appliances for refrigerating, ventilating, cooking, dishwashing, or laundering; or outdoor equipment or furniture.

Under the ACV descriptions, ISO does help a business by valuing "Stock" that you have sold but not delivered at the selling price (less discounts and expenses you otherwise would have had).

However, if you have unsold finished goods, they will be valued at ACV. Therefore, you must add either the **CP9930 Manufacturer's Selling Price (Finished "Stock" Only), CP9905 Distilled Spirits and Wines Market Value,** or **CP9931 Market Value Stock endorsement**. Otherwise, you will forever lose the difference in value between ACV and your cost of selling.

You may be thinking you have Business Income coverage, so you may be inclined to believe you do not need to worry about that. However, you will see when we address Business Income in Chapter 6 that you need to address the loss of income for completed but unsold goods on your property coverage.

Your glass will be valued at the cost of replacement with safety-glazing material if required by law.

The form discusses the valuation of Tenants' Improvements and Betterments, but we will discuss this in Chapter 9.

REPLACEMENT COST VALUATION

Believe it or not, there is a lot of confusion surrounding the term Replacement Cost. In the policy, Replacement Cost (RC) valuation is simply defined as "Replacement Cost (without deduction for depreciation)." However, the following does clarify what it means:

The insurance company will not pay more for loss or damage on a replacement cost basis than the **least** of **(1), (2)** or **(3)**, subject to **f.** below:

(1) The Limit of Insurance applicable to the lost or damaged property;

(2) The cost to replace the lost or damaged property with other property:
   a. Of comparable material and quality; and
   b. Used for the same purpose; or

(3) The amount actually spent that is necessary to repair or replace the lost or damaged property.

> (6) The cost of repair or replacement does not include the increased cost attributable to enforcement of or compliance with any ordinance or law regulating the construction, use or repair of any property.

In other words, they will replace what you had with something comparable. If you have a brick building with a wooden joisted roof and asphalt shingles, that is what you get. However, suppose you build using an all-metal building structure because it is quicker and less expensive. In that case, the insurance company will only pay for the lower cost of replacing the block/wood building with the metal building of the same square footage. If you want to build bigger, even if the larger building costs less than the original brick/wood building, it does not matter; the insurance company will pay out the *lesser* amount.

In discussions with business owners about what they would do should they have a catastrophic disaster, some will say that they would *"take the money and run!"* This is usually when the business owner is near or past "retirement age" and may not have any heirs to pass the business onto, so they do not want to go through the aggravation of rebuilding and reopening when they would eventually want to sell shortly after that. However, when asked if they would like to have rental income when they are retired, their eyebrows rise in curiosity.

If they want to do this, by designing the policy to rebuild their build to today's code, they can see that they can easily rent the building out for above market value. The only caveat, the tenant must be similar in operations as the policy states that it must be "Used for the same purpose."

On the other hand, many business owners have separate corporations or LLCs that own the building they occupy. In that case, the building's purpose is a rental building, so renting it out to others is the same purpose, even if they are not in the same business as you.

However, in either case, you should discuss that with the

insurance company beforehand to eliminate pushback should a disaster happen.

Replacement Cost Valuation does not apply to personal property of others; contents of a residence; works of art, antiques or rare articles, including etchings, pictures, statuary, marbles, bronzes, porcelains, and bric-a-brac; or "Stock," unless the "Including Stock" option is shown in the Declarations.

The form also clarifies that for Replacement Cost Optional Coverage, your tenants' improvements and betterments are not considered the personal property of others. Personal property of others is usually settled on an Actual Cash Value basis.

You may initially decide to claim for loss or damage covered by your insurance policy on an Actual Cash Value basis instead of on a replacement cost basis. If you elect to have loss or damage settled on an actual cash value basis, you may later still make a claim for the Replacement Cost Valuation. This Optional Coverage provides the option of later choosing the Replacement Cost valuation only if you notify the insurance company of your intent to rebuild within 180 days after the loss or damage.

It is recommended that you notify the insurance company in writing that you intend to rebuild and request the Replacement Cost Valuation before the 180-day mark post-disaster if you have not started rebuilding. Doing so will preserve your right to rebuild and receive the Replacement Cost valuation later on.

During the discussions about what business leaders intend to do post-disaster, some business leaders would want to build at a new location as their location has constraints as to being the most efficient for them. Others have said that they want to move due to reducing property taxes or more accessible access to the workforce or transportation. The policy does state that if you rebuild at a new location, the amount the insurance company will pay is limited to the cost which would have been incurred if the destroyed building had been rebuilt at the original premises.

Ordinance or Law Issue

> (6) The cost of repair or replacement does not include the increased cost attributable to enforcement of or compliance with any ordinance or law regulating the construction, use or repair of any property.

This policy limitation is effectively an exclusion and creates considerable confusion. Because of this clause, there are coverage issues when you rebuild or replace your property, and you must meet current building code requirements. We will discuss ordinance, law, building codes, etc., in more detail in Chapter 4.

Between this ordinance or law clause and the "lesser of three options" we discussed before, you may realize that Replacement Cost does not mean the insurance company will pay for the total cost of a brand-new building. It does not mean they will pay for new state-of-the-art equipment to replace decades-old machinery. This limitation clearly means Replacement Cost will pay for reconstructing the identical building that existed before the disaster, with new materials, or to replace your equipment with something as close to the original as possible.

In other words, Replacement Cost will pay for the property *as was* and not *what it needs to be* (or you want it to be), subject to the coverage limit on the policy and any other terms and conditions in the policy.

However, to clarify, the policy does provide a small amount of Ordinance or Law Coverage for each described building in the policy. It provides for the lesser of $10,000 or 5% of the Limit of Insurance applicable to that building. This addresses only minor Ordinance or Law issues, nowhere near what you may need to rebuild an entire facility. Plus, it applies to building only, so no equipment updates. It also does not provide any coverage or money to pay for the additional costs to comply with any changes in building codes, laws, etc., that are put in place after the disaster.

Because of this, you should do some leg work and investigate what codes, ordinances, and laws you will need to comply with the repair of your building or construction of a new building. Please note that if your building is damaged enough, you may lose its "grandfathering" and become subject to repairing or rebuilding under the new building construction rules.

There was a significant number of Ordinance or Law issues with Jack's situation. We mentioned that Jack had to have a sprinklered spray booth, and the new one cost $350,000. However, in the Ordinance or Law Chapter, we will discuss how Jack needed $578,000 to bring his new building up to code.

AGREED VALUE OPTIONAL COVERAGE

Notice the section header says Agreed Value *Optional Coverage* and not Agreed Value *Valuation*. Agreed Value is a little bit of a misnomer. It is not a separately defined valuation. It does not mean that the insurance company agrees to pay you the total Agreed Value limit listed in your policy and not evaluate if the costs of repairing or rebuilding are less than the policy's limit.

Agreed Value Option simply removes the Additional Condition of Coinsurance, so it does not apply to any Covered Property to which the Agreed Value Optional Coverage applies on the declaration page. The Agreed Values Option "states that the insurance will pay no more for loss of or damage to that property than the proportion that the Limit of Insurance under this Coverage Part for the property bears to the Agreed Value shown for it in the Declarations." In other words, if the valuation clause is ACV, they will pay the same depreciated value percentage. If RC, then they will pay replacement cost valuation. All Agreed Value does is remove the Coinsurance Clause.

COINSURANCE CLAUSE

We will take a quick pause from Valuations to discuss the Coinsurance Clause as it is misunderstood and misexplained by many insurance agents and therefore misunderstood by many business leaders.

> a. We will not pay the full amount of any loss if the value of Covered Property at the time of loss times the Coinsurance percentage shown for it in the Declarations is greater than the Limit of Insurance for the property.

You may have heard someone say that they were told they were "underinsured" after a loss and therefore did not receive what they felt that they should have received, even when they had a coverage limit greater than the amount of the loss. That is the effect of the Coinsurance Clause. When a Coinsurance percentage is shown in your Declarations, the insurance company is trying to force you to pay for enough coverage that represents the total value of your Building's or Your Business Personal Property's actual valuation, whether it is ACV or RC.

Insurance companies calculate your premium using the rough formula:

$$\text{Limit} \times \text{Rate} = \text{Premium}$$

The Rate that insurance companies charge for coverage contemplates that the overwhelming majority of losses will be small. As a business leader, you take on risks every day you are in business, so you may want to gamble and assume that any claim will be smaller than a fully catastrophic total loss. Therefore, you feel that you should only purchase a smaller limit of coverage and risk not being paid for the total loss.

However, insurance companies factor into their rates that they will still have to pay for a certain amount of more minor claims, and if you are not insuring 100% of your building, they are not receiving 100% of the premium that they need even for the small claims.

Therefore, ISO placed the Coinsurance Clause as a mechanism to force you to insure the total value or become Co-Insured with the insurance company and participate in the smaller claims.

The percentage of the claim that the insurance company pays is not the Coinsurance Percentage on the policy, as some agents state.

For example, the percentage is not where $100,000 fire and 80% Coinsurance Clause would cause the insurance company to pay 80% or $80,000. It is a minimum insurance requirement. If you meet the requirement, your claim will be paid in full; if you do not, a formula will determine the percentage amount the insurance company will pay.

In April 2020, just after COVID-19 started, an owner of a hotel that was forced to cease operations due to the virus wanted to reduce his premiums to conserve cash. From March through June 2020, this was a frequent topic with business leaders. The owner was also going to take advantage of what he saw as a prolonged shutdown to make some improvements that would take nine to 12 months to be completed.

During the conversation on ways to cut costs, the owner steered the conversation to "stripping the policy down," as he put it. However, there were first things that reduced the premium but did not affect coverage. He did this by taking his general liability rating basis to $0 revenue and his workers compensation to $40,000 of payroll, the payroll of the maintenance person "only." He was willing to pay a potentially large premium audit bill if the actual sales/revenue and payroll were higher than what they were changed to, as this meant the hotel was open and operating. These were "rating basis" premium changes and not coverage changes.

The owner then shifted to coverage changes. The owner said he would send the registration plates back to the state for the two hotel shuttles to remove those vehicles' coverage. The owner was willing to risk the damage to the shuttle should something happen while they were parked in the parking garage. As there were no plates and the keys were locked in his safe at his home, he felt little risk of something happening and did not want to insure them.

But then the owner wanted to reduce his building insurance limit from $18,000,000 to $5,000,000 as that was the amount of the loan he had outstanding, and that limit "would satisfy the bank." He believed that nothing would happen since the building had a sprinkler system and was an all-concrete block and steel building. He certainly did not contemplate the possibility of his maintenance person starting an $840,000 fire while making lunch in the kitchen as he proceeded to deep fry some French Fries while the fire suppression system was turned off due to the renovations.

We will go through the scenario that would have played out if the business leader had changed the limit on his policy. And no, the insurance company would not add Agreed Value to the policy at a $5,000,000 limit.

> a. We will not pay the full amount of any loss if the value of Covered Property at the time of loss times the Coinsurance percentage shown for it in the Declarations is greater than the Limit of Insurance for the property.

The policy goes on to say that due to the Coinsurance Clause, the insurance company will determine the amount to be paid, using the following steps and formula:

> (1) Multiply the value of Covered Property at the time of loss by the Coinsurance percentage;
> (2) Divide the Limit of Insurance of the property by the figure determined in Step (1);
> (3) Multiply the total amount of loss, before the application of any deductible, by the figure determined in Step (2); and
> (4) Subtract the deductible from the figure determined in Step (3).
>
> We will pay the amount determined in Step **(4)** or the Limit of Insurance, whichever is less. For the remainder, you will either have to rely on other insurance or absorb the loss yourself.

When the adjuster showed up to start adjusting the fire, he brought in a contractor specializing in commercial fire restoration. While the owner, GM, and myself, and the adjuster discussed the fire and the adjustment process, the contractor measured the entire building. The contractor was doing this to create a building reproduction/rebuild cost estimate for the entire structure and not just the damaged area. (Once again, you should now be hearing the ominous, impending *"duunnn dunnn... duuuunnnn duun..."* theme music of Jaws approaching playing in your head.)

The following week, the adjuster met with everyone again and handed the insured a check for $400,000 to start the repairs. During the discussion, the adjuster pointed out that the business owner had $18,000,000 of building coverage with an 80% Coinsurance Clause and that the contractor estimated the building to be $20,618,557. The owner proceeded to exclaim, *"That's way too high!"* But when it was explained to the owner that 80% of $20,618,557 (being $16,494,845) is less than his limit of $18,000,000 and that there would be no "Coinsurance Penalty," he understood that the insurance company would have to pay 100% of the claim costs. The adjuster went on to state the same.

However, we will suppose that the building limit was changed from $18,000,000 to $5,000,000 in coverage per the business owner's request. If that was done, this is what would have happened to the claim settlement:

The RC value of the property was:	$20,618,557
The Coinsurance percentage for it is:	80%
Your Limit of Insurance for it is:	$5,000,000
The Deductible is:	$5,000
The amount of loss is:	$840,000

Step (1): $20,618,557 × 80% = $16,494,845

(the minimum amount of insurance to meet your Coinsurance requirements)

Step (2): $5,000,000 ÷ $16,494,845 = 0.303

Step (3): $840,000 × 0.303 = $254,625

Step **(4):** $254,625 − $5,000 = $249,625

In this example, the insurance company will pay no more than $249,625 for the $840,000 loss. The remaining $590,375 is not covered. In other words, the hotel owner would have to pay $590,375 as he became "Co-Insured" with the insurance company and decided to take some risk by not insuring to a limit close to the valuation value of the building. However, this fire could have done more damage, and the insured could have been out of millions of dollars in either a more significant "partial" loss or a total loss.

Be careful. Some agents will change your Coinsurance percentage to 100% and may even tell you that you are 100% covered. This subtle change in percentage tends to be overlooked by business leaders and often not explained by agents.

Moving from 80% Coinsurance to 100% Coinsurance reduces your rates and, therefore, your premiums by 10%, which makes them "more competitive." However, the net effect of a 100% Coinsurance Clause on this example would mean that when the hotel owner insured his building at $18,000,000, he would have received only $733,320 of the $840,000 ($106,680 shortage). Therefore, the perceived premium savings will yield a shocking lower claim payout if you are not 100% insured to value.

When initially insuring this hotel, Marshall-Swift estimating software generated a Replacement Cost estimate of $19,850,000. The building owner said that it was an all-concrete and block building and that it would not be destroyed and wanted to stay with $12,000,000 of coverage, the amount he initially paid for the hotel. After explaining the Coinsurance Clause, he at least agreed to allow the policy to be issued with $18,000,000, the lowest limit the insurance companies were willing to accept.

Keep in mind, the value that the insurance company uses in the Coinsurance Clause is determined at the time of the loss. If you spent $10,000,000 to build the building within the last year, when the loss occurs, it would most likely cost more to rebuild nine months or two years down the road, so a 100% Coinsurance Clause will become a problem.

It is better to give yourself a margin of error and use a 95%, 90%, or 80% Coinsurance Clause. That is unless you can negotiate to have the Agreed Value Option added to your policy.

Margin Clause

There is another big issue you must watch out for, and that is the *Star Wars*-sounding **CP1232 Margin Clause** endorsement. Many employers blanket their multiple locations, so it becomes difficult for the insurance company to use the Coinsurance Clause when calculating the combined building value compared to a single location. Therefore, it was possible to cheat on some on each insured property as you would have the policy's total limit to respond to the loss. Many business leaders and insurance agents have figured this game out, so the insurance industry created the Margin Clause to put this practice in check.

Essentially, the Margin Clause converts overall blanket limits to specific per building limits by placing a maximum on the amount payable for loss to each building and the contents for each building shown in the endorsement schedule. When you insure your property on a blanket limit for all locations, the insurance company has you sign a Statement of Values used to calculate the total blanket limit. The Margin Clause now makes the Statement of Values part of your policy. In other words, the limit for each Building or BPP on the Statement of Values is used when calculating the maximum amount that the insurance company will pay. A 110% Margin Clause means that they will pay out no more than 110% of the limit you stated on the Statement of Values. A 125% Margin would mean 125% of that location value.

When reading complete policies as part of a Coverage Analysis, insurance companies have used a 100% Margin Clause. This means they will not pay out more than the limit you placed on the Statement of Values. Doing so basically wipes out any advantage of a blanket limit. If you undervalue a location, even by accident, it could cost you significant dollars.

Therefore, it is essential to look for a Margin Clause being applied to your Blanket Property Limits. When comparing insurance company quotes, you may see the same Blanket Limit. Adding a Margin Clause does not only potentially reduces coverage, it also reduces your premium. A 105% Margin clause would lower your property premiums by 7%, and without knowing its presence, you may believe you have a "better deal" due to the lower premium. However, it could come back to haunt you when you suffer a disaster.

The Margin Clause also does not provide any relief of clerical errors. When reviewing documents as an expert witness, there was a $91,000,000 replacement cost valued building on the Statement of Values but listed at $9100000 ($9,100,000). Therefore, please be extra cautious when completing, signing, and submitting a Statement of Values to the insurance agent.

FUNCTIONAL VALUATION

Replacement Cost is the cost of repairing or rebuilding "as was" before the loss. The Coinsurance Clause means you must insure the structure on your policy to be within that percentage of the actual cost to repair or replace the "as was" structure at the time of the loss using comparable materials. The fact that you *choose* to replace with less costly materials is not contemplated in the policy language for these two items.

Therefore, it is conceivable that the combination of these two factors, *Replacement Cost* and *Coinsurance Clause*, could force you to insure your building on your policy at a limit that does not make financial sense. If you did not do so, your risk is being penalized on a claim that is not a total loss. For example, business leaders have purchased former steel manufacturing plants constructed with hand-made decorative brick, over-engineered steel, massively high ceilings, etc. Then others have purchased Great Depression-era or previously built buildings and renovated them to work for them today. However, they would never rebuild the building "as was"; they would construct something that is, well, more *functional* for them. Plus, the cost of rebuilding them as they were, or replicating them to match, would be prohibitive.

There are also times that a business leader's equipment may be replaced less expensively due to the nature of its construction, manufacturing, or new technology.

If you are thinking that replacing or repairing what you have "as was" is not exactly what you would rebuild or replace with today, Functional Valuation may make sense for you. We will look at **CP0438 Functional Building Valuation** and **CP0438 Functional Personal Property Valuation Other Than Stock**. Although they sound similar, they are different.

Functional Building

When you chose to have Functional Building Valuation for your building, the endorsement does many things that would benefit a business leader when they rebuild their facility. But the requirements insurance companies ask the business leader to comply with and provide, plus the effect on your premium rates for you to use this valuation will now be discussed. First, the endorsement removes the Coinsurance Clause from the specific building described on the endorsement.

Second, if you *contract* for repair or replacement of the loss or damage to restore the building listed on the endorsement for the *same occupancy and use, within 180 days of the damage, and* unless you come to an agreement, the insurance company will pay the *least* of the following:

    a. The Limit of Insurance is listed on the endorsement that applies to the damaged building.

    b. In the event of a total loss, the cost to replace the damaged building *on the same site*, or on a different location if relocation is *required* by an ordinance or law, with a less costly building that is functionally equivalent to the damaged building;

    c. In the event of a partial loss:

        1. The cost to repair or replace the damaged portion of the building with less costly material, if available, in the

architectural style that existed before the loss or damage occurred; and
2. The amount you actually spend to demolish and clear the site of undamaged parts of the building (subject to some ordinance or law limitations).
d. The amount you actually spend:
1. That is necessary to repair or replace the lost or damaged building with less costly material if available; and
2. To demolish and clear the site of undamaged parts of the building (subject to some ordinance or law limitations)

If you do not repair or replace, the insurance company will pay the smallest of the following:
- The Limit of Insurance listed on the endorsement as applicable to the damaged building;
- The "market value" of the damaged building, exclusive of the land value, at the time of loss; or
- The amount it would cost to repair or replace the damaged building on the same site, with less costly material in the architectural style that existed before the damage occurred, less allowance for physical deterioration, and depreciation.

The policy then defines "Market Value" as the price that the property might expect to realize if offered for sale in a fair market.

Some of the advantages of this valuation are that it provides coverage for Ordinance or Law within the limit on the policy: Loss to the Undamaged Portion of the Building, Demolition Cost Coverage, and the Cost to Reconstruction in Compliance with Ordinance or Law. These items we will describe in detail in Chapter 4, but for this endorsement, the limit you must use and list on the endorsement must include at least the following:
- The cost of building your facility, including all of the necessary Ordinance or Law requirements such as, but not limited to: sprinkler systems, alarms, changes in materials, heating and ventilation requirements, foundational requirements, American with Disabilities requirements, etc.
- The cost of demolishing any undamaged, residual structure and disposing of it at an approved waste site.

You will need to make sure the limit you use as your Functional Value is greater than what you expect the cost of the new building would be to be built on a cleared, already prepared building site. And, you should add in additional costs associated with demolition and debris removal.

This form includes the costs associated with constructing a new building "as needs to be," including compliance with the ordinances or laws at the time of the loss (or endorsed to cover post-loss code changes). Because of this, insurance companies will typically require the business leaders to provide them with a written plan. The plan would detail the type, size, and materials used to what the business expects to construct as a new building with the necessary additional costs associated with clearing the site and building the facility. Therefore, it will take some effort to add this valuation endorsement to your policy.

Another thing to keep in mind is that the insurance companies will add an extra 30% to the building rate when calculating the premium as the form waives the Coinsurance provision. The insurance company will have to pay for the total cost to repair partial losses and include code issues required to be complied with even after a small loss. As we discussed, the Coinsurance Clause was created to enable the insurance company to receive enough premium to cover both catastrophic *and* partial losses. As the value you list on the Functional Valuation endorsement will be lower than the full "as was" valuation, the insurance company will collect an extra rate to offset the lower value used so that they can pay for the partial losses.

Functional Personal Property

Unlike the Functional Building, Functional Personal Property requires you to schedule the *specific items* that this will apply to, as Coinsurance would not apply to those items.

Under this valuation, if you repair or replace the item, the insurance company will pay the lesser of the following amounts:

a. The Limit of Insurance you provided and scheduled on the endorsement for the lost or damaged item(s) of personal property.
b. The cost to replace, *at the same location*, the lost or damaged item(s) of personal property with the most closely equivalent property available; or
c. The amount you actually spend that is necessary to repair or replace the lost or damaged item(s) of personal property.

Therefore, you can purchase something used or new that works for you so long as it costs the same or less than what you scheduled the item(s) for, but you must do so at the same location at the time of the loss. Functional Valuation restricts you from repairing at your original site.

If you choose not to repair or replace the item(s), the insurance company will pay the smallest of the following amounts:
a. The Limit of Insurance you provided and scheduled on the endorsement for the lost or damaged item(s) of personal property;
b. The "market value" of the lost or damaged item(s) of personal property at the time of loss; or
c. The amount it would cost to repair or replace that part of the item(s) of personal property that is lost or damaged with material of like kind and quality less allowance for physical deterioration and depreciation.

The policy then defines "Market Value" as the price that the property might expect to realize if offered for sale in a fair market. Many business leaders have older, usable equipment that they may not use the equipment very often, but they are not ready to replace the items. If damaged or destroyed, they would prefer to receive funds to purchase something better should a covered loss happen to the equipment, and therefore would be happy to receive market value for the items.

Ken Clifton, CCF Industries

Halfway through the process of rebuilding, Ken's large claims specialist adjuster for the insurance company told us that Ken's disaster was one the most complex that he had dealt with in his 40-year career.

It is hard to forget the approach and landing in snow-covered Ogdensburg, New York, across the river from Ottawa, Canada, on April 4th, 2014. I was there to conduct a risk and culture assessment of a manufacturing firm that one of my clients was purchasing. Leaving Pittsburgh at 5:30 am and 58-degrees and arriving at 10 am at the 23-degree Ogdensburg was a bit of a shock. On approach, you could see the still-frozen St Lawrence River as we turned to land. It is memorable for two reasons: one, it is not too often you get to sit in the co-pilot seat of a twin-engine propeller commuter plane; and two, for the terrible event that unfolded that day.

After landing, as everyone does, you turn on your phone during taxiing. There were almost a dozen missed calls from Ken and my office. Just as the ground crew was opening the door, my phone started to ring. It was Ken, who was about to fly back from a golf trip that had been cut short. He informed me of what just happened. As soon as the passengers were escorted into the terminal, it was necessary to quickly go to the airline desk and attempt to make arrangements to fly home that evening to meet with Ken as soon as possible. There were no available flights till the following day. As Ken was to arrive till late afternoon that day, he said to just fly back in the AM and meet with him mid-afternoon. However, the CEO of the Pennsylvania-based manufacturing conglomerate was already in Ogdensburg for the acquisition meetings. After hearing about what happened to Ken on the drive to the plant, he volunteered to cut his trip there short and drive me home late that afternoon. He even took me to the Pittsburgh airport to get my car, where we arrived close to midnight.

Ken had turned a hobby into a successful, growing business. He started in 1995 making custom cabinetry while working from his family's garage. Due to Ken's keen attention to detail and the quality of his work, his reputation was becoming well known, and his business began to grow quickly. Ken then moved to a new location for a few years but quickly outgrew it and then made the jump to his current location in Apollo, Pennsylvania. At the time, Ken had grown to a 33-employee operation in a 19,000 square foot facility. You can tell it was a great place to work as the employees worked side by side through the reconstruction and reopening process. But we are getting a little ahead of ourselves.

Pulling up to Ken's plant at 8 am the next day, you could see that the entire facility was still smoking. A fire truck and crew were winding up their hoses as they watched to see if the fire would flare-up. Standing off to the side were Ken and his brother, Dale.

No sooner did the conversation start when a car pulled up, and a gentleman got out, put on a hardhat and reflective vest, and proceeded to go under the "Police/Caution" tape and into the carnage. Ken had to ask him who he was because it was a protected site at the time, and no one other than the fire marshal and their staff were allowed to go in.

Ken had been waiting for the local security person to return from having to go to the restroom down the street as the closest open place was a mile down the road.

It turns out the gentleman was an OSHA inspector who saw the fire on the news the night before. He decided to inspect when he saw one of Ken's employees talking to the TV reporter, commenting that it must have gone up quickly due to the amount of chemicals they had in the building. Of course, the fire had probably nothing to do with all of the wood and sawdust that a wood custom, dovetail draw box manufacturer would have on-site (hopefully, you caught the sarcasm.)

The OSHA inspector proceeded to tell us that he needed to know how much flammable liquids and chemicals they were storing and if Ken was storing them properly or improperly. He continued to describe the purpose of his inspection, but the discussion was about to be cut short when he said he was also "to see if there's an *opportunity* to assess a fine or penalty." Very quickly, Dale grabbed his brother and pulled him away. The separation allowed me to explain to the inspector that they were not going to answer any questions at this time and that he was not allowed into the site until the fire marshal released it. If he did enter, we were instructed to call the police as it was a protected site.

What had transpired was pretty interesting. When we initially met Ken, he was concerned about employees becoming injured, especially with the power equipment in his facility. Ken engaged us eight months before the fire to improve his safety procedures. Fortunately, one of which was an evacuation plan. Ken's fire alarm system did not have any local audible alarm. As part of their new evacuation plan, our safety professional placed air-compressed horns throughout the facility mounted on the wall so employees could use them to alert everyone if there was a fire.

Well, at one point that morning, the horn went off. Marianne, the office manager, explained that she initially wondered who decided to have yet another evacuation drill as they had just installed the plan three weeks before and had already run four drills. Marianne proceeded to walk out to the door to the rendezvous site, and she saw everybody running, not walking to it. She turned and saw all the smoke billowing from the facility.

The forensics showed it was not one big thing that went wrong that caused the catastrophic fire, but many little things. Their procedure was to sweep up in the morning to collect any dust that settled on the floor and onto the equipment overnight before they turned on the dust collection system and proceeded to work.

One of an employee's duties is to use an air hose from the compress to blow off the excess varnish from the metal filters from the air filtration system in the spray booth. This involves taking the filters down, placing them on the table, and blowing them off.

However, the dust collection system had already been turned on. That was because an employee who did not finish a project the day before decided to show up early that morning to start.

The problem started when the employee did not ground himself as he should have. As a result of this oversight, an electrostatic discharge or spark went from the air nozzle to the metal screen filter and caused the screen to catch fire. There was quite a bit of varnish and loosened particles on the filter to add fuel to the fire.

The employee quickly left the spray booth to grab a fire extinguisher but left the door open. As he was heading back, the fire suppression system, much like a huge ABC fire extinguisher mounted to the roof of the spray booth, discharged improperly. Only one suppression head in the back of the booth fired, and it came out like a cake with extraordinarily little powder. This created a rush of air that caused the burning sparks to fly off the screen and out of the booth, and the dust collection system quickly sucked in the burning particles.

Once the sparks were in the dust collection system, they ignited all of the dust in the ducts of the dust collection system. The Fire Marshall believes that the rapid expansion of heated air cracked open the dust collection duct pipes that went through the building's attic, allowing the fire to escape the metal duct. Rather than having the particles sucked into the outside vacuum system designed to suppress any fire inside it, the escaping burning particles caused the timbers and joists of the roof and ceiling to catch fire.

In less than 10 minutes from the ignition spark, the fire was out of control, and the roofline started collapsing.

During the Coverage Analysis, it was necessary to work with Ken to estimate the building's Replacement Cost valuation limit and add in for the additional covered property needing to be included in the building's insurance limit. As part of the Additional Covered Building, the foundations (including one for the CNC - Computer Numerical Control - laser machine and one for the cyclone vacuum outside), spray booth, and all of the dust collection system equipment and ductwork were included in the definition of a building.

With all of the items, Ken's building limit went from $1,330,000 to $2,100,000.

There was a need to change the business income and extra expense limit to be much more substantial and closer to what he needed, as you will see in Chapter 6 relating to business income issues.

There was a significant amount of Ordinance or Law issues. Still, as you will see in Chapter 4, things went unaddressed during the analysis, which became compounded when Ken decided to increase the size of his building to accommodate the growth he was expecting to regain. As mentioned before, every claim has a lesson to be learned.

Unfortunately, even after asking Ken if the limit was correct, he did not feel a need to increase the amount of BPP. As previously mentioned, no catastrophic claim ever goes perfectly.

What was learned from Ken's unfortunate fire and looking back at the other claims was that business leaders know what they have paid for what they own, or in the case of Ken, all the equipment in his shop. The problem is that business leaders do not necessarily know what it will cost to replace everything at today's prices. Also, business leaders may buy equipment used or at auction and do not know the total cost of purchasing that same piece of equipment new from the manufacturer. This led Ken into thinking his $1,600,000 of BPP coverage would be more than enough to replace everything, as he felt he had $1,400,000 to $1,500,000 in equipment and some inventory. In the end, Ken needed closer to $1,900,000 to $2,000,000 in funds to replace his equipment.

Based on my hobby, which is woodworking, I suspected that Ken might need more BPP limits and tried to discuss that with him. As I recently bought a SawStop table saw similar to Ken's ones in his facility, Ken said he paid $2,600 for his "newest" table saw. While researching the various models a few months prior, the local store had Ken's comparable unit for sale at $4,450. When you multiply that out over the number of units Ken had and then factored the same concept over all the other equipment he acquired since 1995, the difference can add up to be a significant dollar amount. It turned out to be much more than he was allocating in his estimate to start the policy.

Moving forward, we make the following recommendation to business leaders. Instead of just creating your Excel spreadsheet of equipment you buy and give it to your accountant for the *Depreciation Schedule* for tax purposes, you should take that schedule and make an *Appreciation Schedule*. You take the list of your stuff, enter the date you bought it, and apply the inflationary percentage each year so that you are closer to the total BPP limit you will need. Then in the future, you would periodically revalue your items with more reliable data, enter that new valuation date into your spreadsheet, and apply the inflation amount from that point.

Sometimes, using this kind of documentation is needed to get an insurance company to agree to use Agreed Value Coverage.

Debris Removal

This chapter has focused on the types of valuations and the limit of insurance you need based upon the valuation you choose to have for your covered property. However, there is one more wrinkle, and that is the cost to remove debris from your site after a disaster. Think about it. You will have to pay a contractor to scoop up all the damaged property, place it into dumpsters, have the dumpsters hauled to a landfill, and then pay the landfill to accept and dispose of the materials. This becomes expensive.

With any limit you chose for your covered property, you need to factor in some amount for Debris Removal. The most the insurance company will pay for the total of direct physical loss or damage *plus* debris removal expense is the Limit of Insurance applicable to the Covered Property that has sustained loss or damage. In other words, the most they will pay for the covered property is the limit on the declaration page.

However, there are two caveats to Debris Removal. First, the insurance company's will pay for debris removal expense is limited to 25% of the direct physical loss or damage to the Covered Property. Second, they include an additional $25,000 for debris removal expenses. However, this $25,000 is for each location and any one occurrence of physical loss or damage to Covered Property. In other words, the 25% *is not* in addition to your building limit. However, the $25,000 *is* in addition to your policy limit. It is essential to pay attention to include an additional amount to your limit of covered property as the removal and disposal of Ken's building, and BPP was $122,000.

Also, Debris Removal does not apply to costs to:
- Remove debris off property that is not insured under this policy or property in your possession that is not Covered Property;

- Remove debris of property owned by or leased to the landlord of the building where your described premises are located, unless you have a contractual responsibility to insure such property and it is insured under this policy;
- Remove any property that is Property Not Covered, including property addressed under the Outdoor Property Coverage Extension;
- Remove property of others of a type that would not be Covered Property under this Coverage Form;
- Remove deposits of mud or earth from the grounds of the described premises;
- Extract "pollutants" from land or water; or
- Remove, restore or replace polluted land or water.

In other words, if they are not insuring it, they will not pay to remove it.

The last three are important to pay attention to as after water is used to extinguish the fire, it is common for mud to cover the grounds of your facility and your neighbors. If the water causes pollutants to become washed into the ground, or neighboring streams or property, you may need to address this issue with a pollution liability policy.

MYTH BUSTING...

Over my 30-plus years of providing Risk Management and Insurance Program Design for business leaders, a common myth that many business leaders are lead to believe, or are allowed to believe incorrectly, is related to Umbrella Policies. The myth is that an Umbrella Policy provides excess coverage and fills in the "gaps" over ALL your insurance policies, including your property policy. Unfortunately, Umbrella Policies are liability policies and only provide excess over the liability policies that you request, and the insurance company accepts and specifically describes in the Schedule of Underlying Policies and Coverages. Therefore, your property coverage limits must be enough to take care of your specific loss, all while meeting the terms and conditions of your policies that may limit any such coverage payout. Your umbrella policy will not help you.

EXPECT THE UNEXPECTED...

Murphy's Law states: *If anything can go wrong, it will.*

Business owners, being risk-takers, do not want to pay more for their insurance than they must as they tend to believe that they will not need it. Many of the interviewed business leaders argued with their agents over the value used for their building(s) as they knew the higher the value, the more they would pay in insurance. However, when their disaster struck, they wanted every dollar that they could find in coverage.

We discussed adding in an additional coverage limit for the Debris Removal costs paid within your building and business personal property coverage limits. What you may not think about is when there is a significant, widespread disaster event that causes material or labor shortages. When there is a shortage, the law of supply and demand will cause prices to go up significantly. This is seen in areas affected by a hurricane, wildfire, tornado, or flooding. Following Hurricane Sandy, several of the business leaders talked about delays in hiring contractors to repair or rebuild buildings. Due to the extra costs of shipping materials into the area from other parts of the country, there was a significant increase in building material costs.

As the Coinsurance Clause is calculated at the time of the actual event or loss, the effect of surging material and labor costs usually does not play into the Coinsurance Calculation after the disaster. When you go to rebuild, the problem becomes the limit on your policy is still the most the insurance company will pay for rebuilding, replacing, or repairing your building and equipment. If there was a surge in material costs, your property policy fails to factor in the increase in material costs. You would need to request your agent to increase your policy limits accordingly.

ISO does have an endorsement **CP0409 – Increase in Rebuilding Expenses Following Disaster**, where you can choose a percentage of your building coverage limit to be an additional coverage limit available for construction cost spikes. Suppose you choose a 25% limit on the endorsement, and you have a $1,000,000 building, you would have an additional $250,000 available for the construction cost price spike when a hurricane strikes.

The endorsement allows 20% of your additional amount can be used for Debris Removal and Increased Cost of Construction from ordinances or laws. In this example, you can use up to $50,000 (20%) for Debris Removal and $50,000 for the Increased Cost of Construction. However, any amount used for Debris Removal and Increased Cost of Construction come out of your additional amount and are not in addition to it. If you use $25,000 for Debris Removal and $50,000 for the Increased Cost of Construction, you would have $175,000 to cover the additional construction costs due to the Hurricane.

The declared disaster that causes the construction costs to increase must also be a covered cause of loss in your policy. Therefore, you will most likely need flood coverage on your policy when construction costs spike from a hurricane when you rebuild from the tornado that destroys your building.

A declared state or federal disaster must be the direct cause of your construction cost surge, and the disaster must occur in a close timeframe to your catastrophe. The question will become, suppose your fire is five months after the hurricane occurred, will the insurance company state this endorsement will still apply or not? It is conceivable that an insurance company might determine you had ample time to increase the limit on your policy to allow for the new, higher replacement costs, and therefore, this endorsement no longer applies. At some point, the new higher prices after a large disaster become a new reality: when costs do not go down to pre-disaster costs. When this occurs, you will need to insure to higher coverage limits that amount before your claim occurs.

The problem becomes when large-scale material cost increases are unexpected or inflationary and not disaster-related. The impact of COVID-19 drove demand up for construction materials, while it also negatively affected manufacturing and distribution of supplies. The pandemic led to a 56% increase in lumber costs and a 20-25% overall increase in raw materials.[13] The pandemic also affected supplies of raw materials and machinery. Because of this, many businesses became at risk by not having enough property limits or enough business income coverage due to delays the pandemic caused in rebuilding or reacquiring BPP. More on this in Chapter 6.

Therefore, if you can afford some extra premium, you may want to increase the limits on your policy to allow for unexpected material and labor surges beyond the inflation guard limit in your policy. Otherwise, when material and labor costs escalate, you will have to hope you remember to increase your policy limits before something happens to your property, regardless of its reasons.

TAKEAWAYS/LESSONS LEARNED

Insurance is based on the law of large numbers. Every year many businesses have to pay premiums for property coverage so that the insurance companies can afford to pay the claims of those few that have property claims that year. Insurance companies also must collect premiums to pay for small to large claims to catastrophic claims.

Everyone understands that insurance companies will only pay what they are contractually obligated to pay, or as some put it, the least that they legally must pay. And the insurance industry designs the coverage forms that are used.

As you are now seeing, you must pay attention to your property limits and valuation need when the insurance agent designs your insurance program. It would help if you overstated your limits some to cover additional costs associated with clearing the old building and constructing the new one as those costs are covered but come out of your property insurance limits. It would also help if you thought about what you want your business to look like on the other

---

[13] https://ccorpinsights.com/domestic-materials/

side of a disaster and have that vision planned in advance so that your policy can adequately respond to your rebuilding and reopening desires.

As you can see from the Claim Adjustment Process, you need to pay attention to what valuation you chose to have on the policy and what Coinsurance percentage is used should you not receive Agreed Value. And do not allow someone to let you believe 100% Coinsurance is the same as Agreed Value. You should also decide whether you should use an inflation guard percentage in your policy valuation and factor in additional limits available for disasters that affect large areas.

- Take the Master List of all the items you identified and uncovered.
- Determine if there are items that you may want to handle separately, specifically as ACV or Market instead of RC.
    - Then identify if those items or buildings should have a Functional Valuation.
- Determine the value for each.
    - For RC, try to determine the cost to purchase new, or take the original value and date purchased, and use a formula to increase it for inflation.
- Separate the special items out
- Tally the Building, BPP, and PPO values, and separately list the items for Functional Valuation.
- For Building & BPP, specialized companies can help businesses determine ACV, RC, or Functional Values needed to be more adequately insured. One of the services we commonly see is Industrial Appraisal Services, but many others are out there.

Chapter 4

To Rebuild, or Not to Rebuild? That is the Question…

You briefly met John back in the Introduction. John was the prior machine shop owner that became the GM of another machine shop. John became one of those affected by the scary failure statistic when he was forced to sell the business 16 months after his grand reopening.

John conveyed his very tragic story over an hour and a half lunch. John's 47-employee operation in southwest Pennsylvania that he built from scratch over 32 years, a business that enabled him to put three children through college, and had two of them working there, and that he was planning on perpetuating the business to his children; that business was gone. You heard how John poured in his life savings, even sold his family vacation home on Hilton Head Island for more cash, all to save his business for his family. With no family business to support them, each family member had to find new career paths. The only thing John, his wife, and his children had left was the building he was renting to the new machine shop owner, albeit at a lower than typical market monthly rents.

John went on to provide the details of how an electrical short in one of his CNC machines apparently ignited an oil-mist collector, and there possibly could have been some chips and dust from machined magnesium in that machine at the time, creating a small explosion that generated a spreading fire throughout the non-sprinklered shop. It is believed that the machinist left the machine on after leaving for a dentist appointment and did not return as expected. Therefore no one noticed it had not been powered down.

During that lunch, John commented about several things that caused him to pour his life savings into his business to rebuild and reopen:

First, for his 50,000 square foot facility, he was about $375,000 short of funds for rebuilding his building. He had not been aware that they should potentially address several issues under Property Not Covered: mainly the building and machinery foundations and groundwork.

Second, issues were surrounding his Business Income Coverage, one of which was waiting for a little over four months to be able to have access to the site due to an ongoing "arson" investigation that was eventually dropped. The cause of the fire was not easily determined, and the questions relating to possible accelerants in the machine were put to rest. The investigators did not initially understand that magnesium dust and chips are highly flammable, not to mention borderline explosive. More of the story will be addressed in Chapter 6.

Third, there was a significant shortfall relating to the additional costs to construct the new building to current codes. Unfortunately, John was not able to get a code variance when rebuilding. When John outgrew his prior facility, he was "lucky" to find an existing building that previously housed a wholesale distributor recently moved to a larger facility. This saved him the time and aggravation of building a new facility, and being less costly to acquire this location than to build a new building was financially beneficial.

The problem became that the repurposed facility was not sprinklered; therefore, adding a sprinkler system would cost almost $500,000 by itself. With changes due to ADA, the new facility access ramps and bathroom layouts added about $40,000 to the building. There were some other items relating to the building and exhaust systems, but it was a little over $600,000 in code-related changes that he had to find a way to fund when all was said and done. As a result, John had to borrow money and use personal cash to cover the $975,000 shortage that his insurance program design had left him. That shortage was 26% of his costs for the new building.

Not to be redundant, but for redundancy's sake, and the fact that repetition is an excellent way to learn, you should take the time to understand *what is* and *what is not* covered in your policy coverage forms. Do not simply focus on the main covered property headers are of Building, BPP of PPO. Look at the limitations, or "exclusions," in all insurance policies.

Once again, highlighting that the **CP0010 Building and Personal Property Coverage Form** states that Replacement Cost will repair or replace your building *as was* and not *as needs to be*. If the paraphrased "we are not going to pay for code issues" limitation in the Building and Personal Property Coverage Form was not clear enough for you to understand the insurance industry does not pay for code issues. The insurance industry used redundant redundancy to further explain it by placing Ordinance or Law as the first exclusion in the **CP1030 Causes of Loss – SPECIAL Form**.

Welcome to the Department of Redundancy Department.

Ralph Sitterson, the current Vice President of Loss Management at the Keystone Insurers Group and former Senior Vice President of Claims for the W. R. Berkley Mid Atlantic Insurance Group, saw thousands of property claims over his distinguished career. Ralph stressed that "the impact of the broad exclusions surrounding Ordinance or Laws are a significant reason why so many businesses struggle to rebuild their facilities. Many business owners believe that they are 'grandfathered' and do not realize that all bets are off after a loss. They can be facing tens to hundreds of thousands of dollars, to even millions given their situations, and it does not take a total loss to trigger a significant code loss."

Like John, when already facing the challenge of rebuilding their facility, many business leaders are surprised to learn that 15% – 30%, or more, of their new building's costs are not covered. During your diaster's insurance adjustment process meeting is not a good time to find this out. There are significant costs necessary to bring a new building "up to code" that are either not covered or significantly underinsured by their insurance program design. Because of these limitations and exclusions, you need to understand what is necessary to bring your facility up to the current code should you ever have a disaster. However, once you have done so, the insurance industry does provide endorsements to allow you to purchase what you need.

The three ISO endorsements are **CP0405 Ordinance of Law Coverage**, **CP1531 Ordinance or Law – Increased Period of Restoration**, and **CP0426 Ordinance or Law Coverage for Tenant's Interest in Improvements and Betterments**.

During a Coverage Analysis, when discussing what a business leader intends to do post-disaster, it is necessary to determine what is necessary to meet ordinances or laws should a business want to rebuild and reopen. Often during this analysis, a business leader may state that they have Ordinance or Law coverage. This is true, in essence, as there is some coverage in the **CP0010 Building and Personal Property Coverage Form** that provides the lesser of $10,000 or 5% of the Limit of Insurance applicable to that building to pay for code issues. It may be true as many insurance companies have "Property Enhancement Endorsements," which provide some coverage, maybe $10,000, $50,000, or $100,000. Clearly, these are token amounts of coverage meant to make you feel comfortable with your insurance program. Whereas so many businesses fail despite being insured, this is proof that most Enhancement Endorsements will tend to fall drastically short of what you *actually* need. Not only that, but your Enhancement Endorsement may also fail to address all the Ordinance or Law issues that you will face.

Tony Vecchio, Tony's Auto Care

On Sunday, June 10th, 2004, Tony Vecchio, the owner of an eight-employee operation in Ruffs Dale, Pennsylvania, was sitting in a little restaurant across the street from his repair facility when the waitress rain over and said, "Tony, your building has smoke pouring out of it!"

It seems a friend of Tony had his vehicle failed inspection Saturday, and he needed his car as quickly as possible so he could drive 30 miles down the PA Turnpike to a construction job he was working on Monday. To help his friend out, Tony came in Sunday morning to weld a patch to cover a hole underneath the floor of the pickup truck. After welding a new plate onto the bottom of the pickup, the last thing needed so that the vehicle would be able to pass inspection, Tony waited and performed his 45-minute flash watch before he went to grab some lunch across the street. A flash watch is required to make sure that there are no hidden, smoldering fire issues occurring.

Half an hour later, the waitress came running to Tony, yelling that smoke was pouring out of his building. The fire company could get the fire under control, but not before the roof fell in and bowed the front wall out and caused several courses of cement block to fall to the ground.

Fortunately for Tony, he was able to find an auto repair facility not even half a mile down the street that had recently shut down. Even the vehicle lifts were still in that building. Although it was only two-thirds the size he needed, it enabled him to start working with the tool and equipment sales representatives. Luckily, Tony had all the tools and equipment he required within three weeks. The insurance adjuster mentioned that this was one of the quickest temporary location re-opening he had ever seen.

Tony was friends with another repair garage nearby that would perform Tony's state vehicle inspections until Tony got his inspection license approved at his new operations. All told, although he was not able to return to his building for almost nine and a half months, the claim did not go completely smooth.

Remember in the **ISO CP0010 Building and Personal Property Coverage Form,** the main sentence that drives everything is:

A. **Coverage** - We will pay for **direct physical loss** of or damage to **Covered Property** at the **premises described in the Declarations** caused by or resulting **from any <u>Covered Cause of Loss</u>**.

In the **CP1030 Causes of Loss -Special Form**, the policy form starts out defining Covered Cause of Loss:

> When Special is shown in the Declarations, Covered Causes of Loss means direct physical loss unless the loss is excluded or limited in this policy.

Then under Exclusions:

> We will not pay for loss or damage caused directly or indirectly by any of the following. Such loss or damage is excluded regardless of any other cause or event that contributes concurrently or in any sequence to the loss: **a. Ordinance Or Law.**

As previously mentioned, the very first exclusion is ***Ordinance Or Law***, and it is pretty broad. The exclusion clearly states that the policy does not cover anything regarding the enforcement of, or compliance with, any ordinance or law that regulates the construction, use, or repair of any property. This exclusion pertains to:
- The requirement to tear down any property,
- The cost of removing debris is not covered,
- Whether the loss results from an ordinance or law that is enforced even if the property has not been damaged,
- The increased costs incurred to comply with an ordinance or law in the course of construction, repair, renovation, remodeling, or demolition of property, or removal of its debris, following a physical loss to that property.
    - This one is focused on bringing any covered property "up to code" as well as any delays in construction due to the additional time needed to repair or replace the covered property to the current code requirements (Business Income issue)

In Tony's restoration, the building's front wall was damaged to the point that it would have to be reconstructed. Add that to the damage to the roof, and the combination of these two led the local code enforcement officer to explain to Tony that he would have to tear down and rebuild the entire building. In addition, during the reconstruction process, the movement of the front wall cracked the front foundation, and therefore the whole structure would have to be rebuilt from the ground up. Therefore, looking at the Ordinance or Law exclusion, you can see that the costs to tear down and dispose of the undamaged porting of the building, the three walls, and 65% of the foundation, would have been excluded for Tony unless the policy was changed.

When you are driving down the road and notice these damaged businesses, you will see the standing portions of the building, sometimes even some roofline. But when the amount of damage is significant enough, the code enforcement officer/engineer will have to determine what may be safe to rebuild upon and what may not be safe and therefore removed. This will lead engineers to state that the unsafe portion will need to be torn down and disposed of. Thus, in most fires that lead to rebuilding, there are undamaged portions of the structures that will be excluded.

To address this exclusion, ISO created CP0405 Ordinance of Law Coverage form that addresses three main issues:

- **Coverage A – Coverage For Loss To The Undamaged Portion Of The Building**
- **Coverage B – Demolition Cost Coverage**
- **Coverage C – Increased Cost Of Construction Coverage**

Coverage A – Coverage For Loss To The Undamaged Portion Of The Building

First, a building must sustain direct physical damage from a covered cause of loss. When that happens, the insurance company will pay under Coverage A for the loss in value (the Valuation you chose) of the undamaged portion of the building as a consequence of being required to comply with an ordinance or law that requires demolition of undamaged parts of the same building.

You will see the word required/requirement in this form as they will only apply to codes, laws, regulations, ordinances, etc., that are in place that necessitate compliance.

When you purchase this coverage, they will pay within the Limit Of Insurance applicable to the damaged covered building. Therefore, Coverage A does not increase the Limit of Insurance you had on the policy when the disaster occurred.

Tony's contractor estimated the cost of the undamaged foundations and walls to be around $204,000 of the $423,000 needed to rebuild. Therefore, imagine rebuilding a facility if the insurance company does not pay for 48% of your construction costs.

Be wary; you will note that the Building and Personal Property Coverage Form does not include any coverage for the Undamaged Portion of the Building. Also, many Enhancement Endorsements that include Ordinance or Law coverage may provide a combined single limit that applies to all three A, B, and C Ordinance or Law coverages we are discussing. This can leave you significantly short of coverage when there are significant costs associated with the value of the undamaged portion of the building that must be torn down (Coverage A). Plus, the costs of tearing the undamaged portion down and disposing of it (Coverage B). This combined limit often does provide a large enough amount to cover A, let alone B, and nothing, if anything, would be left for Coverage C. Other Enhancement Endorsements may only increase the Coverage C for Increase Costs of Construction will be addressed shortly.

Coverage B – Demolition Cost Coverage

When a building sustains direct physical damage from a covered cause of loss, the insurance company will pay under Coverage B the cost to demolish and clear the site of *undamaged* parts of that building because of a requirement to comply with an ordinance or law that requires demolition of such undamaged property.

It goes on to say that the Coinsurance Additional Condition does not apply to Demolition Cost Coverage.

For Tony, the building contractor gave him a bill for $38,000 to tear down and dig up the undamaged portion of his building.

Fortunately, during the Coverage Analysis, comparing and contrasting insurance companies and their coverage forms and property enhancement endorsements, Tony decided to pay about a thousand dollars more in premium to select an insurance company that met the minimum limits of all the coverages Tony needed. The insurance company's program provided the Full Building Limit for Coverage A and $75,000 combined for Coverage B & C. Had Tony chosen to remain with the prior program, he would have had only $50,000 of Ordinance or Law coverage. You probably think that $50,000 is greater than $38,000, so he would have been OK. But that is not the case. The other insurance company's Enhancement Endorsement had a combined $50,000 coverage for A, B & C, leaving Tony $192,000 underinsured ($204,000 Undamaged + $38,000 Tear Down = $242,000 code loss − $50,000 Coverage = $192,000). It would have been an amount that Tony and his family would have struggled to be able to pay.

Returning to the situation with Kirsopp Auto Body, there were a significant number of Ordinance or Law issues. We mentioned that Jack needed a sprinklered spray booth which cost $350,000, as well as Jack needing $578,000 to bring his new building up to the current code. We will shift to Coverage C – Increased Cost Of Construction Coverage to address these types of issues. It is important to learn how to have your insurance policy pay for the necessary improvements to your building to meet current construction codes after a covered claim occurs.

Coverage C – Increased Cost Of Construction Coverage
When a building sustains direct physical damage from a covered cause of loss, the insurance company will pay under Coverage C the increased cost necessary to comply with the minimum standards of the ordinance or law. It includes:
- To repair or reconstruct damaged portions of that building; and/or
- To rebuild or remodel undamaged portions of that building, whether or not demolition is required.

However, Coverage C applies only if the restored or remodeled property is intended for similar occupancy as the current property unless such occupancy is not permitted by zoning or land use ordinance or law. The insurance company will not pay for the increased cost of construction if the building is not repaired, reconstructed, or remodeled.

The form also states that the Coinsurance Additional Condition does not apply to Increased Cost of Construction Coverage.

When a building is damaged or destroyed, and Coverage C applies to that building and loss, Coverage C will also pay for the increased cost of construction, as well as the repairing or reconstruction of the following, subject to the same conditions discussed above:

1) The cost of excavations, grading, backfilling, and filling;
2) Foundation of the building;
3) Pilings;
4) Underground pipes, flues, and drains.

In essence, these four items are deleted from Property Not Covered. Still, only with respect to the coverage described in this Coverage C. Therefore, when you are rebuilding, and code dictates that you must tear out your undamaged foundation and excavate to install a new foundation and new pipes, Coverage C can provide coverage for those items. However, it is preferable not to rely on Coverage C to solely provide coverage for these items. That is because if the disaster actually damages your foundation and underground piping, Coverage C would only pay for the changes you would have to make to comply with code changes. Therefore, if they were damaged and needed to be replaced, Coverage C does not completely help; these items should be added as covered property.

Even if you do not plan to rebuild following a catastrophe, you should pay attention to these coverages and the Ordinance or Law exclusion. Many minor, covered damage to property incidents have led to a significantly Increased Cost of Construction due to compliance with code issues. Not too long ago, a vehicle driven by a person that had a medical episode went through the front entrance of a retail store. The replacement of the front entrance led to triggering building code issues such that they required the business owner to add a ramp and handicap automatic doors for a cost of $32,000. Then in another instance, there was a fire in a hotel kitchen, resulting in the kitchen being gutted. Everything needed to be replaced, which in turn triggered the code to require the kitchen and restaurant to be sprinklered with a more robust system for a cost of $318,000 as they had to install a more extensive water line 800-feet down a hill to the main water line which ran along the highway. It was necessary to do that to have a large enough diameter water line to accommodate the new sprinkler system's water supply requirements; the larger diameter pipe allowed for the additional gallons per minute flow required by building ordinances.

The senior claims manager of a larger national insurance company conveyed a similar story as a warning to business leaders that it does not take a significant physical disaster to have a financial disaster. She explained that a vehicle drove into a restaurant and did about $90,000 worth of damage, stretching from the corner of the building to the front entrance, which was about one-third of the way down the restaurant's front. The insurance policy covered the damage to the walls and door but would only respond to $50,000 of the restaurant's local code enforcement officer requirements to now meet current fire and ADA laws. The restaurant owner was required to install a sprinkler system for the entire facility and install new access ramps and entrance doors. Since they were by the entrance, they were also required to widen the hallway width, and make the bathroom ADA compliant. All of these code and law issues exceeded $600,000. The owner could not recover enough from the driver as the driver had legal minimum limits of liability coverage and no additional assets to pay for the damages. The restaurant owner was unable to secure a loan to pay the $550,000 for ordinance improvements. Therefore, he had to sell his building to a local property owner so that the repairs could be paid for and keep his restaurant open. However, during this process of trying to settle claims, selling the building, and then making the required repairs and keeping the restaurant closed for almost five months, the claims manager stated that the restaurant later closed due to the reduction of patrons visiting the establishment.

Jack Kirsopp, Kirsopp Auto Body

In the case of Kirsopp Auto Body, as to Coverage C-Increased Cost of Construction, the biggest issue was that Jack's building was in a 50-year flood plain, as the McLaughlin Run Creek ran through the valley just across the street. Therefore, Jack had to elevate the building two feet above the flood plain to rebuild, a total of almost seven feet higher than the original ground floor. The foundation was damaged beyond repair. Because the foundation, piping, and grading were added to Covered Property, the building limit was going to pay the costs to replace the existing foundation.

What was not known, because the valley was a stream bed formed during the last ice age, was that the soil on the bottom of the valley was too soft and could not be adequately compacted. Several of the buildings in the valley have large settlement cracks in them.

To enable Jack to rebuild his building, the contractor had to drill caissons, which are large concrete piers, into the ground as much as 18 feet below the floor of the new building to hit the solid rock that allowed the building could be supported appropriately. This added a little over $75,000 to the cost of the foundation system. Unfortunately, this was not contemplated when estimating the ordinance or law coverages needed during the Coverage Analysis. Without Coverage C, the additional costs for the foundation caissons would not have been paid.

After the fire, but *before* Jack rebuilt, one of the other things that occurred was *Jack's* municipality decided to pass an ordinance *after* the fire that required businesses to have a particular quality aesthetic image when they built their facilities. Being an upscale community, the municipality wanted a say in how a business looked in their community.

Therefore, Jack could not rebuild with an ordinary, plain brick-and-steel building as he had before. Jack needed more of an ornate, decorative facade. This code change added about $60,000 in additional costs for the decorative block the municipality required Jack to use on the front, street-facing side, which needed to be more ornate and apparently "better-looking."

Unfortunately, back in 1995, the CP0405 Ordinance or Law Coverage edition did not pay for post-loss ordinance or law changes. However, that option is available today, and you should choose it as Jack's fire was not the only one where the local municipality changed the code after a loss.

However, even if it did cover the new ornate block, unfortunately, Jack did run out of Ordinance or Law Coverage C, based on the initial estimates of needing $475,000. When it was all said and done, to be off a little over $100,000 in the scheme of a $3.5 million total fire, Jack was happy and in "hug" mode. By the way, Jack and Gale's daughter, Lori, became the company's third owner in 2019. A happy ending.

Ken Clifton, CCF Industries

As mentioned, the insurance company's Large Claim Property Adjuster said that Ken's fire and rebuilding were among the most complex claims he had the pleasure of adjusting. There were multiple investigations into the cause of the fire in addition to the Fire Marshall's. Ken's insurance wanted to determine if there was any ability to subrogate against the fire suppression contractor for improperly installing and maintaining the fire suppression system. And then, the investigation by the fire suppression business's insurance company took the longest as that insurance company needed to defend the contractor as best as possible. Because of these investigations, the site was not released for almost four months.

At that point, the contractor started to clear the site, perform excavation, install new piping, and pour the new foundation. They began to erect the new steel building in September. It was erected entirely and skinned (no doors or windows yet) around the middle of October. But late September through early October was a stormy period. As a result, the ground was a pool of mud, which made finishing the erection of steel and installing the roof and side panels incredibly difficult. Then mid-October started one of the coldest and longest winters in Pittsburgh's history. There were several inches of snow on the ground before Halloween.

This created problems because the mud inside the building had frozen and made it difficult to pour the floor or excavate the piping. They had to come in and remove several feet of the ground to backfill inside, place the gravel bed and finally pour the floor. The weather was the main reason for delaying the project to the point that it took just a hair shy of 52 weeks to complete the entire structure for or Ken and his team to move back in 12 ½ months after the disaster.

And yes, it was quite expensive to rebuild. During the Coverage Analysis and designing of Ken's insurance program, it was identified that Ken's building was undervalued, although he did increase his coverage limit. Adding the CP1415 Additional Building Covered Property endorsement was also necessary. The building's definition was expanded to include the existing spray booth, the dust collection system and ductwork, and the foundations for the building, and a piece of machinery.

We invited the local code enforcement officer to meet, allowing for the identification that a newly built facility would require a different, more expensive fire suppression spray booth. In addition, to the entire new facility now being required to be sprinklered to code, it was also identified that the dust collection system would also require a fire suppression system with alarm sensors inside of it. Without defining the dust collection as covered building property, the Increased Cost of Construction Coverage would not have applied to those costs as they would not have been covered as building items. The ductwork would have been BPP as they could be removed and moved to a new location, and Coverage C does not apply to BPP.

When added up, the estimated amount of code issues was somewhere in the range of about $500,000. So, that is what was included on Ken's policy for Coverage C - Increased Cost of Construction. The ballpark estimates were $210,000 for the sprinkler system, $100,000 for the more robust spray booth, $75,000 for the dust collection system upgrades, $50,000 for alarm system upgrades, all of which were rounded up to $500,000 as a cushion.

What was not known, nor did the code enforcement officer identify it, was that today's new buildings are required to be much more airtight than older buildings. Due to these energy-efficiency reasons, Ken would have to install a much larger HVAC system, especially since the air/heat exchange/makeup unit, where exiting air helps pre-condition the air coming in for energy savings, and would drive up costs. The larger heat system also required a more extensive gas line, which had to be installed via a trench cut across the parking lot and bored under the road to the far side where the gas mainline was located. All of these items added significantly to the total cost of rebuilding. They added an extra $205,000 in costs or approximately $140,000 over the $500,000 that was estimated.

Fortunately, Ken's building was increased enough to cover the cost of rebuilding as-was, plus the additional costs of $500,000 of the $640,000 he needed to bring it to code. In the scheme of an $8.3 million disaster, $140,000 was close enough for Ken to afford to rebuild. Adding the **CP1531 Ordinance or Law – Increased Period of Restoration** form is discussed in Chapter 6, the delays in reconstruction due to all the extra code work needed were also addressed.

Outside of the Business Income changes made and discussed in Chapter 6, the Coverage Analysis and insurance program changes filled the holes that Ken's prior agent left in his insurance program to the amount of $1,277,000. Without these changes, Ken could not have afforded to rebuild, and without the business income changes, he would not have been able to rebuild, reopen and survive.

One of the complexities not anticipated was that before rebuilding, Ken decided to increase the square footage of his building from 19,000 to 23,000-square-feet. As the building increased in size, you would expect an increase in the new code costs for the building. However, the additional square footage took the code requirements up a level. There was a disproportional increase requirement for HVAC size and airflow capabilities and additional air exchange requirements. Therefore, the insurance company had to figure out how much more HVAC and sprinkler changes were costing due to size and building code for the larger footprint. When it was all said and done, they determined that even at the same 19,000 square feet, they still would have exceeded the $500,000 of Coverage C – Increase Cost of Construction.

The additional square footage required a larger HVAC Unit and Air Exchange Unit, which added almost $22,000 to the cost of purchasing and installing the system. These were not paid for by the insurance company under Building coverage. Because of this, it is recommended that you have a separate estimate for the construction costs of a new building of the same size prepared and approved by the adjuster before construction if you plan to increase the size of your structure.

The coverage forms **CP1531 Ordinance or Law – Increased Period of Restoration** will be addressed in Chapter 6 on Business Income Coverage, and **CP0426 Ordinance or Law Coverage for Tenant's Interest in Improvements and Betterments** and will be addressed this in Chapter 10 relating to Tenant Issues.

TAKEAWAYS/LESSONS LEARNED

As we pointed out, insurance companies will only pay what they are contractually obligated to pay, and the insurance industry designs the coverage forms used. Therefore, it is critical to pay attention to the details.

Even a partial loss can trigger ordinance or law requirements to make significant improvements. Therefore, even if you do not intend to do a complete rebuild from a disaster, you need to pay attention to the Ordinance or Law exclusion and available coverage forms you can add to pay for costly upgrades from partial losses.

As you can see from the Ordinance or Law exclusion and coverages available, you will now need to start to look at what needs to change should you have to do significant repair or even rebuild.

- Determine what ordinances or laws your municipality follows.
- Does the municipal code require tearing down an undamaged portion of a building if a certain amount is damaged?
- Take the Master List of all the items you identified and uncovered and mark any item you believe will need to be upgraded due to an ordinance or law.
- Reach out to your local code enforcement office and discuss what would have to change should you decide to build a new building today compared to how your building is built. You may have the same conversation with a contractor should they be familiar with building a facility for your type of operation as some codes are occupant specific.
- Talk to a building contractor to find out how much it might cost to tear your facility down and have it disposed of – Coverage B.
- Determine an estimated cost of each change – Coverage C.

To Rebuild or Not to Rebuild, THAT is the Question

Chapter 5

Know what they *Giveth*, but also know what they *Taketh Away!*

Pittsburgh, Pennsylvania

On June 2, 1998, a storm system spawned nearly 50 tornadoes stretching from New York to South Carolina, including eight in southwestern Pennsylvania. It was one of the most significant tornado outbreaks in Pennsylvania history. An EF-1 with wind speeds of 110 mph, one of those tornadoes, tore a 32-mile path through Allegheny and Westmoreland Counties. That tornado caused 50 injuries and damage to dozens of homes and businesses.

But what it also caused was widespread power outages. Anthony, the owner of a printing company, called about a week after the tornado hit, asking if our insurance program would cover his loss of power. I asked Anthony to clarify what was going on and why did he ask about our policy. Anthony said he was already closed for a week and was told not to expect to be open for several more days. He was upset that his insurance agent told him that his business income coverage would not cover him as the damage that caused the power failure did not happen on his premises. Therefore, he was calling multiple insurance agents to see if they provided coverage for what he was going through; and offered that he would change insurance agent to obtain the coverage.

It was almost two weeks before Anthony's power was restored. Then he found out that some of the production equipment in his shop ceased working after the power was restored. The presses were

Know what they *Giveth*, but also what they *Taketh Away!*

operating when the power abruptly stopped, which caused damage to some of their motors and electrical controls. The insurance program his agent had designed did not cover any of these issues. Anthony estimated the cost of the repairs, lost business, and payroll he paid to his 13 employees at $95,000. The amount ate up over half of his line of credit and created a severe cash flow problem for months.

When reading the declination letter from the insurance company, they were referencing a specific exclusion - **e.- Utility Services.**

To refresh, one of the issues that you will face with the ISO **CP0010 Building and Personal Property Coverage Form** is the Covered Cause of Loss.

> A. **Coverage** - We will pay for **direct physical loss** of or damage to **Covered Property** at the **premises described in the Declarations** caused by or resulting **from any <u>Covered Cause of Loss</u>**.

The ISO **CP1030 Causes of Loss-Special Form**, the policy form starts out defining Covered Cause of Loss as:

> When Special is shown in the Declarations, Covered Causes of Loss means direct physical loss unless the loss is excluded or limited in this policy.

Then under Exclusions:

> We will not pay for loss or damage caused directly or indirectly by any of the following. Such loss or damage is excluded regardless of any other cause or event that contributes concurrently or in any sequence to the loss.

Just so you are aware, the focus will be just on the **CP1030 Causes of Loss - Special Form** policy as it is the most commonly used form in the industry. There are also other causes of loss forms, the **CP1010 Causes of Loss - Basic Form** and the **CP1020 Causes of Loss - Broad Form**. These two forms specifically describe the covered causes of loss, whereas the **Special Form** generally lists what is excluded.

The Special Form is an important document filled with extensive lists of both exclusions and limitations. It is incredibly detailed and comprehensive to a point where the 5,842 words long form would be almost 55 pages in this book itself. Therefore, it would be an extremely long read to address each Exclusion and limitation and provide examples of exclusions that are most likely to cause a business to have trouble surviving a catastrophe. However, you should review your policy coverage forms and endorsements as separate standard ISO exclusions and/or unique "manuscript" exclusions are sometimes added. By "manuscript," we mean the policy language written by the insurance company specifically for your business.

With regards to Anthony's situation, this is the exclusion and how it led to the insurance company denying Anthony's claim:

Utility Services Exclusion

This Exclusion relates to the failure of power, communication, water, or other utility service supplied to your described premises, however it is caused, if the failure originates away from your described premises. It also excludes if the loss of utility originates at your described premises, but only if such failure involves equipment used to supply the utility service to your described premises from a source away from your described premises.

Loss or damage caused by a surge of power is excluded if the surge would not have occurred but for an event causing a power failure.

Loss or damage caused by a surge of power is excluded if the surge would not have occurred but for an event causing a power failure.

But suppose the failure or surge of power, or the failure of communication, water, or other utility services, results in a Covered Cause of Loss. In that case, the insurance company will pay for the loss or damage caused by that Covered Cause of Loss. In English versus Insuranceese, if the lack of power or the power coming back starts a fire, there would be coverage for the fire. You can read the story of the Candle Company in the Additional Case Studies in Chapter 6. The fire started when the power returned to their facility after it was interrupted by a contractor cutting down a tree which caused a branch to sever the power line.

Communication services include but are not limited to Internet access or access to any electronic, cellular, or satellite network.

Communication services include but are not limited to services relating to Internet access or access to any electronic, cellular, or satellite network.

When meeting with Anthony and reviewing his situation, several coverage options may have covered the damage to his equipment and the impact on his cash flow and profitability. The damage to his equipment may have been covered by endorsement **CP0417 Utility Services – Direct Damage**. This form pays for loss or damage to covered property caused by an interruption in utility services. You must identify the utility services you cover: water supply, communication supply, and power supply, including whether or not you want to include overhead transmission lines for the communication and power supply. Overhead Transmissions lines are those giant, very tall towers that usually have blinking lights on them so low flying aircraft do not crash into them at night.

Also, the damage must result from a direct physical loss or damaged by a covered cause of loss. This form will also cover both the damage from the sudden loss of power or a power reduction, commonly referred to as a brownout.

The related coverage form, the **CP1545 Utility Services – Time Element,** was designed to address your business income and/or extra expense needs from a suspension of operations caused by an interruption to utility services to your premise from a direct physical loss or damaged by a covered cause a loss. Once again, you must identify what utility services you are covering, such as water supply, communication supply, and power supply, including whether or not you want to include overhead transmission lines for the communication and power supply. Even with that, there still is usually a waiting period before coverage kicks in.

This is yet another example of why doing a thorough Coverage Analysis is necessary to determine what coverages you want to specifically address when there are limitations or exclusions in a policy.

Earth Movement Exclusion

> Earthquakes, including tremors and aftershocks and any earth sinking, rising or shifting related to such an event; landslide, including any earth sinking, rising or shifting related to such event; Mine subsidence, meaning subsidence of a man-made mine, whether or not mining activity has ceased; Earth sinking (other than sinkhole collapse), rising or shifting including soil conditions which cause settling, cracking or other disarrangement of foundations or other parts of realty. Soil conditions include contraction, expansion, freezing, thawing, erosion, improperly compacted soil and the action of water under the ground surface.
>
> But if Earth Movement results in fire or explosion, the insurance company will pay for the loss or damage caused by that fire or explosion.
>
> But suppose volcanic eruption, explosion, or effusion results in fire, building glass breakage, or Volcanic Action. In that case, the insurance company will pay for the loss or damage caused by that fire, building glass breakage, or Volcanic Action.

As you can see, the definition within the Earth Movement Exclusion is quite extensive. However, the coverage forms that ISO provides is very specific – *Earthquake and Volcanic Eruption*. It is not an *Earth Movement* endorsement.

- **CP1040 Earthquake and Volcanic Eruption Coverage with Percentage Deductible**
- **CP1028 Earthquake and Volcanic Eruption Coverage with Flat-Dollar Deductible**
- **CP1045 Earthquake and Volcanic Eruption Coverage (sub-limit form with Percentage Deductible)**
- **CP1029 Earthquake and Volcanic Eruption Coverage (sub-limit form with Flat-Dollar Deductible)**

They only add back coverage for earthquake and volcanic action in all of these forms, meaning the eruption explosion or effusion of a volcano. They also state that all events that occur within seven days of the initial event will be considered a single event.

You should also pay attention as you must decide to either include or exclude masonry veneer should your building have a bricklayer outside of either a block or structural frame wall. The form excludes the veneer if not chosen to be included. The form also excludes damage caused by a title wave or tsunami, even if attributable to an earthquake or volcanic eruption.

The Earthquake and Volcanic Eruption Coverage forms will also extend to business income and extra expense.

However, you must choose a limit of coverage to include on this form. It does not simply add earthquake or volcanic eruption as a covered cause a loss to the limit of the described covered property.

Water aka Flood Exclusion

In September 2004, Hurricane Ivan struck the nation's East Coast and drenched the Pittsburgh region, hitting some areas particularly hard. As the *Pittsburgh Post-Gazette* reported[14], "Where I'm sitting right now, there was seven feet of water," recalled Mary Ellen Ramage, Etna Borough manager. "We lost everything [in the borough offices], and while we had nothing — no phone, no fax, no electricity — we had over 400 homeowners and

---

[14] https://www.post-gazette.com/local/north/2014/09/18/Hurricane-Ivan-10-years-later-Pittsburgh/stories/201409180035

businesses — 25 percent of our community — who needed us to respond. That's an unbelievable task when you have nothing."

This water exclusion can be one of the costliest exclusions that exist in your property policies. There are a lot of common misperceptions with regard to water and flood. Although floods, hurricanes, and storm surges hit the media and the Weather Channel, the damage caused by water leaking through failing roofs and flashings and walls and foundations causes significant costly repairs that are not covered by insurance.

George was the owner of a manufacturing company in eastern OH. One day, he noticed the minor sagging of a floor where there seemed to be isolated water seepage through the wall, but only in the absolute most severe rainstorms. This seepage occurred for more than a year. On the other side of the wall was the employee parking lot. George assumed that although the parking lot mostly sloped away from the building, that there was just so much rain that it somehow still came into the building. But as it was not every rainfall and quickly cleaned up, he did not think much of it. When George noticed the sagging, he contacted a building contractor who scheduled an appointment the next week to inspect and assess what was going on. Before the contractor arrived, around 35 feet of the wall came down, damaging equipment and parked cars and causing a significant portion of the roof to sag.

George did not realize that the downspout from the roof that came down between the building and parking lot had become clogged underground where it joined the main drain pipe to the under the parking lot dry sump. The drain pipe broke, and water began washing away the soil under the foundation, George's facility, and the parking lot.

As it was clear that the erosion occurred over a prolonged period, the insurance company cited this Water Exclusion and a few others to clarify that they were not going to pay for the repairs to the building that totaled over $400,000.

As you will see, the exclusion for water is comprehensive:

➢ Flood, surface water, waves (including tidal wave and tsunami), tides, tidal water, overflow of any body of water, or spray from any of these, all whether or not driven by wind (including storm surge);

➢ Mudslide or mudflow;

➢ Water that backs up or overflows or is otherwise discharged from a sewer, drain, sump, sump pump, or related equipment;

➢ Water under the ground surface pressing on, or flowing or seeping through:
- Foundations, walls, floors, or paved surfaces;
- Basements, whether paved or not; or
- Doors, windows, or other openings; or

➢ Waterborne material carried or otherwise moved by any of the water referred to in (1), (3), or (4), or material carried or otherwise moved by mudslide or mudflow.

This exclusion applies regardless of whether any of the above, in (1) through (5), is caused by an act of nature or is otherwise caused. An example of a situation to which this exclusion applies is the situation where a dam, levee, seawall, or other boundary or containment system fails in whole or in part, for any reason, to contain the water.

Over 20% of all filed FEMA flood claims are from property owners not inside high-risk flood plains.[15] FEMA estimates that 50% of all structures flooded each year are not in flood plains[16]. In the flooding in Etna, most of the structures flooded were not in the defined flood zone.

Sal was an owner of a wholesale distribution operation in the North Hills of Pittsburgh, just above the town of Etna, when the

---

[15] https://www.fema.gov/media-library-data/1510759434562-dfb20c9a88200a9b6eae4a8e26443b75/FactSheet_Flooding_Am_I_At_Risk.pdf

[16] When referring to a property as being "in a flood plain", it is the general term to describe those that are located in Special Flood Hazard Areas (SFHAs).

flooding devastated the area. Sal had reached out to the association he belonged to, the SMC Business Councils, who recommended he reach out to us for assistance.

Sal was looking for help as he had received notification from his insurance companies that his business had no coverage for the almost $1 million of inventory in his basement. Sal was confused as he purchased two flood policies. One with the National Flood Insurance Program (NFIP) policy with a $500,000 Building Limit and a $500,000 Contents Limit, and another $1 million flood policy with his property insurance company. Because Sal had a policy with the NFIP, his **CP1065 Flood Coverage Endorsement** was written on an excess basis. Despite both policies, the NFIP and insurance company informed Sal that he had no coverage.

Within the terms and conditions of the property insurance policy's Flood Coverage Endorsement, there is an "other insurance clause." The clause stated that the property insurance company *will only pay for the amount of loss in excess of what the maximum limit that can be insured under a NFIP insurance policy, whether or not such coverage was obtained.* In this case, the property insurance company stated that the NFIP maximum limit is $1 million, a combination of $500,000 for building and $500,000 for contents. Therefore, as the total limit of the loss was below that maximum NFIP limit, the property insurance company's policy did not apply.

The recommendation at that time was for Sal to seek out legal counsel for two reasons:

- First, the maximum limit that can be insured under the NFIP for contents is $500,000, so maybe the insurance company was misinterpreting the coverage. Maybe a jury or judge would side with the business owner that the property flood policy should start after the $500,000 for contents and not the combined $1,000,000 limit ($500,000 for building and $500,000 for contents).
- Second, the insurance agent's proposal stated that the NFIP would respond to the BPP in the business's basement. The problem is an NFIP policy excludes any contents in any level that is below ground level or partially below ground level.

Sal's basement level was about six feet below ground, and there was a downwards ramp that enabled a truck to back up to the basement to be loaded. Therefore, as every exit from the lowest level of the business owner's building required some vertical "climbing" to get to ground level, the NFIP policy would not cover the basement contents (except for some mechanicals).

Fortunately, Sal's legal action was successful against both the property insurance carrier and the agent, and he recovered almost $700,000 after legal costs. Otherwise, Sal stated he would more than likely had to file bankruptcy to try to have some time not have to deal with debt until he could recover.

If his agent had not made an error in the description of coverage, the business owner would still have been out $500,000 from the NFIP coverage. Sal's legal argument was that if informed that the NFIP policy would not have covered the contents in the basement, they would not have stored inventory there.

You should pay attention to the Flood Coverage Endorsement as the Coinsurance Condition may apply. Also, the flood endorsement limit is typically both an occurrence limit and an annual policy aggregate limit, so you may not be able to have enough coverage should you have multiple events in one policy period.

Although debris removal is covered, it does not increase the limit on the endorsement, nor does debris removal cover the cost of removing deposits of mud or earth from the grounds premise. It would only cover the cleanup of the earth (soil and rock) inside of your premises.

Business leaders routinely state that they do not need flood insurance when their building is at a decent elevation higher than the bottom of the hillside or mountain that they are on. However, flash flooding causes significant damage to businesses every year. Flash flooding is where there is so much rain that the sheer volume of water starts to build upon itself to create rivers of water that flow down the streets or crevasses of the hill. This effect is why FEMA sites so many buildings that most floods are outside of flood zones.

Imagine your building is about 200 above the river, but the top of your hill is still 150 feet above you. The question is, when would a torrent of water gushing down the street and demolishes your building be covered and or not covered?

Water rushing down the street and into three buildings housing an automotive repair shop, a real estate office, and a beauty shop next to each other were severely damaged in two different events over 18 years.

Providing support to several automotive industry associations, I was requested to serve as an expert witness regarding three property owners suing one insurance company when that second torrent of water destroyed their buildings.

In the late 1990s, about 5.5 inches of rain fell in an hour. The flash flood went into their buildings damaging equipment in the auto repair facility and the beauty shop and real estate office furnishings, filling those two facilities' basements. Because of this, all three purchased flood insurance after that event.

Fast forward to a few years ago when a 36-inch water main line broke, sending a torrent of water down the street and damaging or destroying over a dozen structures. All three businesses happened to have the same insurance agent and insurance companies. All three filed claims with their NFIP flood insurance policies, and they received denials from the NFIP flood insurance program.

Therefore, all three filed claims with their property insurance company. The adjuster read the Water/Flood Exclusion paragraph (1), where they saw "surface water" was excluded and denied coverage for businesses. Unfortunately, the newly trained adjuster did not understand that you have to read the entire Exclusion and context. The full exclusion is "Flood, *surface water*, waves (including tidal wave and tsunami), tides, tidal water, overflow of any body of water, or spray from any of these, all whether or not driven by wind (including storm surge)." As you can see, these are whether driven events, not intended to exclude a water main breakage event.

All the other properties received payment for their damages from their property insurance company, and the insurance company realized the mistake after receiving suit papers and paid the claims.

You may also recall Hurricane Katrina and Superstorm Sandy both effectively destroyed a significant number of properties and businesses that were not necessarily in a *Special Flood Hazard Area*, as well as many that were not insured. Therefore, do not assume that not being located in a *Special Flood Hazard Area* means you are safe.

More Water Exclusions

Continuous or repeated seepage or leakage of water, or the presence or condensation of humidity, moisture, or vapor, occurs over a period of 14 days or more.

Water, other liquids, powder, or molten material that leaks or flows from plumbing, heating, air conditioning, or other equipment (except fire protective systems) caused by or resulting from freezing is excluded. However, coverage is afforded if you do your best to maintain heat in the building or structure; or drain the equipment and shut off the supply if the heat is not maintained.

Boiler & Machinery / Equipment Breakdown Exclusion

It would be best to tackle the next three together: Artificially generated electrical disturbance, mechanical breakdown, and an explosion of steam boilers:

Artificially generated electrical disturbance (power surge) Exclusion

Artificially generated electrical, magnetic or electromagnetic energy that damages, disturbs, disrupts, or otherwise interferes with any electrical or electronic wire, device, appliance, system, or network; or device, appliance, system, or a network that is utilizing cellular or satellite technology is excluded.

For this Exclusion, electrical, magnetic, or electromagnetic energy includes but is not limited to: electrical current, including arcing; electrical charge produced or conducted by a magnetic or electromagnetic field; Pulse of electromagnetic energy; or electromagnetic waves or microwaves.

But if fire results, the insurance company will pay for the loss or damage caused by that fire.

But if fire results, the insurance company will pay for the loss or damage caused by that fire.

Mechanical breakdown Exclusion

Mechanical breakdown, including rupture or bursting caused by centrifugal force, is excluded. But if mechanical breakdown results in an elevator collision, the insurance company will pay for the loss or damage caused by that elevator collision.

Explosion of steam boilers Exclusion

An explosion of steam boilers, steam pipes, steam engines, or steam turbines owned or leased by you or operated under your control. But if the explosion of steam boilers, steam pipes, steam engines, or steam turbines results in a fire or combustion explosion, the insurance company will pay for the loss or damage caused by that fire or combustion explosion. The insurance company will also pay for loss or damage caused by or resulting from the explosion of gases or fuel within the furnace of any fired vessel or within the flues or passages through which the gases of combustion pass.

The ISO endorsement **CP1046 Equipment Breakdown Cause of Loss** eliminates these exclusions with some exceptions regarding these three exclusions. The insurance company will not pay for damage to covered equipment undergoing pressure or electrical testing, nor will the insurance company cover wear and tear or other corrosion, decay, or deterioration unless a "breakdown" occurs.

The insurance company defines breakdown as a direct physical loss that causes damage to Covered Equipment that necessitates the repair and replacement from the failure of pressure or vacuum equipment; mechanical failure, including rupture or bursting causing by centrifuge, will; or electrical failure including arcing unless the loss or damages otherwise excluded.

A breakdown does not mean a malfunction, defect, erasure, errors, limitations, or viruses in computer equipment and programs;

leakage of any valve, fitting, shaft; damage to any vacuum tube, gas tube, or brush; damage to any structure foundation supporting a piece of covered equipment; the functioning of any safety or protected device; where the cracking of any part of an internal combustion gas turbine exposed to the products of combustion.

You can also purchase a sub-limit for the release of ammonia contamination or other hazardous substances due to a covered event.

Covered Equipment includes equipment built to operate under internal pressure or vacuum, electrical or mechanical equipment that uses in the generation, transmission, or utilization of energy; communications equipment; and computer equipment, that is, your programmable electronic equipment that is used to store, retrieve, and process data, and associated peripheral equipment that provides communication input and output functions or auxiliary functions.

Even with the availability of this coverage form, it is recommended that you analyze your situation as there are insurance company-specific coverage forms available, sometimes referred to as Boiler and Machinery policies, that can be much more comprehensive in coverage and better suited to your potential claim. It is vital given the potential costs and expense of repairing and replacing your equipment from elevators to production machinery to your heating and air conditioning system.

However, preventive maintenance and inspection are critical to prevent you from having a breakdown and having a breakdown not covered by your policy.

There is a very large printing company with well over 150 employees, and they have a 10 Color Web Press that prints over 80,000 sheets of paper an hour. The cost of just this one press is north of $10,000,000. After performing the Risk Management & HR Assessment, it was necessary to change how they addressed part of their preventative inspections: i.e., they started to perform thermal imaging of their facility as well as their equipment. When inspecting this press, they noticed that the primary motor seemed to be running at a much higher temperature than other motors. They reached out to the German manufacturer, who agreed to manufacture and ship a new motor which took six and a half weeks to arrive. The day before the planned shutdown to replace the motor, the motor seized up, and the damage was beyond repair. Had they waited till the motor failed and then replaced it, they would have been unable to use this press for that six-and-a-half-week timeframe. Yes, this may have been a covered mechanical breakdown claim, but with the business printing 24/7, there was no way to make up the amount of printing their most significant machine outputs. They would have had many upset customers due to production delays, even if outsourcing whatever production they could. They would have had a long-term financial impact of losing customers, something that would be uninsurable.

Wear and Tear/Poor Maintenance Exclusion

Wear and tear, rust or other corrosion, decay, deterioration, hidden or latent defect, or any quality in the property that causes it to damage or destroy itself is excluded.

However, if these excluded causes of loss result in a "specified cause of loss" or building glass breakage, the insurance company will pay for the loss or damage caused by that "specified cause of loss" or building glass breakage.

"Specified causes of loss" means the following: fire; lightning; explosion; windstorm or hail; smoke; aircraft or vehicles; riot or civil commotion; vandalism; leakage from fire-extinguishing equipment; sinkhole collapse; volcanic action; falling objects; the weight of snow, ice or sleet; water damage.

The Exclusion for wear and tear is the one that causes the most angst with business leaders. Insurance adjusters often cite it as a reason why coverage for a breakdown of a piece of equipment or machinery is not covered. Wear and tear are also not defined as covered in an equipment breakdown policy, as discussed before. Therefore, you must keep detailed records about the purchase, maintenance, preventive maintenance, and repairs you have made regarding any of your property. The better the case you can make as to the quality of your maintenance reduces the likelihood that an insurance adjuster will use "wear and tear" as the cause of the damage or loss and exclude the loss.

The reason for prefacing earlier that the seizure of the printing press motor most likely would have been a covered mechanical breakdown claim is that there was no apparent cause of the seizure of the motor. The motor was sent to the manufacturer, who did not provide a reason. Due to the nature of the event and the fact that the printing company has four large presses from that manufacturer, the manufacturer chose to provide them with a replacement motor but not pay for the labor. Plus, the printing company not only replaced the motor while they were down, but they also performed the scheduled preventative work at the same time. Therefore, they did not feel a need to file a claim.

There have been similar events where the insurance company and manufacturer inspected and stated that the business had not adequately maintained the lubrication of the machine. Therefore, the insurance company would not cover the event, and the manufacturer says that they are not responsible for the costs of repairs due to the business's "poor maintenance." Had poor maintenance been the cause and this incident was deemed not to be covered, between the cost of the motor and the loss of revenue, the total impact on the printing company would have exceeded $1,000,000.

A significant claim adjustment problem occurs when the contractor performing the repairs incorrectly reports to the insurance company that the cause of the damage was due to "wearing out." Sometimes, the contractor is more focused on getting in, finishing the repair, and moving off to their next job as quickly as possible. Insurance companies often follow the lead of the repair contractor's description of what happened as the contractor is supposed to be the "expert." Therefore, it is not the insurance company looking to avoid paying a claim, and it is the "expert" that causes the incorrect diagnosis.

For example, a client had a multi-million-dollar piece of equipment cease to work, and the failure of one part caused other damages resulting in almost $180,000 in repairs. The contractor wrote in their report that the drive shaft that extended from the motor to the equipment to make the machine work had "wore out," and that is why it broke. After much discussion, the business insisted that they had done preventative maintenance over the years and believed they replaced it a few years ago, plus the part's life expectancy was a decade or more. However, when the insurance company asked for documentation, the business did not have records of it other than a record of the check payable to the maintenance contractor, who was deceased and had not maintained proper documents. Therefore, no evidence of the prior replacement of the part was found.

We suggested that a metallurgist analyze the shaft for any issues. The examination determined that the driveshaft was undoubtedly newer, but more importantly, it had some imperfections in it that caused it to fail. Therefore, with that documentation, the insurance company paid the breakdown claim.

Collapse Exclusions

Following the wear and tear in terms of maintenance exclusion is Collapse. Collapse is included in any of the following conditions of property or any part of the property: an abrupt falling down or caving in; loss of structural integrity, including separation of parts of the property or property in danger of falling down or caving in; or any cracking, bulging, sagging, bending, leaning, settling, shrinkage or expansion as such condition relates to these.

However, if collapse results in a Covered Cause of Loss at the described premises, the insurance company will pay for the loss or damage caused by that Covered Cause of Loss.

This exclusion does not apply to collapse caused by one or more of the following: the "specified causes of loss"; breakage of building glass; the weight of rain that collects on a roof; or weight of people or personal property.

However, the form does give back coverage under the **Additional Coverage, Collapse** for an abrupt collapse. It is defined as an abrupt falling down or caving in of a building or any part of a building with the result that the building or part of the building cannot be occupied for its intended purpose, but for limited causes only:

    a. Building decay that is hidden from view, unless the presence of such decay is known to an insured prior to collapse;

b. Insect or vermin damage that is hidden from view, unless the presence of such damage is known to an insured prior to collapse;
c. Use of defective material or methods in construction, remodeling, or renovation if the abrupt collapse occurs during the course of the construction, remodeling, or renovation.
d. Use of defective material or methods in construction, remodeling or renovation if the abrupt collapse occurs after the construction, remodeling or renovation is complete, but only if the collapse is caused in part by: a cause of loss listed in a. or b.; one or more of the "specified causes of loss"; breakage of building glass; weight of people or personal property; or weight of rain that collects on a roof.

In addition, the Additional Coverage – Collapse does not apply to the building or structural parts that are showing signs of potential collapse or cracking, bulging, sagging, bending, leaning, settling, shrinkage or expansion. It must abruptly fall with no prior signs of issues. In the example discussed before of the water from the roof and downspout eroding the foundation, the Additional Coverage – Collapse would not apply either as it started to show signs of sagging before collapsing, so it was not abrupt. Going back to the wall collapse due to the water escaping the downspout. As there was a visible sign the floor was starting to sag before the collapse, the Collapse Exclusion also applied.

"Fungus", Wet Rot, Dry Rot and Bacteria Exclusion

Continuing with what are viewed as maintenance or preventative issues, the insurance companies exclude the presence, growth, proliferation, spread, or any activity of "fungus." wet or dry rot, or bacteria. But if "fungus," wet or dry rot, or bacteria result in a "specified cause of loss," the insurance company will pay for the loss or damage caused by that "specified cause of loss."

This exclusion does not apply when "fungus", wet or dry rot, or bacteria result from fire or lightning; or to the extent that coverage is provided in the Additional Coverage, Limited Coverage for

"Fungus," Wet Rot, Dry Rot and Bacteria, with respect to loss or damage by a cause of loss other than fire or lightning.

The exclusion does apply whether or not the loss event results in widespread damage or affects a substantial area.

Now, the limited coverage provided applies only when following a "specified cause of loss" incident or flood if your purchased flood coverage from your property insurance company. This is assuming that you took all reasonable means to clean, save and preserve the damaged property, then this limited amount of coverage is only $15,000.

Once again, it is possible to purchase a separate pollution policy for such damage, but that would need to be purchased from a specialty insurance company. This is highlighted because there have been cases of black mold effectively destroying a building and not being covered.

Pollution Exclusions

Discharge, dispersal, seepage, migration, release or escape of "pollutants" unless the discharge, dispersal, seepage, migration, release, or escape is itself caused by any of the "specified causes of loss." But if the discharge, dispersal, seepage, migration, release, or escape of "pollutants" results in a "specified cause of loss," the insurance company will pay for the loss or damage caused by that "specified cause of loss."

This exclusion does not apply to damage to glass caused by chemicals applied to the glass.

The best course of action with pollutants is to make sure you are following all best practices regarding storage, transport, and disposal of the pollutants. You should also determine if you should purchase a separate pollution policy that provides coverage for clean-up and restoration, as well as third-party damage, should the pollutant migrate to other properties.

Although the big industrial spills tend to be the ones that hit the media, many "smaller incidents" come back to haunt a business leader when they least expect it. As most chemicals are stored and used by manufacturing and construction companies above ground, business leaders believe that any release could be dealt with quickly and inexpensively. They think that their storage containment or handling procedures will keep any incident to a minor clean-up. However, there can be costly clean-up issues when the business leaders sell their property, or a neighbor goes to sell. It is common for a bank to require a Phase I pollution study, and sometimes Phase II, where they take soil samples.

A business owner recently went to purchase a closed 40-plus-year-old motel from the original owners. The business owner was going to tear it down and build a nursing home. During the investigation of the property, Phase I and Phase II were completed. The environmental engineer found pollutants from the swimming pool in the ground, but that was not the biggest issue. They also found other chemicals in the ground that migrated from a neighboring property. The adjacent property was currently tenanted by a large "Lasik Surgery & Eye Care" center, but over 20 years ago, a dry-cleaning operation was located there. The estate of the dry clean store owner sold the location to a local business owner for cash to be a rental property. As the current neighboring property owner did not cause the pollutants, she was found not to be liable in court for the damage at the motel property. Still, she will now face high clean-up costs when she goes to sell the property. However, the current motel owner now had to pay to have the contaminated soil removed and disposed of. The effort involved tearing down the old motel, excavating the parking lot, trucking out over 100 dump truck loads of soil, and acquiring clean fill to replace the removed, contaminated soil. When it was all said and done, the cost of remediating was $2,700,000, which was more than the location was worth.

Dishonest or Criminal Act Exclusion

Dishonest or criminal act (including theft) by you, any of your partners, members, officers, managers, employees (including temporary employees and leased workers), directors, trustees, or authorized representatives are excluded. This includes when the person(s) was(were) acting alone or in collaboration with each other or with any other party; or theft by any person to whom you entrust the property for any purpose, whether acting alone or in collaboration with any other party.

This Exclusion does not apply to acts of destruction by your employees (including temporary employees and leased workers) or authorized representatives, but theft by your employees (including temporary employees and leased workers) or authorized representatives is not covered.

With over 30-plus years in this industry, it never ceases to amaze me how people could get away with it for prolonged periods before being caught. In interviewing business leaders and insurance adjusters, all these businesses had two things in common: one, the business leaders thought they had solid policies and procedures in place to prevent such a situation, or at least would quickly identify that something was going on; and two, the business leaders believed the employee(s) in those positions could be trusted entirely.

There was the case of a high-end retail store in an affluent area of a city, where they lost power one day. The electricity utility informed them that power would be restored in the evening or even the next day. Therefore, the owner sent everyone home. The owner stayed for a little to do some work while his laptop battery lasted and was just about to leave when the power came on unexpectedly. He proceeded to call employees back to their store, and while waiting for them to arrive, he counted and set up the cash register drawers. While balancing the one drawer, he noticed that one drawer was $220 over with cash. He proceeded to go through the transactions and saw a special-order item return noted in the system, and not returning the funds to the customer would explain the overage. As special-order returns required that the customer's information be entered, he went into their system to see who it was so he could return their money. He quickly noticed that the person who had "made the return" happened to be a friend that had died three years previously. Therefore, the owner promptly recognized that there was something shady going on.

When the office manager arrived, he had her "set up the cash drawers," and she said everything checked out. He asked her to step away from her desk. That is when he found the $220 shoved in a folder off to the side. At that point, he notified the authorities.

Afterward, his accountant started going back through the records to help provide the documentation for their Employee Theft Coverage claim. It turns out that the office manager had been skimming cash from the store every day for such a long period that the accountant stopped counting once he hit the business's $250,000 limit for employee dishonesty coverage that they had. It turned out that over several years, she had built the skimming practice to an average of over $1,000 a day. You may be wondering how someone could steal that much from a single store, but when you factor that the store did over $10,000,000 in revenue a year, and over 30% of their income was from cash transactions, it was not hard. Just Google "largest employee embezzlement ever," and you will see case after case. One website lists 25 Examples of Embezzlement and Workplace Theft: Forging Checks, Cashing Customer Checks, Faking Vendor Payments, Over-billing Customers, Theft of Customer Card Data, Padding an Expense Account, Double-Dipping, Using a Company Credit Card For Personal Use[17].

Now skimming over time usually does not always end in a business leader filing bankruptcy. However, according to the Association of Certified Fraud Examiners, 30% of bankruptcies involve employee theft, and 22% of fraud cases involve losses greater than $1,000,000[18].

False Pretense Exclusion

Back in 2018, while speaking at a conference, I met the sales manager of a large west coast company that makes custom CNC machinery who shared the story of how they received an RFQ inquiry for a new custom machine from a repeat customer from the United Kingdom. After emailing back and forth for a few weeks, the

---

[17] https://smallbiztrends.com/2019/09/embezzlement-examples.html
[18] https://www.acfe.com/article.aspx?id=4294968471

customer digitally signed the purchase order but asked that the equipment be shipped to their new production facility in Hungary. The manufacturer shipped and invoiced their customer. About a week later, the customer reached out to ask what the invoice was for as they did not order, nor do they have any other facilities. Even though they could intercept the shipment and have the equipment returned, it did not matter much as the custom CNC machinery had no other potential buyers.

The duped manufacturer said that the exchange of emails for the order was not unusual given the eight-hour time difference. However, if they added an established, known contact verification via a simple phone call, they could have averted this. The sales manager went on to say that they eventually salvaged some of the machine for some parts, but they still lost over $100,000 in non-reusable components, labor to build, and shipping. Voluntary parting with any property by you or anyone else to whom you have entrusted the property if induced to do so by any fraudulent scheme, trick, device, or pretense is excluded. There has been a significant increase in the number of businesses duped into providing products or services to people who provided false or promised payments, particularly phone orders using credit cards or email.

This is especially true for "hackers" manipulating emails that appear to come from a boss or coworker requesting help. Most people believe that they can spot these emails: the ones with bad grammar and misspelled words. However, business leaders continue to convey story after story of how they or employees fell prey to these scams. The reason being, most fraudulent emails are no longer full of poor grammar and misspelled worded emails; the effective ones are akin to the best marketing emails that are designed to elicit a response and get you to take action.

But the more significant issue is that there have been "hackers" who intercepted and manipulated legitimate emails that convey purchase orders. There have been businesses that ship the goods and never receive payment from their "existing" client or invoices for actual goods or services where someone changes the terms of payment to a falsified bank account for EFT payment.

Know what they *Giveth*, but also what they *Taketh Away!*

Sometimes, the scam goes beyond the computer. The City of Ocala, in central Florida, had someone posing as an employee of the construction company performing a project for the city, was able to dupe a city employee into changing banking for the construction company, and that led to the city sending a payment of $742,376.73 to a fraudulent bank account[19].

Some of this may fall into the world of Cyber Insurance, but some happen right in your facility. However, you may want to know that some insurance companies already have customized property endorsements to provide coverage for such an occurrence. Still, with the increase in the frequency of these events, it is more difficult to obtain, and frequently they will only provide a small sub-limit of coverage.

More Exclusions...

As mentioned earlier, these are not all of the exclusions or limitations in the **CP1030 Causes of Loss - Special Form** referred to incorrectly as the "All-Risks" coverage form. There are many exclusions: governmental action; nuclear hazard; delay, loss of use or loss of market, smoke, vapor or gas from agricultural smudging or industrial operations; smog; settling, cracking, shrinking or expansion; nesting or infestation, or discharge or release of waste products or secretions, by insects, birds, rodents or other animals. Some exclusions apply to all Covered Property. Some apply only to Covered Personal Property, such as the exclusions of dampness or dryness of the atmosphere, changes in or extremes of temperature, or marring or scratching. Sometimes, suppose an excluded cause of loss results in a "specified cause of loss" or building glass breakage. In that case, the insurance company will pay for the loss or damage caused by that "specified cause of loss" or building glass breakage the insurance company will not. Then there are times that things are covered, but then a dollar limitation kicks in for specific items: furs, fur garments and garments trimmed with fur; jewelry, watches,

---

[19] https://www.ocala.com/news/20191028/ocala-police-scammers-swiped-nearly-750000-from-city

watch movements, jewels, pearls, precious and semiprecious stones, bullion, gold, silver, platinum and other precious alloys or metals; or stamps, tickets, including lottery tickets held for sale, and letters of credit.

If you are like some other business that goes through a disaster, one of the biggest issues you may face in rebuilding and reopening will be the $2,500 limitation for patterns, dies, molds, and forms. You may purchase enough Personal Property of Others coverage limit to pay for what you believe the value of the patterns, dies, molds, and forms of your customers to be, but the Causes of Loss - Special Form loss limitation kicks in. Without addressing the limitation with an insurance company-specific endorsement, it could leave you trying to come up with tens or hundreds of thousands of dollars to reimburse your customers. And NO, your General Liability or Umbrella will not help you either as there is a Property in the Care, Custody, or Control exclusion in those liability policies.

Even More Exclusions + Pandemics... In addition, the argument over whether a virus causes Direct Property Damage always plays out in the courts and takes years to conclude. The other Exclusion that also creates an issue that has a financial impact on pandemic claims being paid for by a Business Income policy is the mandatory endorsement of **CP0140 Exclusion of Loss Due to Virus or Bacteria**. Even if the courts deem that a virus does cause property damage, this endorsement's sole focus is to exclude a virus from being covered on the Buildings and Business Personal Property Coverage Form or the Business Income and Extra Expense, including Civil Authority's action.

During a Coverage Analysis, it is necessary to take the time to review a complete policy with all forms and endorsements. When the insurance company recognizes a risk within your business, they agree to insure by adding one of the hundreds of endorsements to specifically provide coverage of the property item or cause of loss. However, there are times the insurance company recognizes a risk within your business that they DO NOT want to insure and by adding one of dozens upon dozens of endorsements to expressly exclude a property item or cause of loss from being covered. That is the starting point to understanding what risks may need addressing, both from a policy and procedural standpoint and a coverage standpoint.

However, it is interesting that when reviewing proposals, business leaders receive that list the primary coverages of Building, BPP, BPPO, Business Income, General Liability, etc... These proposals highlight what coverages were added by endorsement, typically through the insurance company's general Enhancement Endorsement. What is surprising, too few references any exclusions within a policy. It is like they ignore the exclusions or limitations that may impact your ability to receive insurance proceeds from an event that occurs and financially affects your operations.

TAKEAWAYS/LESSONS LEARNED

Here is a question to ask yourself: What do Donuts, Swiss Cheese, and Insurance Policies have in common?

HOLES!

You buy insurance to pay your claims; why would you not want to know when you will be writing the check to settle your claim instead of the insurance company cutting you a check? Therefore, it is important to understand what the insurance company *Giveth* and what they *Taketh Away*.

Insurance companies will only pay what they are contractually obligated to pay, or as some put it, the least that they must pay per the contractual amount. And the insurance industry designs the coverage forms that are used.

You must review your coverage forms to see what is covered and what is excluded.

- Review the Master List of all the items you identified that you want as Covered Property, and determine if any limitations in your policy would lead you to fail in meeting your needs or legal obligations.

- Review the exclusions within your policy and create a list of exclusions that you need to have addressed to receive enough proceeds to rebuild and reopen.
- If the coverage endorsement added to your policy can only add the coverage with a sub-limit, determine what the sub-limit covers (Building, BPP, PPO, and Business Income) and make sure you purchase enough to pay for what you need.

Know what they *Giveth*, but also what they *Taketh Away!*

Chapter 6

Cash Flow is King!

The four most expensive words in the English language are, 'This time it's different.' – Sir John Templeton

You own or run a business with employees, property, and equipment, not because it is your hobby or you like to sit back and watch, but because you do it to *make money*. Money, particularly an ongoing cash flow, is needed to pay for your employees' payroll, mortgage, or rent, buy materials, and pay bills. And then, hopefully, you make a profit to cut through all the hassle to make having employees, paying bills, and owning stuff worthwhile. Profit pays YOU!

With a solid cash flow, you can do all kinds of things.

Without money, well, nothing happens. No one gets paid. YOU do not get paid. And then you are broke…

When done right, Business Income Coverage can provide that cash flow needed to keep your business *in business* during your darkest hours after a disaster.

When not done right, well, you become a statistic.

Remember, over 50% of businesses either do not reopen or close within three years of reopening.

Do you want to base your outcome on a flip of a coin, or would you rather know NOW whether or not your Business Income Plan Design will be there when you need it?

John's Machine Shop

We are going to revisit John. John was the prior machine shop owner who became my client's new GM after losing his business and pouring his family's life savings back into it to keep it afloat. John had to borrow and use personal cash and sell the family's vacation home, all to cover the $975,000 shortage that his Building and Business Personal Property insurance program design left him. But that was not the whole story.

You may recall an earlier discussion about John's disaster experience; there was a reference to his Business Income Coverage issues.

Before changing agents, John had a Business Income and Extra Expense Insurance program that provided him with $4,000,000 for his $7,000,000 a year revenue business. When taking "insurance bids" from several insurance agents, the program he accepted was lower in premium than his prior program, but he believed it provided more coverage. The new program included *12 Months Actual Loss Sustained Business Income and Extra Expense Coverage*. The agent explained that if John needed more than $4,000,000 for his business income loss, the proposed policy had NO DOLLAR LIMIT. John liked that as he was uncertain that the $4,000,000 would be enough for his growing company.

You may also recall that one of John's issues following the fire stemmed from it taking over four months for John's contractor to have access to the site to start the construction process due to an ongoing possible subrogation claim investigation eventually was dropped. Due to this delay in cleaning up and breaking ground, by the time they completed the rebuilding, it was just a little over 11 months from the time of the fire to the doors reopening. John received his lost profit and enough money to pay for his ongoing expenses during the rebuilding, with not one employee missing a paycheck. Sound like a successful outcome? Not really...

Issue #1

John personally owned the building and was receiving $40,000 a month in rent from the business. He had a Triple Net Lease with his business, where his business would pay for and provide the insurance. He was to *"name John _____ as additional insured on the General Liability and Property Insurances."*

John's *12 Months Actual Loss Sustained Business Income and Extra Expense Coverage* did not include Rental Income. As John was listed as an Additional Insured on the policy and not a Named Insured, he would not receive the direct benefit of the property policy. Therefore he would not have received rental income even if the policy included Rental Income in the Business Income definition. Having John as Named Insured and including Rental Value in the Business Income Definition would have worked. However, insurance companies do not like to add an Individual as a Named Insured to a business's policy for fear of being pulled into personal liability issues or other properties or operations owned by the individual.

Although the lease said that the business was to pay rent even if unusable, John did not receive a dime after the disaster. The state's case law states that if the building is not tenantable, the tenant cannot be forced to pay rent. Even though the lease agreement said that the business was to continue to pay John, the appropriate endorsement **CP1503 Business Income – Landlord as Additional Insured (Rental Value)** was not added to provide payments for rent to John instead of the state law. John did not disclose the lease requirements to the agent, nor did the agent ask for a copy of and read the lease agreement.

Therefore, John did not receive any rent following the fire and was personally out $400,000 over those ten additional months. Plus, since the rent was not a Necessary Ongoing Operation, the business also did not receive funds from the insurance company to pay for the rent.

Issue #2

All other Ongoing Expenses were paid during those 11 months.

John started purchasing new machines shortly after the fire. He even rented a temporary location for a year, about two weeks after the fire, to have somewhere to work from (Extra Expense).

However, it took anywhere from four to eight months for the new CNC Machinery to arrive. While John could not make parts or not produce enough parts for himself as equipment was coming, he attempted to order parts from other machine shops, who would send them to him for inspection, and then John's business would ship them out. But as he would have to approach other machine shops for their pricing, he missed many bid deadlines and lost much business. John also did not understand that they could price the parts as if they were making them, and the Extra Expense Coverage would take care of the difference in price between what they would sell it for and what it cost to acquire. Therefore, John was higher in bid more often than he would have been before the fire.

However, even if John bid at the same price as if he was making the parts, the delays in finding a shop with the capacity to make parts for him created issues and missed deadlines, and a lot of missed work.

In addition, John also effectively lost two to three weeks of production during the move back to his new building.

John's business was operating at about 40-45% of the pre-fire work when he had the reopening party. Thus, understanding Extra Expense coverage better may have enabled John to keep more of his clients.

Issue #3

After the 11th month mark, John reopened, and his coverage shifted from Business Income and Extra Expense to his Extended Business Income Coverage. The policy continued to provide funds to fill the cash flow shortage to cover lost profit and all ongoing expenses, including all his employees' payroll. But at the 12-month mark, the wheels fell off the wagon.

The *12 Months Actual Loss Sustained Business Income and Extra Expense Coverage* form did include a 60 Day Extended Period of Indemnity (aka Extended Business Income coverage). Typically, after John reopened, the insurance company would continue to pay the lost profit, and ongoing expenses would be covered for 60 days. However, this specific insurance company's coverage form restricted the business income coverage claim to 12 months after the covered loss occurred. So, even though John was only 25 days into his 60 Day Extended Business Income Period, his Extended Business Income coverage ceased at 25 days.

Because of this, John would no longer have a cushion to protect his cash flow after the 12-month mark. John would not receive payment for 60 to 90 days post shipment on the orders he made and shipped in that first month he reopened. John started hemorrhaging cash to pay the bills, pay the payroll, and stay open. John also figured, at best, he was at 50% of revenue at the end of the 12-month mark. Not wanting to risk losing good employees during a low unemployment period, John kept the employees on despite the revenue shortage, all while hemorrhaging more money.

Even if John had the full 60 Day Extended Business Income, he believed he might have been close to 55% of pre-disaster revenue as the end of what would have been 60 days.

John was forced to sell many months later when his revenue slowly climbed to only 70% of the pre-disaster revenue range and was not increasing as rapidly as John initially believed it would.

Some of the post-fire problems were: John lost clients to competition and was unable to woo them back; John had more debt load (and it snowballed); he had to charge more to make profits on the parts, and that made him less competitive; even though he did start to lay off employees after a few months, he still had a few too many employees on staff at the end. Because of John's Optimism, John never laid off enough staff to be profitable as he anticipated more business in the future and did not want to go through the hiring and training of new employees.

Had John remained with the previous insurance company and the $4,000,000 of coverage, which was later clearly determined not to be enough to "keep the doors open with the same operation before the fire" as John put it, two things may have occurred:

- John may have more quickly come to the financial conclusion that he needed to correct his financial ship much earlier, and maybe, he would, unfortunately, have had to lay

off unnecessary or excessive employees do so much earlier; and
- John's prior insurance program had a 120 Day Extended Business Income Coverage on the Coverage Enhancement Endorsement, which may have bought John more time to woo clients back. He could have laid off unnecessary employees and done so more quickly during the period he was closed or partially operating, thereby saving his business income coverage limit closer to reopening and the Extended Business Income period.

You probably have the same question when John told the story: did he sue his agent? Yes. However, you should be aware that the proposal from the new agent clearly showed the 12 Months limitation and the 60 Days Extended Business Income, both of which affected the outcome and eventual failure of this business. Because of the proposal highlighting the coverage terms, John lost his lawsuit directed at his insurance agent.

What this teaches is that protecting your cash flow is the most vital thing you need to do. When designing your insurance program, if you guess wrong and do not buy enough Building insurance coverage, you can build a smaller building with the funds you do receive. If you have enough coverage to protect your cash flow of income, you can finance the shortage of coverage through a loan and build your building back to the size you had before. If you do not have enough coverage to protect your cash flow of income, you will not be able to finance any shortage and will hemorrhage cash trying to keep your business afloat.

More scary statistics:
- 66% of small to medium-sized businesses lack proper Business Interruption Insurance[20],

---

[20] https://www.insurancejournal.com/news/national/2015/09/02/380367.htm

- 90% of businesses without Business Interruption Insurance Fail[21]

You can buy all the equipment, inventory, and computers your business needs, but you cannot hire anyone to make things or stock the shelves without income to pay the people. How long can you afford to keep the doors open, ship and sell goods, and pay employees without any funds coming in?

Face it, you are in business to make money, therefore, protecting your money, or in this case, your cash flow, is the most important thing you need to do.

You can buy all the equipment, inventory, and computers your business needs, but you cannot hire anyone to make things or stock the shelves without income to pay the people. How long can you afford to keep the doors open, ship and sell goods, and pay employees without receiving any funds?

You may be asking yourself if these businesses had business income coverage, how did they go out of business? The 66% of businesses that lack proper Business Interruption insurance is not too far off from the 50% statistic of businesses that fail to reopen or fail within two years of reopening. The 90% of businesses that fail that do not have Business Interruption insurance is akin to another statistic – 90% of startup businesses fail[22]. It appears that restarting after a disaster is somewhat similar to that of starting a new business with two exceptions: one, assuming you have property insurance, you do not have to buy all the materials and equipment that a startup would; two, you may have some returning customers, and therefore you may not be starting with no revenue.

Therefore, if they did have Business Interruption insurance and still did not make it, the only thing that makes sense is that they did not understand *How Much* or *How Long* they would need their Business Interruption insurance.

---

[21] https://www.fema.gov/media-library-data/1441212988001-1aa7fa978c5f999ed088dcaa815cb8cd/3a_BusinessInfographic-1.pdf

[22] https://fortune.com/2014/09/25/why-startups-fail-according-to-their-founders/

Cash Flow is King!

Both insurance agents and their clients misunderstand business Income. This leads to agents being unable or unwilling to explain and help calculate the correct coverage amounts and give options to business leaders so that they can survive a catastrophic event.

Chapter 1 outlined the reasons WHY there are so many post-disaster business failures. Although these are a repeat, there are a few that are specific to Business Income. It is worth reviewing those from the list:

- Most agents do not fully understand what it takes for a business to survive while being closed and attempting to reopen from a disaster.
- Most agents do not fully understand what it takes for a business to survive while being closed and attempting to reopen from a disaster.
- Business leaders often believe that they will be back in business faster than it will take them to do so.
- Business leaders often believe that they will be back in business faster than it will take them to do so.
- Business leaders struggle to perceive how much Extra Expenses will be incurred to keep the doors open and retain as many customers as possible.
- Business leaders think all or most of their clients are loyal and will return as soon as their doors open.
- Financial industry terms that accountants and business owners use are different in the "insurance" world. For example, the cost of goods sold and net income mean two different things in each world.
- Many business owners are reluctant to share their "financial picture" with insurance agents as they feel that their information is "private."
- Business leaders and agents do not like to have a conversation about uncomfortable topics like the business's

death and, more importantly, what the plan is when something happens.

So, ask yourself, *are you willing to flip that coin?*

For you to understand **How Much** or **How Long**, meaning **How Much** money will you need to pay for everything, including yourself, and **How Long** you will need that cash flow to last, here are a few questions that you need to answer:
- *If everything is destroyed, will you want to reopen?*
  - If you are reading this book, it will be assumed that it is a YES!
- *Which will take longer to occur, rebuilding your building or replacing your Business Personal Property (BPP), equipment, and production machinery?*
  - Some businesses will need 18-20 months or more when they order the production equipment as it will need to be manufactured, delivered, installed, and operational.
  - And before you say it, it will take more than six months to build your building (more to follow)
- *How long is your sales life cycle?*
  - There are businesses that from the time they first speak to a prospective client (or significant portion of their client base) until they can make their product and get paid by the client, or the client can use and pay for the service, is six to nine months to even a year or more. Some businesses are event-based and may need 18 months to 2 years to rebook their facilities.
- *Are you truly unique, or can others provide at least a comparable good or service to your clients while you are closed?*
  - This is not saying that the other options would not be as good or more expensive than yours, nor further away from needing more lead time. But, in general, do your customers have options?

- Status quo becomes your enemy when trying to woo customers back.

BUSINESS INCOME AND EXTRA EXPENSE COVERAGE FORM

What you need to protect your cash flow is Business Income Coverage. The **ISO CP1030 Business Income (and Extra Expense) Coverage Form's** Insuring Agreement states:

> We will pay for the **actual loss of Business Income** you sustain due to the necessary **"suspension" of your "operations"** during the **"period of restoration"**. The "suspension" must be caused by **direct physical loss** of or **damage to property at premises which are described in the Declarations** and for which a Business Income Limit of Insurance is shown in the Declarations. The loss or damage must be caused by or result from a **Covered Cause of Loss**.

We discussed the **Direct Physical Loss** and the **Damage to property at the premises described in the Declarations** in Chapter 2. This Direct Physical Loss requirement is why insurance companies stated that the Business Income insurance policies did not cover the pandemic of COVID-19.

There are several new key terms and phrases from this insuring agreement that is important to all business income losses:
- Actual loss of Business Income;
- Suspension of Operations;
- Period of Restoration.

Actual Loss of Business Income

This is where the financial and the insurance world start having different terminologies. You will now see that there is essentially a misunderstanding that Business Income Insurance protects your

Gross Income or Total Revenue. It protects your Business Income, the *How Much*...

> **Business Income** means the:
> a. Net Income (Net Profit or Loss before income taxes) that would have been earned or incurred; and
> b. Continuing normal operating expenses incurred, including payroll.
>
> For manufacturing risks, Net Income includes the net sales value of production.

> **3.** Loss Determination
> a. The amount of Business Income loss will be determined based on:
>   1) The Net Income of the business before the direct physical loss or damage occurred;
>   2) The likely Net Income of the business if no physical loss or damage had occurred, but not including any Net Income that would likely have been earned as a result of an increase in the volume of business due to favorable business conditions caused by the impact of the Covered Cause of Loss on customers or on other businesses;
>   3) The operating expenses, including payroll expenses, necessary to resume "operations" with the same quality of service that existed just before the direct physical loss or damage; and
>   4) Other relevant sources of information, including:
>   (a) Your financial records and accounting procedures;
>   (b) Bills, invoices and other vouchers; and
>   (c) Deeds, liens or contracts.

Your Business Income is your **Net Income** - *Your Net Profit (or Loss) before Income Taxes* - PLUS necessary, normal operating expenses that will need to be continued, including all payroll.

Therefore, Net Income in the business income policy is not the same as it is in your financials, in that Net Income usually is revenue less Cost of Goods Sold. In other words, most businesses include the labor costs in the Cost of Goods Sold, which generally means deducting payroll costs when arriving at Net Income on your business's financial, but with insurance, you would not remove the costs associated with labor.

When you have a Business Income loss, the insurance company will use a Forensic Accountant to pour through your financial records and calculate your Business Income loss. They will calculate your Net Income (or Loss) and review contracts and other documentation to determine the necessary continuing operating expenses that need to be continued. These would include payroll, contracted minimum utilities, and software subscriptions, or those expenses that would not continue, such as rent that is not contractually obligated to continue or costs of shipping goods.

Therefore, your Business Income is the Net Income *Profit* or *Loss* before the catastrophe and all necessary ongoing expenses. As for John's machine shop, the rent payments to John were not necessary nor required, nor were they covered. But as all payroll and other ongoing expenses were covered and paid while John's facility was being rebuilt, and he moved into the new facility with all of his machinery to operate, it actually masked the pending fiscal cliff that John went off.

Another point of difference is that if you are not operating, there will be expenses that you will no longer need to pay for: the costs of shipping your products, utilities (unless you are on minimum use contracts), services that you subcontract out, allowances for returns, and anything else that does not occur since you are not operating. If those items do not occur, you do not need the revenue associated to pay for those expenses. This is why the Business Income policy does not protect your revenue or income. Instead, it protects your Net Income (essentially Gross Revenue less Cost of Goods Sold) and then less anything non-continuing, unnecessary expenses.

Steve the Candle Maker

Steve's fire was a particularly challenging one. Leaving the office early and heading towards home as the fire would take a few more hours to be extinguished, Steve suggested it would be better to grab something to eat before driving that evening to meet with him, as well as the two owners. While on the way to business, cresting the peak of a large hill in Southwestern Pennsylvania that was some 30-plus miles away from Steve's facility, you could clearly see the massive, black plume of smoke in the distance.

The owners had built a successful 40-employee operation that manufactured scented candles and potpourri that my wife loves and still buys frequently. Although the owners were active in the business, all my business dealings were with Steve, the CFO, as the owners relegated the insurance purchasing and management to Steve.

During the day, a contractor trimmed trees about a mile down the road and cut a branch that brought down the power line, resulting in the candle company losing power. Steve was told it would be several hours before they could restore power, and since they could no longer maintain the heat to the paraffin wax, it would start solidifying. As a result, they would not make candles that day as it takes time to re-melt. Therefore, they sent the employees home for the day.

Since they did not have power, Steve decided to get a haircut and then eat. While eating lunch just down the street, one of the waiters came and said, "Steve, there's smoke coming out of your building."

When power was restored, based on the forensics, a significant power surge caused sparks to fly out from the power line both inside and outside the building.

Now, this was an all-steel building of about 15,000 square feet that was also sprinklered. However, the underside of the roof was insulated and had a protective fabric material to keep the insulation in place. The fabric material that held the insulation in place was supposed to be fire-retardant. Over time, it lost its chemical properties and became highly combustible. Such an insulation

Cash Flow is King!

system is no longer allowed by building codes. The sparks ignited the fabric and quickly engulfed the roofline, causing the roof to sag and then collapse, breaking the sprinkler system.

The burning material was dropping to below and ignited all the boxes used for packaging and shipping of the candles, plus the flammable paraffin wax itself, which fueled the fire. It was complete devastation.

The closest temporary facility that they could find, because there were no other sprinklered facilities available within 25 miles that would accept them as a tenant due to the volatile nature of the manufacturing process for their products, was over the state line. As they were a tenant in their building, and since the landlord decided that he was no longer going to rebuild the structure and sold the cleared lot, in essence, their temporary move became a permanent one.

The biggest challenge they ran into was that 20-plus years ago, businesses typically used a "tape" backup system for their computer systems, a cassette with a magnetic tape inside it that looked like the old 8-Track cartridges. They only had three tapes for their backup system and rotated them. Each morning, Steve would remove the overnight completed backup and replace it with the one he brought in that morning from home; the most recent backup he just pulled out would go into the safe, and then he would place the one from the safe in his briefcase to take home that night.

Well, when Steve went to lunch, he left his briefcase on his desk. The ensuing fire not only destroyed all three backup tapes but also all their paperwork.

Compounding the problem was Steve, being a CPA, also took care of filing their taxes. Their financial records were either in the computer system, which now had no backups or were destroyed with all the paper in file cabinets. When it came time for the insurance company to adjust their business income claim, it was exceedingly difficult, which certainly compounded the problem.

Steve's biggest problem was providing documentation supporting the cost of the financial loss so that their Business Income and Extra Expense policy would pay. Although the insurance company retained copies of the Business Income Worksheet prepared and provided to the insurance company every year, no one had a copy of the financial documents that would support it for the insurance company. Not even the insurance company premium auditor. Nor did the insurance company request a copy of their financials when the insurance underwriter reviewed the Business Income Worksheets.

Steve had to request copies of their tax records from the IRS, which took months to obtain, and the most recent tax return was from almost two years prior as the most recent year was not yet filed as Steve had filed for an extension. In essence, the most recent tax return was from financial data 18 months before the fire.

When all was said and done, that inability to have clear financial records caused them to most likely not receive as much money as they should have from their business income claim. The sad part was that there was an inability to demonstrate the significant growth that they were experiencing. Therefore the insurance company could not fully or adequately trend the Business Income loss.

The advantage of finding a new, temporary location that became their permanent one was that they did not have exceptionally long downtime. In fact, according to Steve, it took them a little less than two months from the fire to get new equipment and stock needed to start being able to make and ship their candles and other items.

The lessons learned from this disaster were:

The first was to obtain a copy of the financials used in completing the Business Income Worksheet and store them in a locked filing cabinet at our office or secure folder on our computer server. This is especially important when a business does not use an outside accounting firm with copies of financial records.

The second lesson highlighted the importance of a proper Computer Recovery Plan and a solid systemwide backup. Today this is even more critical with all the Ransomware encryption events occurring. When this disaster occurred, the common question on an insurance company questionnaire was to ask if the business kept a copy of their computer backup off-premise, which Steve said he did.

And the third, starting from that point, I realized that questionnaires and checklists did not go far enough. It was always necessary to go a step further and ask more questions, such as digging deeper into a businesses' processes and going through examples and scenarios to clear what is occurring. For example, sticking with computers, understanding how the system is backed up, what information is backed up, and when are complete system and daily backup of recent system changes are made. Knowing this is critical to make sure that there must be a recent backup off-premise at any given moment and that at no point were all the tapes in the same place at the same time. It is also essential to dig deeper to determine the business's ability to restore after a computer virus. You may need to access clean, viable backups that predate the introduction of the virus as any reinstallation cannot include files that were compromised, and the virus would not be reinstalled and reactivated.

Unfortunately, many businesses using today's cloud-based backup systems believe they are fully protected. However, when we asked questions and went through scenarios, we identified critical data that was not backed up or did not have isolated complete system backups archived. Not having clean, isolated archived backups could mean a business may have corrupted backup files. So, by reinstalling the backups, a ransomware event could be retriggered. With corrupted backups corruption, you must pay the ransom as you no longer have viable backups or pay your employees to recreate your data.

While reviewing a business's computer systems, these discussions were even more critical during COVID-19 and the business employment changes that following it. COVID-19 greatly increased the number of permanent remote employees, or those that work in a hybrid model of working from both the office and their home.

Many businesses with Employees who work remotely often come too late when they realize the data on the remote computers were not correctly backed up. Many businesses' computer systems became more vulnerable to attack as businesses needed to allow more remote access to their internal systems. By allowing more access, computer hackers could easily access their systems because accessibility was not appropriately controlled. In other words, a User ID and a Password are not enough to protect your systems today. Additional security measures such as Secondary Protocols are critical.

Jack Kirsopp, Kirsopp Auto Body

As it was alluded to in the intro and the adjusting process, not everything went very smoothly. There were days that Jack was quite happy with us and days that he was not. One of the times that Jack probably wanted to "deck" me was after the adjuster finished explaining to Jack how they were going to adjust the loss almost about a month after the business was closed. Now, to clarify, Jack would not hurt anyone; he was expressing frustrations. You may recall, the Building and BPP discussion went well, but then it went "south" rapidly when the adjuster told Jack to put all the employees on unemployment rather than continuing to pay them.

During the Disaster Planning/Business Income Analysis, Jack was quite clear that good body shop employees and mechanics are hard to find. One of Jack's questions was, "How do we make sure that they're taken care of?" Therefore, regarding his business income coverage, we made sure that there was enough coverage limit to include all of Jack's payroll – or "ordinary payroll," as it is called – for all his employees. The goal was to ensure no limitations or restrictions in the policy relating to his employees receiving wages.

The adjuster was attempting to mitigate the cost of loss for the insurance company, but that was not an acceptable option. For the nine and a half months it took to release the site, design, and rebuild his business, none of Jack's employees ever missed a paycheck.

Making sure there was enough coverage, *How Much*, until Jack reopened, he reopened with one less employee. While getting paid to stay home, one employee took his wife to stay with his parents in Florida during the rebuild and decided to stay there. Interestingly enough, Jack reopened with one less employee and still had the same amount of output that he had before.

The ISO CP0030 Business Income (and Extra Expense) Coverage Form clearly states that it includes payroll. However, some insurance companies change their coverage form to limit "Ordinary Payroll" to not being covered or covered for only a certain number of days. The Ordinary Payroll limitation is quite common on Business Owner Policies. It is also common in policies that use *12 Months Actual Loss Sustained Business Income and Extra Expense Coverage* form to provide the Business Income coverage. "Ordinary Payroll" is typically defined as employees other than officers, executives, management personnel, and contract employees, and sometimes includes employees that you could not operate without (a.k.a. where you cannot hire a replacement for that person). A restaurant's Head Chef would not be ordinary payroll as Head chefs are imperative to a restaurant and sometimes are even management. But with the local restaurant I tried to help, the insurance company would not include the wife of the Head Chef when the business owner tried to claim she was the "maître de," even though they were a family-oriented Italian restaurant. The insurance company believed that people did not come to eat at the restaurant because of the "maître de" and that a replacement "maître de" was a "host" that could be easily replaced through proper hiring and training.

Because of this, be cautious of "ordinary payroll" limitations or exclusions. They may not be as transparent as having an **ISO CP1510 Payroll Limitation or Exclusion form** on your policy. The discussion on this topic will continue in the next chapter.

Suspension of Operations

You would think that *Suspension* of your *Operations* would be self-explanatory, but due to various reasons, ISO does need to define both.

"Suspension" means:
   a. The slowdown or cessation of your business activities; or
   b. That a part or all of the described premises is rendered untenantable, if coverage for Business Income Including "Rental Value" or "Rental Value" applies.

"Operations" means:
   a. Your business activities occurring at the described premises; and
   b. The tenantability of the described premises, if coverage for Business Income Including "Rental Value" or "Rental Value" applies.

All this means is that there needs to be *both* a reduction in your business activities or inability to perform any business activities, *and* the impact on your activities must occur at your physical location described in your policy.

A contractor may perform all their revenue-generating business activity away from their premise as they may construct, repair, or install components or equipment of a structure. Therefore, while completing a building, if there is a fire that damages or destroys the structure, the contractor would not be able to have an unendorsed Business Income policy pay for the loss of profit or any ongoing expenses like payroll. The contractor would be out of the business income and profit due to not completing the construction. This type of construction risk is better addressed through a Builders Risk that includes coverage for Overhead and Profit for that building under construction.

Your unaltered Business Income policy will not respond to your largest client or supplier/vendor having a fire. Their Suspension of Operations will impact your ability to generate revenue or profitability.

Although discussed later in Chapter 9, ISO did create several endorsements to fill in the holes from your offsite operations or the impact from key vendors or clients having a catastrophe:

- CP1501 Business Income from Dependent Properties Limited International Coverage
- CP1502 Extra Expense from Dependent Properties Limited International Coverage
- CP1506 Off-Premises Interruption of Business – Vehicles and Mobile Equipment
- CP1508 Business Income from Dependent Properties – Broad Form
- CP1509 Business Income from Dependent Properties – Limited Form
- CP1534 Extra Expense from Dependent Properties

Period of Restoration

The Period of Restoration is the trigger when the Business Income Coverage starts and ends. It is part of the conversation of *How Long* you will need your Business Income Coverage to last. There is also quite a bit of confusion relating to the period that a Business Income Policy pays:

"Period of restoration" means the period of time that:
a. Begins:
    (1) 72 hours after the time of direct physical loss or damage for Business Income Coverage; or
    (2) Immediately after the time of direct physical loss or damage for Extra Expense Coverage;
caused by or resulting from any Covered Cause of Loss at the described premises; and
b. Ends on the earlier of:
    (1) The date when the property at the described premises should be repaired, rebuilt or replaced with reasonable speed and similar quality; or
    (2) The date when business is resumed at a new permanent location.

> "Period of restoration" does not include any increased period required due to the enforcement of or compliance with any ordinance or law that:
> (1) Regulates the construction, use or repair, or requires the tearing down, of any property; or
> (2) Requires any insured or others to test for, monitor, clean up, remove, contain, treat, detoxify or neutralize, or in any way respond to, or assess the effects of "pollutants".
>
> The expiration date of this policy will not cut short the "period of restoration".

There is confusion when coverage starts.

The Period of Restoration does not start immediately. There is a waiting period for coverage to apply, sort of like a "timeframe" deductible. It usually is 72 hours or three days. The thought process is that a business should catch up from a short period of being closed from minor events like a summer storm that causes a temporary blackout. Business leaders are familiar with having a deductible when they have a property loss to their Building or BPP but seem to expect immediate coverage with their Business Income Coverage. That typically is due to the waiting period for the policy coverage to start is usually not listed in proposals or policy declaration pages but is built into the policy. Just so you are aware, you may reduce or eliminate the waiting period but need to do so by an endorsement and usually an additional premium charge.

There is confusion when coverage concludes.

The Period of Restoration does end abruptly and not when business leaders believe it should. The common misperception is that the Period of Restoration does not end until you return to pre-disaster operational levels and revenues, which is not the case. The Period of Restoration ends as soon as you have repaired or replaced your Building and Business Personal Property. In other words, the Period of Restoration ends when you have the *ability to resume all of the activities* you performed before the disaster. It does not matter if you are not operating at the same *activity levels* as before the disaster. The policy does go on to state that the Period of Restorations ends:

- The date that the property *should have been* repaired or replaced with reasonable speed.
- The date that you resume business at a new *permanent* location.

Also, the Period of Restorations does not include:

- Any delays in construction from having to comply with Ordinances or Laws.
- Any delays due to you having to have the property cleaned or treated due to any pollutants.

You can add the **CP1531 Ordinance or Law – Increased Period of Restoration** to extend the timeframe to allow for the additional time needed to comply with the codes.

The graph below depicts the Business Income Coverage, the first of the entire Business Income (and Extra Expense) Coverage Form that we will go through and build on. Business Income is specifically designed to pay for the Net Profit (or Loss) and ongoing expenses assuming a complete shutdown from the time of the Covered Cause of Loss until you can or should have been able to reopen.

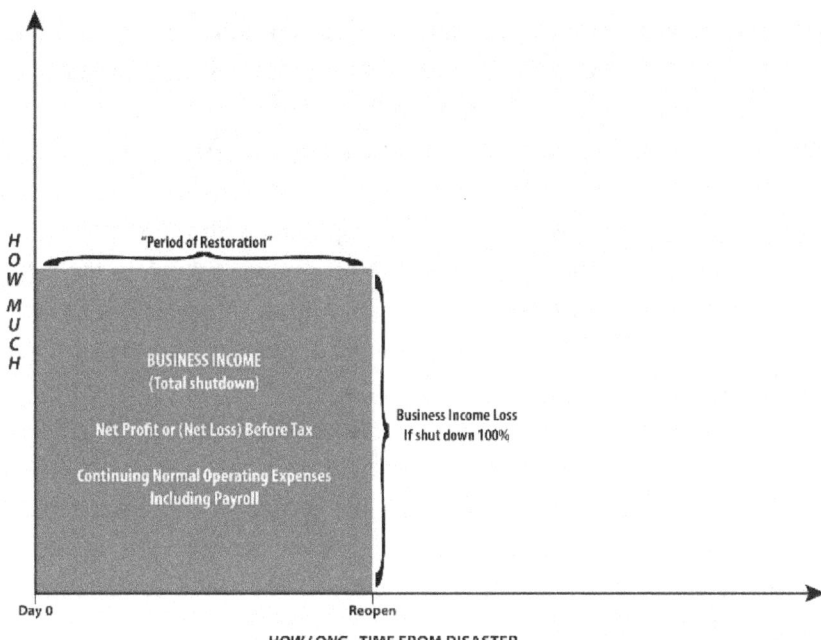

HOW LONG - TIME FROM DISASTER

To determine *How Long* you will need to have your Business Income coverage to last, you should consider how long you believe it will take to rebuild your facility, plus factor in any normal delays that may occur. As you may recall, during several examples, the stories showed that it might have taken months for the site to be released post-fire due to multiple investigations as to the cause and origin of the fire and possibly who was to be to blame for the fire. If someone other than the insured were to be at blame, that party would need time to investigate to defend themselves from the pending legal actions that may ensue.

During the interviews, there was one that their investigation timeframe lasted nine months as the local authorities and insurance company suspected it was arson. The local authorities took six months to determine the fire was intentionally set but also stated no evidence to point to who committed the arson. Therefore, they concluded their investigation and did not file any charges. They released the site, and then the insurance company proceeded to perform their own investigation to see if they could find some evidence that the person who set the fire was the business owner. If they could prove the owner committed arson, they would not have to pay the claim. After three additional months of investigation, the insurance company finally came to the same conclusion as the local authorities and agreed to pay the Building and BPP claim and the Business Income.

Being the expert witness in this suspected arson case was rather interesting. The Business Owners Policy had a *12 Month Actual Loss Sustained Business Income and Extra Expense Coverage* endorsement. The insurance company ceased paying for the Business Income Coverage as the coverage limit of 12 months had been exhausted. The insured did repair their facility within six months, but three months *after* the 12 months policy limitation ended. The judge ruled that the insurance company decided to delay construction with their own investigation. Hence, the insurance company owed the business owner coverage for the three-month delay that they caused.

In addition to the investigations, other expected things will occur that will slow down the reconstruction progress that the Period of Restoration contemplates:
- You need to work with an architect to design the new building and create plans,
- Interviewing, bidding, and determining who your General Contractor will be.
- Building permits will need to be submitted and approved.
- The site will need to be cleared of debris and prepared for construction.

These need to occur in an order as each step requires the last action to be completed before it starts. On an expedited basis, this could play out over two to three months, but some of the interviewed cases took upwards of six months due to the complexity of the new building.

To summarize, you should spend a considerable amount of time and due diligence determining your annual Business Income amount. It would help if you researched to determine how long it may take you to repair or replace your facility and all of your equipment. You also need to know if you will have to comply with any Laws or Ordinances that could delay repairs or reconstruction. But we are not finished determining *How Much* or *How Long*...

TAKEAWAYS/LESSONS LEARNED

For Chapters 6-8, the Takeaways and Lessons Learned will be at the end of Chapter 8 as all three chapters tie together to be your Business Income and Extra Expense Program.

Cash Flow is King!

Chapter 7

Retaining Customers is the Key

Now, having gone through what Business Income, the Period of Operation, and the Suspension of Operations are, you would think that *How Much* would be straightforward until you start to contemplate everything you still must pay for while you are closed or impaired during that Period of Restoration:

- Lease and loan payments not settled via building or contents coverage payments.
- Taxes including real estate taxes.
- Payroll.
- Profit (or loses - funded through borrowing or capital infusion).
- **Additional funds that are necessary to keep the business operating in some fashion.**
  - **Rent a temporary location.**
  - **Outsource production.**

The last items, in bold, are items that you would not normally spend money on but are needed. Because of these costs, this is why Extra Expense Coverage is needed to cover unexpected costs from being fully or partial shutdown.

EXTRA EXPENSE COVERAGE

While being closed, the protection of your cash flow is essential. But trying to retain as many clients as you can, is critical. Therefore, you may have to expend cash *beyond* ordinary operating expenses or provide more costly solutions than before the disaster to keep your clients. That is where Extra Expense comes in.

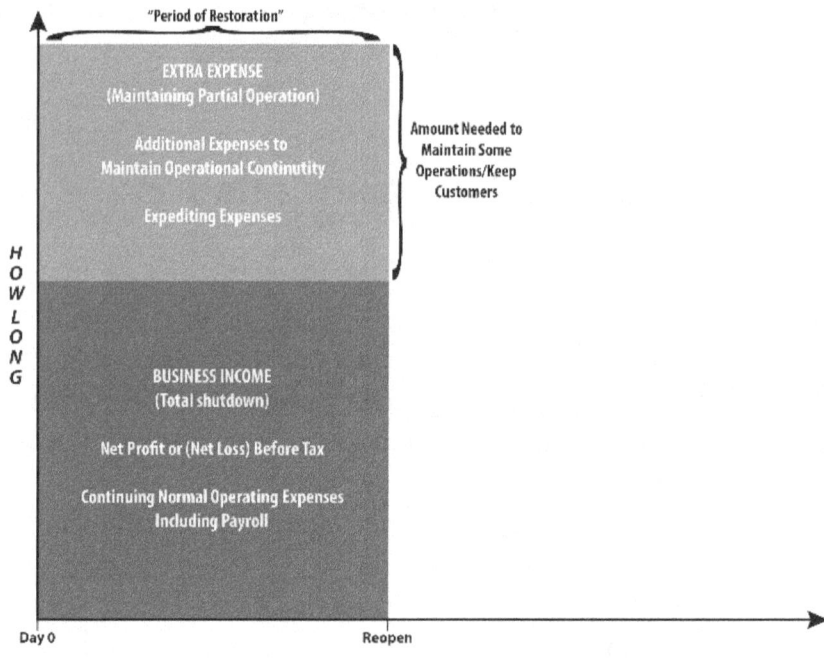
HOW LONG - TIME FROM DISASTER

Extra Expense is the amount of money needed to maintain operations in some capacity and retain your customers. For example, your may need to rent a temporary facility or outsourcing production to a 3rd party company(s). Extra Expense is to minimize the suspension of your business and ***DOES NOT NECESSARILY NEED TO REDUCE*** the actual business income claim that the insurance company pays out.

2. Extra Expense
   a. Extra Expense Coverage is provided at the premises described in the Declarations only if the Declarations show that Business Income Coverage applies at that premises.

> **b. Extra Expense** means necessary expenses you incur during the "period of restoration" that you would not have incurred if there had been no direct physical loss or damage to property caused by or resulting from a Covered Cause of Loss.

> We will pay Extra Expense (other than the expense to repair or replace property) to:
> 1) *Avoid or minimize the "suspension" of business and to continue operations* at the described premises or at replacement premises or temporary locations, including relocation expenses and costs to equip and operate the replacement location or temporary location.
> 2) *Minimize the "suspension" of business if you cannot continue "operations".*
>
> We will also pay Extra Expense to repair or replace property, but only to the extent it reduces the amount of loss that otherwise would have been payable under this Coverage Form.

We will take a quick pause to make the significant point that will hopefully help you realize that protecting your business's cash flow is not a simple process, nor is it readily understood by business leaders. The last workshop I presented before COVID-19 caused conferences and workshops to shift to the virtual universe happened to be on Business Income and Disaster Planning. During the workshop, I asked the attendees: *"Raise your hand if you feel that if you used 100% of your annual gross revenues as a business income limit on your insurance policy, that using that you would cause you to be over-insured? How about properly insured? Or how about underinsured?"*

If you are like 22 of the 23 business leaders, you probably would have raised your hand with *over-insured*.

Therefore, you will most likely find it hard to imagine that for a closed business for 12 1/2 months, the total amount the insurance company paid for business income coverage exceeded their annual revenue for the preceding 12 months before their fire? If you had purchased 100% of your sales as a business income limit, you would have been *underinsured* and ran out of insurance claim money.

Here is an example of an actual event that one business experienced to explain how complicated business income can be.

Ken Clifton, CCF Industries

You may recall that in less than 10 minutes from when the spark occurred that ignited the catastrophe, the fire was out of control, and the roofline started to collapse. Ken's business was destroyed.

There was an extensive investigation. The fire marshall and insurance companies needed to determine the root cause of this fire and any ability to subrogate against the fire suppression contractor who improperly installed and maintained the fire suppression system. Because of this, the insurance companies did not release the site for almost three and a half months.

We also discussed that Pittsburgh had one of the earliest, coldest and longest winters in years. When it was all said and done, it took 12 and a half months to rebuild Ken's building and install all the machinery and equipment, which allowed Ken to return to all of his pre-fire activities.

That was not the most challenging part of his claim saga.

Given the nature of Ken's operations, individual unit dust collection vacuums were not allowed by code. It would have taken six to seven months to acquire and install an extensive enough dust collection system as even a used one was unavailable at that time. Therefore, quickly moving to a temporary location to resume some operations was not doable. To keep his business in operation, Ken had to be very creative.

Ken and his team quickly started to reach out to just over a dozen manufacturers to make his dovetail drawers. Ken needed that number of operations that used multiple types of materials. Not every competitor was able to use the same material, nor did they have enough extra capacity to make as much as Ken needed to complete an entire order.

One of his friendly competitors, some 1,843 miles away in Arizona, did have some extra capacity and room, so Ken outsourced the most significant portion of manufacturing to that location. The product would get made, shipped to his temporary location, inspected, repackaged, and shipped to Ken as he did not want his competitors knowing who his customers were. There significant shipping coming from the Arizona manufacturer, as the drawers required inspecting and reshipping. Due to the amount of shipping costs, it made more sense to send three employees to Arizona to use that facility's equipment to help manufacture the drawers. Those employees could also inspect the work of others as it comes off the line, package it, and ship it under the name of CCF Industries.

Well, in about three months of working in Arizona and with other manufacturers, Ken was able to retain about 60-65% of his clientele-based business. The problem was the insurance company's business income adjuster called Ken at that point and said, *"Hey, Ken, we want to shut this outsourcing down. It costs too much money to outsource all this production. In fact, we are spending $1.37 for every dollar you are selling, so we are paying out a lot of money that is not needed."*

That is when I received a phone call from Kem, who was understandably quite livid and irate (justifiably so). Quickly, it was necessary to arrange a conference call with the adjuster for that same day. During the conversation, the adjuster repeatedly said that Extra Expense Coverage is to minimize the claim. He said that the costs associated with all this outsourcing were inflating the claim costs, not minimizing the loss as required in the policy.

I asked him what policy he was reading because that is not how the policy is worded. The Extra Expense coverage is to reduce the impact of the suspension of Ken's business, not to reduce the insurance company's costs. The coverage is so that you can reduce the impact on the business itself, not the impact on an insurance company.

But yes, outsourcing was quite expensive. Over the phone, everyone could hear the adjuster sift through papers, go quiet for a few moments, then proceed to apologize for the "error." He was confusing the Extra Expense with **Expediting Expenses**.

Within your Business Income and Extra Expense program, the policy will pay for Expediting Expenses, which is the amount of money needed to repair or replace the building and/or contents in a timeframe faster than normal.

For example, your desperately needed equipment manufacturer typically requires nine months lead time to manufacture and deliver the machine. However, for an additional 10% of the amount, they will manufacture the machine, ship it, and install it within six months. The insurance companies will only pay for Expediting Expenses *if* the outcome is expected to reduce the business income loss the insurance company will expect to pay. In this example, if the Expediting Cost of the machine is $20,000, but having that machine sooner will reduce the cost of the Business Income claim by $28,000, the insurance company will pay some of the expediting expenses.

However, we will confuse things a little more. Some insurance companies will add a separate coverage for a small amount of Expediting Expense that you can use at your discretion. That way, you can decide to have your BPP replaced faster, even if it does not reduce the overall costs of the Business Income claim.

Back to Ken's story. About ten months after the fire, one of the local woodworking shops that Ken was outsourcing work to happened to lose one of their largest clients and let some staff go. The owner reached out to Ken and allowed him to rent "part" of the facility and bring some of Ken's employees to work there.

All these actions allowed Ken to increase his production to 65-70% of his pre-fire revenue, which is quite lucky compared to the percentage of business retained by most interviewed businesses during their disaster shutdowns.

During the Disaster Planning/Business Income Coverage Analysis, there was a differing discussion with Ken relating to how much Business Income limit he would need for the Period of Restoration. Ken used to have $300,000 of coverage on his Business Income, with a 1/3-Monthly Limitation. He felt that he could set up shop quickly and just needed some coverage to pay to rent some property somewhere and cover a little bit of what might be a "shortfall of income" or some extra expenses.

Side note: a 1/3 Monthly Limitation is one of the ways to remove coinsurance. There are $1/3^{rd}$, $1/4^{th}$, and $1/6^{th}$ Monthly Limitations. In an effort to remove coinsurance, the insurance company will both limit you as to how much you can receive in any one given month and charge you a higher rate for the coverage. You would multiply the fraction by your limit, and that would be your monthly maximum. In Ken's case, that would have been $1/3^{rd}$ of $300,000, which is $100,000. Your business income limit can last longer if you do not use the full amount in any one month. In other words, you have a $300,000 limit and can use the available limit as long as you need it until you use it up, but you cannot exceed the maximum monthly limit in any one month. Many agents use this limitation to remove coinsurance and avoid having to complete a Business Income Worksheet, but claim time, the use of this limitation typically means that the business owner will be significantly underinsured.

Using the Business Income Worksheet and Ken's financials, we determined that Ken's Business Income for 12 months would be $2,100,000, based on his total revenue and expenses. Estimating for Extra Expense and the Extended Period of Restoration, we suggested Ken use $2,500,000-$2,700,000. Ken immediately felt that even the $2,100,000 was substantially too much and would be too expensive to increase his limits. Therefore, Ken did not want to do that.

Knowing full well that $300,000 would not be enough to keep Ken afloat, even short term, it was necessary to come up with a different solution or have another "confrontation" over **How Much** limit we had on the policy. Because of this, it is essential to proceed to negotiate with the insurance company for one of two things:

- One, provide a *12 Month Actual Loss Sustained Business Income and Extra Expense* policy limit with full coverage for ordinary payroll.
  - Plus, have the underwriter provide a *180 Day Extended Business Income Coverage* also included in the no dollar limit Actual Loss Sustained basis extended past the 12 months.
- Two, if the Timeframe Actual Loss Sustained form was limited to the duration of the coverage, and no more, we could use an 18 Months Actual Loss Sustained timeframe including 180 Days Extended Business Income within that 18 Months.

The underwriter agreed to the first option as there was less risk from the insurance company doing it that way. If the proposal showed no dollar limit, I hoped Ken would not argue about the increase in coverage. Also, so long as Ken could rebuild within 12 months, Ken would have an additional six months to try to bring his business back up to speed as quickly as possible. With either solution, Ken would have been better off than with $300,000.

As we approached the 12-month anniversary of the disaster, it became necessary to occasionally wipe the nervous sweat from my brow as we were running out of time on the 12 Months of coverage for the Period of Restoration. As mentioned before, reconstruction and moving in caused Ken to overshoot the 12 months by two weeks. So yes, there were two weeks of business income coverage that the insurance company did not pay. Therefore, please keep that in mind when it comes to factoring in the timeframe to reconstruct your building, as Ken felt that they could rebuild in six to nine months when I first met him.

When all was said and done, on a $3,000,000 revenue manufacturing business, the total loss of Business Income and Extra Expense, including Extended Period of Indemnity, ended up being $3,800,000 million: 26% more than his annual revenue. The amount was far more than anyone could contemplate based on other cases experienced before or been interviewed since, all because the Extra Expense associated with outsourcing was so significant.

However, after talking to John from the machine shop, he also said that outsourcing what his customers wanted was also rather expensive. You may be asking why $1.35 to $1.40 per $1.00 of a sold product? It has to do with the fact that you will have to buy whatever you have made by someone else at "full retail" price. Even a friendly competitor will not sell anything at a discount or without profit when they could sell their own products for a full price and full profit to their own customers. Therefore, in addition to paying the "full retail" price, you will then pay to have the goods shipped to you so you can inspect and re-label under your name and then pay to ship them again to your client. Having the competitor ship directly to your client would advertise your clients to your competitors and promote your competitors to your client.

You can now see the significant issues: estimated Extra Expense and how much is needed for the Extended Business Income timeframe. With Ken, the Extra Expense was north of $1,000,000 for a business that brought in $3,000,000 in pre-disaster revenue. You might think that is a surprising, staggering number - *it is!* That is the point. The amount you may believe you need to effectively operate with outsourcing production, or buying from competitors and reselling, will be staggering.

As part of the Disaster Planning/Business Continuity planning, it is essential to take the time to analyze what the additional costs of outsourcing may be so you can fund them through the insurance program. You may be thinking that will raise your insurance premiums. Yes, it may, but there are two reasons to do it: one, you will dramatically increase your potential success of surviving a disaster; and two, Business Income Coverage rates are far, far lower than the rates for building and significantly lower than those of BPP. Therefore, you can afford to buy more Business Income coverage.

Going back to the workshop of 23 business leaders, would you now vote by raising your hand with *underinsured?* If that is the case, you are starting to realize the additional costs, the Extra Expense needed to keep as many of your customers, is just as important as the loss of profit and ongoing expenses.

You must do what is necessary to retain as many clients as possible during this recovery period. You may have to outsource the manufacturing of your products to several competitors. You may have to buy materials at retail rates so you can sell at wholesale prices, particularly when your vendors cannot provide you with enough supplies. In the end, Ken retained 60 to 65% of their clients active during the Period of Restoration.

By the way, the one business owner that did not raise their hand until *underinsured* said she assumed it was a trick question and waited till what she figured was my last option, *underinsured*.

We will discuss in Chapter 9 how to determine your limit and minimize the chances that you overshoot or overpay for the coverage.

Now that you are starting to understand Business Income more, you are probably thinking: *OK, I am ready to figure out* **How Much** *we will need*. But there is more. Before addressing that, you still need to understand **How Long**, as **How Long** will also influence **How Much**.

How Long is a little more complicated and therefore where most businesses fail:
- *How Long* will you be shut down?
- More importantly, **How Long** will it take for you to regain your client base and return to a revenue flow similar to before the loss?

Most business leaders will start to rationalize *(optimism)* here that they can repair their building in less than a month. But what if investigators do not release the area for a few weeks. What permits will you need? Will you need engineering work because of possible structural issues? Will you need to do more extensive work because Ordinance or Law dictates that you were damaged enough that you now have to comply? But that is not ***How Long***?

For ***How Long***, you need to start imagining the inconceivable: *the complete destruction of your business*. Most business leaders will begin to rationalize that a total loss is not possible. Ask any of the business leaders who went through a catastrophe if they believed it was possible. They did not. You must think about and plan for the *Worst-Case Disaster* for your Disaster Recovery Plan and when you design your insurance program.

If you are still worried about your premium, you can make changes to reduce your rates:
- You could take a more extended waiting period before coverage starts,
- You can influence the underwriter by sharing your Disaster Recovery Plan to show that you can reduce the cost of the loss as you are ready. The latter goes a long way to earning lower rates (more credits) to afford more insurance.

But before really digging into the ***How Much*** and ***How Long*** discussion, you need to understand one more insurance coverage, as it is just as important as what we discussed so far. It is about the second of those two ***How Long*** questions: ***How Long*** *will it take for you to regain your client base and return to a revenue and profit flow similar to before the loss?*

TAKEAWAYS/LESSONS LEARNED

For Chapters 6-8, the Takeaways and Lessons Learned will be at the end of Chapter 8 as all three chapters tie together to be your Business Income and Extra Expense Program.

Chapter 8

You Reopened, Now What?

Imagine this, you move into your brand-new facility with all the materials and/or equipment needed to perform all of your pre-disaster activities, and you have your Grand Reopening party. You swing open the doors, and what happens? Other than some local customers, friends and family, and the local politicians, who else shows up? Then the following day, you turn on your computer, and the emails for orders and inquiries are nowhere near the level of what they were before the disaster. The phone is not ringing off the hook.

Your Period of Restoration is over; your Business Income Coverage is over.

You have all the stuff you need, so there is no longer any need for Extra Expense.

So, what happens next?

Where are your customers?

What happens to your cash flow?

What enabled Ken to keep the doors open long term was not the unlimited dollar amount during the Period of Restoration. It was the

180 Days that he had for **Extended Business Income Coverage**. In essence, Extended Business Income insures your "cash flow," or in other words, the amount of money you need to maintain operations and pre-catastrophe profitability while your business tries to regain customers or earn new customers and provides you with more time to return revenue to pre-catastrophe levels.

EXTENDED BUSINESS INCOME COVERAGE

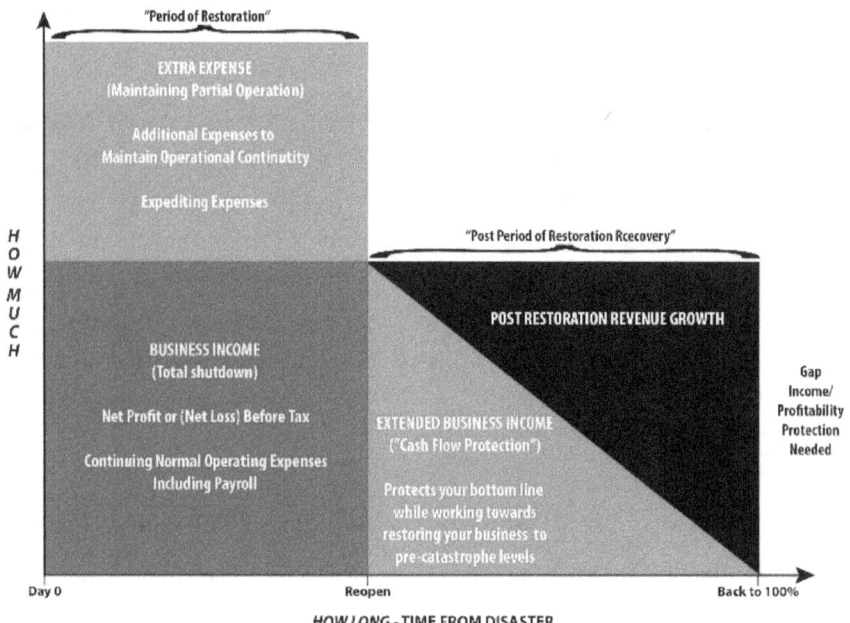

The Extended Business Income Coverage provided Ken six months of coverage to work hard and quickly earn more of his customers back and bring on some new ones. All to get his revenue back to as close to pre-fire as possible and give him time to make adjustments to return to profitability before the Extended Business Income Coverage ended.

At the end of Ken's six months, Ken was running close to 85-90% of pre-fire revenue and was operating at about break-even despite the higher the new debt load.

How did Ken do that? One thing that was not yet explained was that Ken decided to finance some additional equipment purchases. We had a conversation about not reopening as Ken was, but as he wanted to be. He should focus on being more efficient moving forward. Rather than opening as was, but open as Ken wanted to be. Before the loss, Ken would add a piece of equipment and hire a person to operate it when he saw a workstation, and that operator starts to max out in terms of capacity. Having a fresh restart enabled Ken to look at his business as a new slate and determine ways to do things more efficiently. He even worked with a consultant on lean manufacturing techniques. It was Ken's opportunity to reimagine how his business could operate more efficiently and effectively.

Ken purchased a CNC Plywood Panel Saw that helped him reduce wood waste and save a significant amount of time. Before the fire, he had three Panel Saw Workstations where an employee would insert a five-foot-by-five-foot piece of plywood and rough cut the drawer bottoms and panels to about one-quarter to one-half inch of excess. The manual panel saw was not accurate enough to be used in the final drawer assembly. The rough boards would then go to Table Saw Workstations, where the operators cut them to precise sizes. The new CNC panel saw was precise, basically eliminating two Panel Saw Workstations, two Table Saw Workstations, and their respective employees.

You should not feel bad about the four employees, they effectively "quit" during the eight to nine months leading to the remote work at the local workshop. Ken rotated employees through the inspection and shipping operations for when the product came in. Before the fire, Ken significantly focused on safety, even hiring the award-winning Safety and Human Resources firm East Coast Risk Management to cut his employee injury rate by more than 95%. The focus on safety allowed Ken to slash Ken's workers' compensation premium to help pay for Ken's additional coverages. After the fire, Ken became ultra-focused on safety as he never wanted to go through rebuild again. Ken maintained his twice a month safety training and meetings and even started training his employees on their new equipment for two months before they would eventually reopen. All employees continued to receive 100% of pay while only working maybe five percent to fifteen percent of their regular hours. If an employee had more than two unexcused absences, they were terminated. Yes, some people did not show up and did not think of calling ahead to say they were out of town visiting relatives, which would have been allowable. They did not even call to say they were sick; they did not show up for a short shift for full pay.

We are back to imagining this disaster happened to you. You had your Grand Reopening party, doors are open, and what happens next? You have everything you need, except customers. For acquiring customers, what do you need? *Marketing?* You may have that or can create that. *Salespeople?* You have that. *Time?* Now, there is the issue.

You need time to get customers back. Not only that, but you must obtain orders, perform the service or make or acquire the product and ship it, bill the customer, and collect payment. If you are not a retail establishment where you have inventory and get paid as it walks out the door, you usually must bill a customer and receive payment 30, 60, or 90 days later. What happens to your cash flow? When you are short of your cash flow, where do you get money to pay your employees? Pay expenses? Do you need to borrow money to make the bills, and will you have the profits later to afford the payments? If your cash flow is poor, will a bank even loan you money?

It would seem so much easier if you could have the insurance company protect your cash flow *after* reopening. In fact, built into the Business Income and Extra Expense Coverage Form, there is a coverage that can do just that. It is the **Extended Business Income Coverage** part of the policy. As you saw in the last diagram, Extended Business Income protects your cash flow for a defined period of time after you reopen. It is essentially a gap filler between your expected Business Income and how you actually performed during that timeframe after reopening.

> **(3) Extended Business Income**
> **(1) Business Income Other Than "Rental Value"**
> (a) If the necessary "suspension" of your "operations" produces a Business Income loss payable under this policy, we will pay for the actual loss of Business Income you incur during the period that:
> (b) Begins on the date property (except "finished stock") is actually repaired, rebuilt or replaced and "operations" are resumed; and
> (c) Ends on the earlier of:
>   (i) The date you could restore your "operations", with reasonable speed, to the level which would generate the business income amount that would have existed if no direct physical loss or damage had occurred; or
>   (ii) 60 consecutive days after the date determined in (1)(a) above.
>
> However, Extended Business Income does not apply to loss of Business Income incurred as a result of unfavorable business conditions caused by the impact of the Covered Cause of Loss in the area where the described premises are located.
>
> Loss of Business Income must be caused by direct physical loss or damage at the described premises caused by or resulting from any Covered Cause of Loss.

> **(1) "Rental Value"**
> **(a)** If the necessary "suspension" of your "operations" produces a "Rental Value" loss payable under this policy, we will pay for the actual loss of "Rental Value" you incur during the period that:
> **(b)** Begins on the date property is actually repaired, rebuilt or replaced and tenantability is restored; and
> **(c)** Ends on the earlier of:
> **(i)** The date you could restore tenant occupancy, with reasonable speed, to the level which would generate the "Rental Value" that would have existed if no direct physical loss or damage had occurred; or
> **(ii)** 60 consecutive days after the date determined in (2)(a) above.
> However, Extended Business Income does not apply to loss of "Rental Value" incurred as a result of unfavorable business conditions caused by the impact of the Covered Cause of Loss in the area where the described premises are located.
> Loss of "Rental Value" must be caused by direct physical loss or damage at the described premises caused by or resulting from any Covered Cause of Loss.

Therefore, so long as you spend your actual money on necessary ordinary expenses, the adjuster will compare your actual performance with the project monthly Business Income pre-loss, possibly adjusted for trends and financial pro forma. In every one of my clients, the business income adjuster looked at the financials monthly. This is probably due to that being the smallest timeframe a business usually measures financial performance. For example, suppose before the fire, you averaged $50,000 of profit. If, after the disaster, taking your actual revenue and subtracting all necessary ongoing expenses, including payroll, you ended up operating at a loss of $25,000 for that month. In this case, the insurance company would pay you $75,000 in an Extended Business Income payment to get you to the expected monthly profit level.

However, if you have any new expenses after the loss that did not exist before the disaster, those expenses would not be included in calculating any Extended Business Income Payment needs. Using Ken as an example, imagine if his new debt load was $15,000 per month more than pre-fire. If Ken used to have an expected $50,000 profit per month, his new profit equivalent would be $35,000. Therefore, if operating a month at a $25,000 monthly loss, instead of receiving $75,000, Ken would receive $60,000 in Extended Business Income payment. The insurance company would deduct the $15,000 of the new additional debt service. (No, there will not be any math on the final exam.)

You will note that the standard Business Income and Extra Expense coverage form provides the 60 Day Extended Business Income. This can be changed by endorsement or by showing a different timeframe on the declaration page, depending upon each insurance company.

Suppose you happen to look at your insurance policy and see different wording. In that case, the coverage form discussed is the **CP0030 Business Income (and Extra Expense) Coverage Form** with an edition date of 10/2012 (it will most likely show as CP 00 30 10 12 on your schedule of endorsements on your declaration page). If your insurance company uses the 06/2007 or earlier editions, these editions only provided 30 Days.

Now the question for you to answer – *How long of an Extended Business Income period do you need?*

The Unexpected Issues AFTER Reopening

Funny thing, when you boil down human nature, people are creatures of habit. Routines, as some may call it. In general, people tend to continue to do what they were doing until something causes a change in the status quo, and then they look for options. People like to go to the same stores, eat at certain restaurants, have pre-game routines, and even go to the same, or few, vacation spots.

Face it, if you are someone's favorite business to order from, frequent, shop, and you are not open for some time, what do you think your customers may do? Sit back and patiently wait till you can be there for them? Maybe a tiny percentage of customers may wait.

In reality, they will probably look at options. If you frequent a restaurant once a month or multiple times a month, and they are closed for several months, you probably try a few places and eventually find a "new" favorite place to frequent. Then, when you see the old place reopened, you may or may not go back or may go back less frequently. Or possibly, what happened to my wife at our local restaurant happens to you. After it reopened, my wife went to dinner with her mom, sister, and our daughter for a "girl's night out." When I asked her about the restaurant when she got home, she just kept saying the food "was not quite the same," the staff "was not quite the same," and since there were some new people, there was an error her sister's order. On our next "date night," when I suggested we go there as I had not been to the restaurant yet, she said we should go to the other local restaurant we started to frequent. Since then, we did go back but did not frequent nearly as much as we had in the past as we added somewhere else to our routines of favorite places to eat out. When others did the same, you can now see why the business owner eventually had to close.

That is what will most likely happen to your business. You will have to lure your clients back, and if something, even very minor, is off just a little, they will assume that things are different and may or may not continue to use your business. Therefore, you will need to earn new clients. Remember how tight your cash flow was when you first opened your business? You will have to earn new clients with what might be tighter or even more negative cash flow.

If the local restaurant had protected its cash flow with Extended Business Income coverage for a year, the owner felt he might have been able to make it. However, when asked if the owner would have protected his cash flow for two years, he said he believes he would have made it as the first two years were his most challenging years when he initially started the restaurant.

You must look at the type of business you are and how long it took you to build your business, and on top of that, how long it takes you to acquire a client. The local banquet hall, where we have held several events over the years when asked about the timeframe to earn clients they commented that some events, like weddings and graduations, can be booked more than a year in advance. Sometimes they took 18 months or more. We booked our daughter's wedding reception venue 19 months before her wedding. But asking my daughter to imagine if the banquet hall were closed when she started looking, would she have booked a venue based on the renderings and drawings of the finished facility? She said she would have looked elsewhere for fear that it might not be open or not as nice as presented. Therefore, this banquet hall has two years of Extended Business Income coverage.

Bill Coyne, Coyne's Auto

On March 23rd, 2015, Bill Coyne called early in the morning to inform us that his place had caught fire. The two-hour drive north to Edinboro, Pennsylvania, to meet with Bill was scenic and uneventful despite several inches of snow on the ground still. Upon arrival, although the front of the building did not look too bad, only a little smudged and dark from smoke damage, a gaping hole where the garage door used to be, and the front windows were smashed in. But when you went inside, the entire back half of the building and roof were missing. That is where I found Bill. As soon as you saw Bill's face, everyone could see the feeling of being overwhelmed and gut-wrenching concern. Bill was an easy read as we go back for more than 35 years as he was in my brother's high school class.

That morning, Bill arrived to open and start up the three-employee auto repair shop for the day just as his mechanics were about to come.

As usual, the first thing that morning, Bill turned on his computer in the office, which also was the server for his business. Bill proceeded to go into the repair shop area to start the three-day-old Service Area computer. The new computer enabled his mechanics to work efficiently, order parts, and enter work orders.

The day before, Bill had purchased the battery backup system as the computer rebooted a few times each day due to power fluctuations. When he turned on the power, the battery pack somehow created a spark, or it exploded. Investigations determined that the lithium battery was defective.

That immediately started to catch the manuals on fire that he had stored next to the desk for mechanics to research on how to repair things, find part numbers, and so forth for various types of vehicles. By the time Bill responded with a fire extinguisher, it was already too late.

Bill had been a fixture in the community. And although he was a tenant in the building, everyone knew his building as his daughter had painted an incredible mural of all the Pittsburgh Steelers Hall of Fame players on the front of the building.

Luckily, Bill was able to find a building that had just been vacated about two months prior from a tire dealership and was just four miles down the very same road he was on. Bill proceeded to move into his temporary location. Unfortunately, this facility was slightly smaller than what he was used to by almost 200 square feet, which created issues for when he started to restock and buy his tools and equipment, but as it was temporary, he made do.

Working with the Alliance of Automotive Service Providers of Pennsylvania, they could get the state to expedite Bill's vehicle inspection license. The tool manufacturers helped Bill obtain all of the equipment, tools, and everything he needed to be in business in just over two months.

Just after the fire department extinguished the fire, things went crazy. The landlord was in Bill's face demanding Bill, or his insurance company, pay for the repairs because the fire "was due to Bill's operations." The insurance company and the fire investigation confirmed it was the battery backup that started the fire. That meant the Fire Legal Liability (aka Property Damage Liability) coverage on Bills' insurance certificate would not pay the landlord for the building. The insurance company would not pay as Bill, nor his operations were legally liable for causing the fire and resulting damages.

The tricky part came after the building owner informed Bill, thinking that fire legal liability coverage would cover him for *any* fire (and that he was suing). The landlord happened to drop his building coverage due to his misunderstanding of insurance. With the building not going to be repaired any time soon and with the owner unable to pay for any repairs, Bill was informed about three months after the fire that the landlord would not be rebuilding. As there were no other suitable locations for Bill, Bill's temporary location became his permanent new location. By the way, Bill's policy did later successfully defend Bill in court over the Fire Legal Liability lawsuit.

You would think that being in business, with everything he needed just four miles down the same road, was a fortunate outcome that would minimize the impact on Bill's business. But you would be wrong.

Although on the same road, four miles further away from the college town he was located in, Bill had started seeing a significant reduction in client traffic. Bill reached out to some of his customers, and they responded that they felt that he was too far away. Thus, 95% of the college students from the state university stopped using him as he was "too far away" for them to get back to school from dropping off their cars. When the Period of Restoration ended as soon as Bill was in his "new" facility, there was no longer any Extra Expense Coverage to pay for a shuttle service anymore, and the student business dried up completely.

People are creatures of habit and convenience.

The distance to the new location made it worse.

What saved Bill was the 365 Day Extended Business Income Coverage. As was discovered when investigating why Bill had a quick drop in revenue of almost 50%, the phone survey showed why some people were no longer using his services due to the distance and ease of access. This led to going on the marketing offensive to gain new customers. After negotiating with the insurance company for some marketing money, the insurance company agreed to fund the marketing campaign we presented as the insurance company was facing paying the Extended Business Income for up to a year. If Bill could rebuild his revenue base back faster, the amount that the insurance company would have to pay ultimately could be reduced significantly.

Using the client data from Bill's backed-up system, Bill also purchased a list of all businesses and residences within five miles of his shop. This enabled Bill to send out postcards and brochures with coupons in them and invited the prospects to his *Grand Reopening* with *"FREE Hotdogs, Soda, and kid activities."*

Although Bill lost slightly more than half of his customer base for thinking it was too far to drive to get their car fixed, he picked up a significant number of individuals and business customers through the marketing efforts. They included a Saturday open-house grand reopening and coupons for services.

About ten months after the end of the Period of Restoration, the marketing to attract new customers enabled Bill to return to the same revenue he was before, which was 13 months post-fire. At 60 days, Bill would have been at 55% to 60% of income; at six months, Bill was at about 75% to 80% percent.

The first lesson learned here was that just because you have reopened and start to get customers back, cash flow is king. You need to protect the business's cash flow and protect it for as long as you can.

Other lessons learned were improving the marketing process post reopening to attract customers back and making sure that a business extends the Extended Business Income out for a long period as a business can afford. The association insurance program Bill had included 90 Days Extended Business Income. To increase it to 180 Days was a premium change of about one percent a year increase, and going to 365 Days was only an additional few dollars on top of that. Therefore Bill purchased the 365 Days Extended Business Income.

The nice part was that including one year of extended business income was *the* reason why the insurance company was willing to help pay for the additional marketing. Without the extra marketing money, Bill would have struggled to pay for it, and it was needed to attract new customers. Once Bill could regain and rebuild his cash flow to be closer to where he was before, the insurance company would have to pay less. Since the insurance company was looking at a year-long Extended Business Income, they were more than willing to do so because it was a reasonable cost in exchange. Extra Expense ends at the end of the Period of Restoration, so technically, the insurance company would not have to pay for it, but they saw the bigger picture and benefit.

In the end, Bill's Extended Business Income, although the adjuster did calculate it for each of the 12 months after the disaster, was not needed in months 11 and 12.

Last lesson: People are creatures of habits. If something happens to break their patterns, it will affect your business.

You are probably thinking right now, *how long of an Extended Business Income period will I need?* Once again, it depends upon what you do, how long it takes for you to obtain clients and get paid, can you even operate at a temporary location, and how much your customers are creatures of habit. Remember, some highlighted businesses stated that they could not temporarily locate, and others could not relocate anywhere nearby. 30 or 60 Days for Extended Business Income would have been way too short for any interviewed businesses. But if need to still you ask, these would be estimated minimums based on what other businesses have had that were successful:

- Retail: may be the easiest to recover, but 90 days to one year may be enough depending upon competition in the area. The problem is if you have to relocate. 90 to 180 days may be acceptable in the same place, but you may need a year if you

end up located further away. Check your available locations before renewing your insurance or assume the worst case.
- Restaurants: as people like to eat at favorite places, should look to one to two years.
- Hotels & Banquet facilities: 18 months to two years, an event planner has stated that she has seen events planned as much as three to four years in advance, but most seem to be one and a half to two years.
- Hotels that do not have conferences/events: 180 days to one year.
- Manufacturing: can be more challenging to determine. One to two years, or more, may be needed.

To give you an idea that Extended Business Income is important and that longer timeframes are needed, ISO has set rates for a business to extend the coverage to as long as two years. However, some insurance companies can go longer.

No matter what you do, the longer you can protect your cash flow after reopening, the more likely you will survive. Lengthen the Extended Business Income period for a long as you can afford, and factor in the Business Income limit to cover that extra timeframe.

Ways to reduce your Business Income rates to afford more coverage for *How Much* and *How Long* will be discussed later.

Sam's Cabinet Shop

During Ralph Sitterson, Vice President of Loss Management at the Keystone Insurers Group and former Senior Vice President of Claims for the W. R. Berkley Mid Atlantic Insurance Group interview, Ralph conveyed the following story:

"I remember what happened to a gentleman by the name of Sam, who owned a cabinetry shop. Sam had a fire that was not a total loss; however, the rebuild took about ten months. During this time, all the local builders who used this cabinet builder had to find another cabinet maker to fill their orders. Once the cabinet maker who had the fire reopened, he had lost his customer base.

Unfortunately, the business income was only structured to pay until the business could resume normal production. The cabinet maker who had the fire struggled to get his contractors back and was successful in getting only some of them back. Unfortunately, it was too few too late, and the cabinet maker went out of business. It was heartbreaking to see what happened to Sam.

"Sam's story illustrates the importance of having alternative plans to continue operations and finding ways to meet customer's needs through the use of your Extra Expense coverage. It also illustrates the need to have business income structured such that the business income applies after the business has reopened and hopefully until a business returns to normal profitability. Many business owners and agents forget to consider this period when a business owner needs to re-ramp up their business and recover lost clients due to a covered loss. It can take 6 to 12 months to get back to the business income level you were before the loss. Therefore, it is critically important that in considering a loss of income limit that you not only consider the cost to rebuild the building but the time and loss of income that occurs while rebuilding your customer base."

Ralph clarified that the business owner had unused limits of business income coverage. However, the policy no longer had any time available to pay for the business income claim due to the Extended Business Income providing just 60 days of coverage post reopening.

The Manufacturing Dilemma with Extended Business Income

There is a problem, or a "hole," that exists for manufactures between the Business Income Coverage portion of the coverage and the Extended Business Income Coverage. Under the Business Income, the Period of Restoration ENDS when you have replaced all your "stuff" you had before the disaster.

Under Extended Business Income, the coverage BEGINS on the date your property (except "finished stock") is repaired, rebuilt, or replaced, and "operations" can be resumed.

"Finished stock" means stock you have manufactured, which also includes whiskey and alcoholic products needing to be aged, unless there is a Coinsurance percentage shown for Business Income in the Declarations and does not include stock you have manufactured and held for sale on the premises of any retail outlet insured under this Coverage Part.

The cost of making the finished inventory that was waiting to be sold before the disaster, and the items in the process of being produced but not yet finished, are not covered by the Business Income or Extended Business Income coverages. The cost of your labor and additive expenses such as utilities to remake the products and the good in process are not paid for by the Business Income nor Extended Business Income coverages. The Business Income policy coverage form thereby shifts the coverage for the cost of those completed and in-process products to your property policy.

The hole exists because your Business Personal Property covers the actual cost of making your finished goods as well as the costs of goods in process. As discussed in Chapter 3 under Valuations, under the Actual Cash Value descriptions, ISO does help a business by valuing "Stock" that you have sold but not delivered at the *selling price* (less discounts and expenses you otherwise would have had). However, if you have finished goods that have not been sold, they will be valued at ACV, which would essentially be your actual costs to make the product.

Therefore, your Business Personal Property pays for the raw materials and components you need to make your product, as well as your additive costs to make them. As I just reiterated, BPP pays for the loss of profit for goods *sold* and *ready to be shipped*. The hole in the Business Income and Extended Business Income coverages is the *profit* from the *unsold finished* products. The profit from the finished goods not sold destroyed by the disaster will not be paid for by either your BPP or your Business Income, nor will Extended Business Income coverages pay for that lost profit.

However, if you have finished goods that have not been sold, they will be valued at ACV. Therefore, you must add either the

CP9930 Manufacturer's Selling Price (Finished "Stock" Only) or CP9931 Market Value Stock endorsement. Otherwise, you will forever lose the profit, which is the difference in value between ACV and your cost of selling.

Without addressing this valuation, you would be making the product twice for one profit. The hole in coverage becomes a more significant issue if your product has to "age," like alcohol, as the profit from the destroyed aging product is needed to pay for you to make the next batch that will need to be aged. Extended Business Income does not pay for the "aging" timeframe unless you have the Coinsurance percentage removed from your Business Income policy. Therefore, include the aging and finished alcohol sales value into your BPP value and add the ISO CP9905 Distilled Spirits and Wines Market Value coverage form.

LESSONS FROM SUPERSTORM SANDY

The interviews with businesses leaders affected by this hurricane, both the ones that survived and those that did not make it, provided some clear lessons that should be heeded when it comes to planning for disasters that can affect a large area: floods, earthquakes, wildfires, tornadoes, and yes, hurricanes. We already discussed that many of the business leaders stated that they could not reopen following Sandy due to the significant surge in the pricing of building materials and labor costs. The rise of the expenses made it impossible to afford the significant additional costs required to rebuild or repair their facilities. And in some cases, some landlords could not afford to rebuild, causing some businesses to lose their location. Plus, new facilities were not available or were too costly to rent.

The lessons learned relating to Business Income Coverage and disasters affecting large areas are numerous. Sarah owned a diner a block and a half off of the New Jersey shoreline. Like many other business leaders, she was unable to hire a contractor for more than a year. She had to frustratingly wait to begin repairing her building and replacing her kitchen equipment and dining area tables. Because of these delays, many businesses ran out of Business Income Coverage due to either exhausting their available policy limit or, much like Sarah, exhausted their 12 Month Actual Loss Sustained Business Income Period of Restoration of their policy.

What also occurs when there is so much widespread devastation is that not everyone can rebuild and recover quickly for the reasons we just stated. They cannot afford to do so or are unable to find contractors. The problems then compound. With so many other businesses and residences taking years to rebuild, it took years for many people and businesses to return to the area and vacationers to return and rent the homes in the area. After Sarah struggled mentally and financially for almost 19 months that it took to reopen finally, there physically were not enough customers in the area to patronize her diner. Several successful business leaders commented that it took them anywhere from four to six years to have their revenues return to what they had before Sandy. Sarah's potential clientele, unfortunately, took too long to return, and she sadly closed the doors just over a year later.

Therefore, you may want to learn from those affected by Superstorm Sandy and purchase more specific Business Income limits. To survive, you may need to outlast an extended Period of Restoration that will occur in such events. Rather than buying a simple 12 Month Actual Loss Sustained Business Income policy, you should also look to making your Extended Business Income coverage last for as long of a timeframe as you can afford. Some insurance companies offer 18 Month or 24 Month Actual Loss Sustained Business Income policies, but you still need to look at Ordinary Payroll Limitations and the Extended Business Income coverage limitations.

While discussing the benefit of a two-year Extended Business Income Coverage Period, several of those failed businesses commented that they believe they would have made it if they had protected two years of their cash flow. That may be the *Optimism - Behavioral Risk Bias* talking that they may still possess. However, for those who did try to make a go of it, a more extended timeframe of cash flow protection would have enabled them to have an additional two-year head start on rebuilding. They would have had two years of not spending any personal investments or assets they possessed, which they lost while trying to stay open. Sarah burned through her family's cash reserves and their home equity line of credit on top of working 80 plus hour work weeks so that she would not have to pay for another person on staff.

A longer Extended Business Income period would have protected their cash flow, and interestingly enough, they could have even put additional profits in their pockets during that additional Extended Period. The business leaders could have frugally banked those profits, as they did see the delays in people returning to the area. That extra cash may have increased the likelihood that they would have been able to get past time of almost absolutely to no customers to a point where there was a good customer flow, enough flow to help them maintain operations.

TAKEAWAYS/LESSONS LEARNED

Your head may be spinning a little, but we build on a necessary but lengthy conversation when you go through a Disaster Planning/Business Income Coverage Analysis. The ultimate goal of this chapter is to help you determine ***How Long*** and ***How Much.***

- Begin a general plan to rebuild your facility and the expectations in terms of time needed. Talk to a commercial contractor and ask them to estimate how long it may take to plan, prepare, and construct.
- Add time to the contractor's estimate for both general delays in construction, as well as at least two to four months (or more) to have your site released to you.
- Review the Code related items and determine how much extra time is needed to construct your facility to meet new Building Codes.

- Begin to determine your markup for finished goods and estimate the difference in values you have between the costs of your finished goods and your general sales price.
- Look at the Commercial Real Estate websites to investigate comparable properties to determine how much they might be to rent. If there are properties that will enable you to relocate there temporarily, or is there nothing that you can move into? It would also be good to determine if any of these facilities will allow your operations to rent the facility and obtain an occupancy code due to any ordinances.
- What other costs would you incur working from a temporary location that you do not have to pay for now?
- Look at your competition's pricing and determine how much it would cost to purchase from them, and then the costs of shipping to you on an expedited basis.
- Determine the longest timeframe it has taken you to identify a prospective customer to work with, the time that it takes to complete the product or services rendered, and then get paid.
- How many new customers can you adequately begin to work with within any given month? The goal is to determine how long it might take for you to generate revenue from both existing customers and new prospects to return to pre-loss activity levels.

Chapter 9

Do not Run Out of money!

The last three chapters provided an overview of the critical "cash flow" protection coverages needed to help a business survive a catastrophe: Business Income, Extra Expense, and Extended Business Income. We also went through the important concept of the Period of Restoration.

It is essential to understand these concepts with more clarity regarding **How Much** and **How Long** the Business Interruption coverage is needed to protect your business's cash flow. Otherwise, you will become one of those affected by the scary statistic of 50% of businesses not surviving after a disaster.

We have also discussed the reasons **WHY** so many insurance agents and business owners are unable to fully understand the details needed to calculate how much business income coverage is required. It is no wonder **WHY** there are issues: business income and financial terms are different, business leaders generally protect a business's financials, and then there is the dreaded **CP 1515 Business Income Report/Worksheet** that has to be completed to satisfy the insurance underwriters need to verify the amount of coverage being purchased.

As complicated as the worksheet is, every time a business leader goes through this worksheet, they intuitively know that the bigger the number is at the bottom of the worksheet, they will have to buy more business income coverage. They will have to pay more premiums. Business leaders have typically not fully understood the concepts relating to business income since business income is essentially intangible to a business leader and often confusing as you cannot see or touch it. As we discussed in the last chapter, this leads to decisions being made under the influence of the *6 Behavioral Risk Biases* discussed and rationalizing why a business needs a smaller amount of Business Income Coverage at the bottom of that worksheet.

So, even though FEMA states that 90% of businesses fail within a year that does not have business income coverage and are unable to resume operations within just five days[23], business leaders are also influenced by those biases, as well as the quest to reduce their premiums, and actually minimize how much coverage they believe they "must" purchase. Inadvertently, by reducing the very amount of business income coverage they are buying, they are inevitably choking the very lifeblood of what they need to survive after a disaster – their cash flow.

Before determining *How Much* you will need to survive a disaster and explaining the process of completing that dreaded **Business Income Report/Worksheet** to determine *how much,* one crucial concept needs to be understood first.

LIMITING PAYROLL

When looking to reduce the amount of Business Income coverage purchased, it is common for business leaders to add a "limitation" as to the amount of payroll included for certain employees. The **CP1510 Payroll Limitation or Exclusion**, which used to be referred to as the **Ordinary Payroll Limitation** endorsement, is the endorsement that provides that ability. Without the endorsement, 100% of payroll is included. Most often, when the limitation endorsement is used, it is set at 90 or 120 Days.

Just so you are aware, a Business Owners Policy's Business Income coverage typically automatically includes a 60 Day Ordinary payroll Limitation.

Ordinary Payroll means payroll expenses for all your employees *except:* the Officers, Executives, Department Managers, and

---

[23] https://www.fema.gov/media-library-data/1441212988001-1aa7fa978c5f999ed088dcaa815cb8cd/3a_BusinessInfographic-1.pdf

Employees under contract. Therefore, your "ordinary employees" are thought to be, in essence, your "rank and file" employees that could be "easily replaced." The concept of Limiting Payroll would be if your business were unable to operate at all, even at a temporary location, and that you would place these employees on unemployment and rehire them when you reopen. However, many businesses have very skilled employees that they cannot do without, nor would they want to replace.

Therefore, it is common to have a class of employees who do not fall in the standard exception of Officers, Executives, Department Managers, or Employees under a contract you *want* to include in your payroll coverage. If you are going to limit the "ordinary payroll" to a specific timeframe and not specifically identify the employee or class of employees you will keep on the payroll, you may be forced to place them on unemployment. The reason you may have to do that is the insurance company would limit their pay to the number of days identified on the Payroll Limitation or Exclusion endorsement. If you have such employees that you do not want to do without, you would use the **CP1504 Discretionary Payroll Expense** endorsement to specify the certain People or certain Job Classifications that would have different rules apply to them, such as fully including them in your payroll or possibly including them for a different period of time.

On a Business Owners Policy, the Discretionary Payroll Option is included in the coverage form. However, you will need to define the specific limitations you want and make sure that they are specified on the declaration page. You can do so based on either Job Classifications or designated specific Employees.

The reason for the Ordinary Payroll Limitation is reducing how much coverage needs to be purchased. Many business leaders will assume that if it is less than a total disaster, and can reopen quickly. Therefore, they will keep the employees on the payroll during a temporary restoration and not hire and train new employees.

Then, if there is a major disaster, they will pay the employees for a while to give the employees time to find another job. This latter concept is a problem.

In interviews with several business leaders, following their total disaster, they did just that. They kept their employees on the payroll immediately after the catastrophe while working at the temporary location or looking for new jobs. The use of an Ordinary Payroll Limitation created several problems for these businesses:

- If the business was able to operate at a temporary location, at some point, they ceased receiving enough coverage to retain all of the employees as the timeframe for Ordinary Payroll lapsed. Since revenues were not 100% of what they were pre-loss, they had to release employees or suffer a worse financial loss (which some chose to do). On top of that, several business leaders commented that they were even sued for "discrimination" based on who they chose to retain and those they chose to place on unemployment.
- They kept the employees on the payroll immediately after the disaster so that they could find new jobs. Then when they went to reopen, they had already used up all or most of the collective timeframe number of days for Ordinary Payroll. When they went to reopen, they needed to hire and train new employees *before* the actual reopening. It was necessary to hire employees to help them restock and organize their facilities or manufacture their Good In Process back to where they were before the loss. Reminder: costs including payroll of manufacturing Finished Goods damaged or destroyed in the disaster are not included under Business Income. Plus, leading up to reopening, as it took months to rehire and train new employees, businesses need to go through that process so that they *could* reopen and not scare customers away with shoddy service. As the business leaders allowed "their good, loyal employees that they had" to remain on the payroll for 90 days while looking for jobs, they had no days left to pay to hire and train the new employees. Therefore, these businesses had significant payroll expenses that went uncovered.

In the case of the local restaurant we previously discussed that our family frequented if they wanted to include the Head Chef's wife in the payroll, they needed to specifically list her name as included for 365 days of payroll or list Host as being included. More importantly, the restaurant owner felt obligated to pay the Head Chef's wife and other cooks' payroll not to lose them. Plus, as the owner gave his employees paid time to find new jobs, he chewed up most of his 90 days of Ordinary Payroll. This led to paying some new hires out of his pocket and not having enough staff when he reopened. The lack of training time caused issues with customer service, like my sister-in-law's incorrect meal, which led to fewer people returning to use the restaurant, simply because, as my wife said, "it was different." All of this led to a significantly negative financial impact on the owner that added up and later forced the restaurant's closure.

Therefore, if you decided to include a Payroll Limitation or have the limitation reduce on a Business Owners Policy, you must consider the timeframe you will need to recruit, find, hire, and appropriately train new employees. Failure to do so will cause it to be difficult for you can operate once you reopen. Keep in mind that your Period of Restoration ends when you have enough stuff to resume activities. It does not include any additional timeframe needed for finding, hiring, and training enough employees to resume your pre-loss activities; you must be staffed before you have all your stuff. The lack of adequate staffing will not extend your period of restoration.

How Much – **Your Necessary Business Income Limit**

Now it is time to determine *How Much* Business Income Limit you will need to survive a disaster, and the best way of doing so is completing that dreaded **Business Income Report/Worksheet.** Based on completing so many of these over the years, I could pass along some shortcuts that can be used to estimate your required Business Income Limit from your financials. But if you do not understand the Business Income Report/Worksheet and the concepts needed to complete it, there is no way to understand the shortcuts. However, these shortcuts are only used as a quick litmus test to see if a business's Business Income Limit is even close. When conducting the Disaster Planning/Business Income Coverage Analysis, it is best to take the time to complete the worksheet *completely*.

Technically, you do not need to complete every line of the business income report/worksheet, nor do you need to complete both the prior 12 months and estimated future 12 months. Still, you need to complete one entire column that starts with the Gross Sales at the top and ends with the Business Income Exposure for 12 Months. However, if you conduct both manufacturing and non-manufacturing operations, you will need to complete both corresponding columns. You will then need to complete the section that ultimately concludes the Combined Total for all three coverages: Business Income, Extra Expense, and Extend Business Income. The key is being realistic in your data and not rationalizing your financial figures to influence the outcome of the Business Income Exposure for 12 Months or the final Combine Total. Causing the final number to be lower than it should be will come back to haunt you. In other words, do not let *Myopia*, *Optimism*, and *Simplification* influence you.

However, it is recommended that you complete both prior 12 months and future 12 months columns and account for trending. That way, you will have a more accurate business income limit after going through all the various calculations. Also, in every situation, you should adjust for what you expect to happen in the future as the insurance policy will pay the expected loss.

As we work through this worksheet, you will note everything will be done based on 12 months. You should not be making any assumptions about an anticipated timeframe to reopen when completing the Business Income Exposure for 12 Months calculation. So please ignore how long you believe you will be unable to operate due to disaster and how quickly you will return to operations. We will discuss the adjustments for those timeframes later.

CP 1515 Business Income Report/Worksheet (Page 2)

BUSINESS INCOME REPORT/WORKSHEET
FINANCIAL ANALYSIS

	Income And Expenses	12-Month Period Ending:		Estimated For 12-Month Period Beginning:	
		Manufacturing	Non-Manufacturing	Manufacturing	Non-Manufacturing
A.	Gross Sales	$	$	$	$
B.	Deduct: Finished Stock Inventory (at sales value) At Beginning	−		−	
C.	Add: Finished Stock Inventory (at sales value) At End	+		+	
D.	Gross Sales Value Of Production	$		$	
E.	Deduct:				
	Prepaid Freight – Outgoing	−	−	−	−
	Returns And Allowances	−	−	−	−
	Discounts	−	−	−	−
	Bad Debts	−	−	−	−
	Collection Expenses	−	−	−	−
F.	Net Sales		$		$
	Net Sales Value Of Production	$		$	
G.	Add: Other Earnings From Your Business Operations (not investment income or rents from other properties):				
	Commissions Or Rents	+	+	+	+
	Cash Discounts Received	+	+	+	+
	Other	+	+	+	+
H.	Total Revenues	$	$	$	$

First, you will work towards calculating your **Total Revenues** (Line H).

Just like your financial statement, it starts with your **Gross Sales or Revenue** (Line A). This value includes all invoices collected or billed by your business. Therefore, as billed and not collected is included, you will need to add back the total amount of money outstanding in your accounts receivable.

There will be an adjustment for how much your inventory went up or down, affecting the cost basis of your revenue. It is then necessary to adjust your income based on your inventory increase or decrease. In other words, did you effectively sell more goods than you made or purchased during the year or less? You will subtract your **Finished Stock Inventory at the beginning of the year** (Line B) and then add your **Finished Stock Inventory at the end of the year** (Line C). These are your finished inventory values and not goods in the process of being manufactured. It would be best to use your cost basis in these inventory calculations and not your sales price valuations in both cases.

Together these calculate **Gross Sales Value of Production** (Line D).

The next step (Line E) is to deduct certain sales-related expenses such as **Prepaid Freight, Returns and Allowances, Discounts** on goods sold, **Bad Debt**, and **Collection Services**. For Collection Services, this means only the cost of hiring a third party to recover sales proceeds from bad debt. These are removed because if you have no sales, these sales-related expenses did not occur.

At that point, you can calculate your **Net Sales** (Line F) or net sales value of production. To that number, you will be adding **Other Earnings From Your Operations** (Line G), including rents from the property that you occupy. You would not include the annual rental value of other properties as we assume they will not be affected by the destruction of the location we are doing this calculation. When adding these all together, you now have your **Total Revenues** (Line H).

This is also a good point at which you may want to determine the markup of your products, otherwise known as your gross sales profit margin: your gross sales less the cost of manufacturing so that you know how much the profit margin of your goods is. Once you determine your goods' profit margins and apply that to your inventory, you would add that profit margin value into your "stock" or Business Personal Property limits when using a **selling price valuation** endorsement for finished but not sold goods.

Usually, you would complete any worksheet in order. It tends to be easier first to complete the Supplementary Information **Calculation of Cost of Goods Sold** section of Page 5. The final value from this page is needed to be used on the first line of page 3 of the Business Income Report/Worksheet – Cost of Goods Sold (Line I). It would be best to calculate the cost of goods sold using Page 5 of the worksheet because the worksheet does not consider your labor costs as payroll. Remember, payroll is included in the business income coverage calculation. When completing this worksheet, unfortunately, too many businesses take their accounting financial statement and plug in the cost of goods sold from the financials directly onto the Cost of Goods Sold on page three of the worksheet rather than completing **Calculation of Cost of Goods Sold** on page five. This means that most businesses inadvertently reduced their business income to essentially not include payroll, as most businesses include the payroll from the production of goods in their Cost of Goods Sold. Using the financial's value will lead you to have a significant shortage when you need to protect your cash flow after a disaster.

One of the interviewees actually made the mistake of including labor in the Cost of Goods Sold and then later reduced the limit of insurance they purchased by deducting 75% of the Ordinary Payroll from the subtotal, as they added a 90 Day Ordinary Payroll Limitation. The double-elimination of payroll caused them to have a significantly reduced Business Income coverage limit, and they ran out of Business Income coverage much quicker than expected.

CP 1515 Business Income Report/Worksheet (Page 5)

Calculation Of Cost Of Goods Sold	Supplementary Information			
	12-Month Period Ending:		Estimated For 12-Month Period Beginning:	
	Manufacturing	Non-Manufacturing	Manufacturing	Non-Manufacturing
Inventory At Beginning Of Year (including raw material and stock in process, but not finished stock, for manufacturing risks)	$	$	$	$
Add: The Following Purchase Costs: Cost Of Raw Stock (including transportation charges)	+		+	
Cost Of Factory Supplies Consumed	+		+	
Cost Of Merchandise Sold Including Transportation Charges (for manufacturing risks, means cost of merchandise sold but not manufactured by you)	+	+	+	+
Cost Of Other Supplies Consumed (including transportation charges)	+	+	+	+
Cost Of Goods Available For Sale	$	$	$	$
Deduct: Inventory At End Of Year (including raw material and stock in process, but not finished stock, for manufacturing risks)	−	−	−	−
Cost Of Goods Sold (Enter this figure in Item I. on page 3.)	$	$	$	$

This section aims to determine the actual cost of the materials used in making goods and sold throughout the year. Once again, the values used will not include any payroll.

- ➢ **Inventory at the beginning of the year:** manufacturing operations should not include the value of the finished stock on hand, only the raw stock, and stock in process since the BPP coverage will be paying for finished goods. Remember, we already adjusted to the change in the value of finished goods on Page 2, calculating Total Revenue.

- ➢ **(Add) The cost of raw stock purchase during the year:** Does not need to be completed by non-manufacturing.

- ➢ **(Add) The cost of factory supplies consumed:** does not need to be completed by non-manufacturing.

- ➢ **(Add) The cost of merchandise sold:** includes the cost of stock in inventory purchased and held for sale by non-manufacturing operations. But for manufacturers, this includes the costs of merchandise manufactured by other parties but sold by your business.

➢ **(Add) The cost of other supplies consumed** includes the cost of supplies consumed and not made part of your manufactured product. This would consist of disposable safety items like gloves and earplugs, the oil used for machinery, and other consumable supplies used in the manufacturing process that are not inventory. It does also not include items like utilities, as that will be addressed later.

➢ **(Subtotal) The cost of goods available-for-sale**

➢ **(Subtract) Inventory at hand at the end of the year:** remember the cost or value of the finished stock is excluded from this amount for manufacturing operations as your BPP would cover this.

➢ **(Total) Cost of goods sold:** this total would then be carried over to Line I on page 3 of the worksheet.

You can now see why there is confusion between the Cost of Goods Sold for Business Income Coverage and how different it is from the Cost of Goods Sold on your financials.

Do not run out of money!

CP 1515 Business Income Report/Worksheet (Page 3)

Income And Expenses	12-Month Period Ending:		Estimated For 12-Month Period Beginning:	
	Manufacturing	Non-Manufacturing	Manufacturing	Non-Manufacturing
Total Revenues (Line H. from previous page)	$	$	$	$
I. Deduct:				
Cost Of Goods Sold (See page 5 for instructions.)	−	−	−	−
Cost Of Services Purchased From Outsiders (not your employees) To Resell, That Do Not Continue Under Contract	−	−	−	−
Power, Heat And Refrigeration Expenses That Do Not Continue Under Contract (if **CP 15 11** is attached)	−		−	
All Payroll Expenses Or The Amount Of Payroll Expense Excluded (if **CP 15 10** is attached)	−	−	−	−
Special Deductions For Mining Properties (See page 6 for instructions.)	−	−	−	−
J.1. Business Income Exposure For 12 Months	$	$	$	$
J.2. Combined (firms engaged in manufacturing and non-manufacturing operations)	$		$	
The Figures In **J.1.** Or **J.2.** Represent 100% Of Your Actual And Estimated Business Income Exposure For 12 Months.				

Carry over the **Total Revenue** from Line H to this page.

After entering the **Cost of Goods Sold** into Line I, it is necessary to go through the additional items that would be discontinued should your operations be completely closed.

- **(Subtract) Cost of services purchased from outsiders:** (required) these are services purchased from third parties and resold to your customer. You should not include services that you are buying for your use, such as consulting services. You would also include the services that end when your production ceases. You would not include any services that are required by the contract to continue.

- **(Subtract) Power, heat, and refrigeration expenses that do not continue under contract using CP1511 Power, Heat, and Refrigeration Deduction:** (optional) usually, when production ceases, so does the utility cost. You may have some minimum basic charges to maintain service to your site that should be deducted from you to utility costs when entered into this line. However, suppose you signed an agreement for minimum purchase requirements for utilities to reduce your rates. In that case, you will still be contractually obligated to pay for those services and, therefore, should not include them in this line.
- **(Subtract) All payroll expenses or the amount of payroll expenses that are to be excluded using CP1510 Payroll Limitation or Deduction:** (optional) you would only enter an amount should you wish not to include all or some of your payrolls within the calculation. However, you must make sure that the appropriate endorsement CP1511 is added, or you will have potential penalties relating to the Coinsurance clause. Both the ordinary payroll limitation as well as Coinsurance clause will be discussed later
- **(Subtract) Special deductions for mining properties:** you enter the value from the business income report/worksheet from Page 6 on this line.

Business Income Exposure For 12 Months: There are two Line Js for a reason. Some businesses contain both manufacturing and non-manufacturing operations. It is necessary to combine both Line J1's and place them into Line J2. Line J2 represents your 12 months estimate for business income coverage limit.

The next section of the business income report/worksheet is where things become a little bit trickier.

CP 1515 Business Income Report/Worksheet (Page 4)

Income And Expenses	12-Month Period Ending:		Estimated For 12-Month Period Beginning:	
	Manufacturing	Non-Manufacturing	Manufacturing	Non-Manufacturing
K. Additional Expenses:				
1. Extra Expenses – Form CP 00 30 Only (expenses incurred to avoid or minimize suspension of business and to continue operations)			$	$
2. Extended Business Income and Extended Period Of Indemnity – Form CP 00 30 Or CP 00 32 (loss of Business Income following resumption of operations for up to 60 days or the number of days selected under Extended Period Of Indemnity option)			+	+
3. Combined (all amounts in K.1. and K.2.)			$	
L. Total Of J. And K.			"Estimated" Column $	

The figure in L. represents 100% of your estimated Business Income exposure for 12 months, and additional expenses. Using this figure as information, determine the approximate amount of insurance needed based on your evaluation of the number of months needed (may exceed 12 months) to replace your property, resume operations and restore the business to the condition that would have existed if no property damage had occurred.

Refer to the agent or company for information on available coinsurance levels and indemnity options. The Limit of Insurance you select will be shown in the Declarations of the policy.

It is now necessary to gaze into your crystal ball and take your best estimate of what it will take.

> **(Add) (Line K.1.) Extra Expense:** based on the discussions that we just laid out, it may be necessary for you to minimize the suspension of your business and continue your operations by renting a temporary location.
>
> ☐ If you own your location or have contractually guaranteed payment requirements for your old site that you rented, you will need to add in the cost of additional rent from a temporary location. You will need to do two things: one, understand that you will most likely need to sign a lease that is a multiple of a single year, you will need to gauge if you need one or more years while your

facility is being constructed, and two you will need to pay a premium on that as the landlord will not view it as a long-term lease.

- You can consult a real estate property specialist who can provide you with insight into the costs you may incur.

▫ You will need to estimate the additional costs of outsourcing services, production, or acquisition of the product. As was discussed before, you may need to include the costs of having something shipped to you, inspected and packaged, and then sent to your customer potentially on an expedited basis, which is more costly to ship.

- As you may know, the costs associated with buying a product from your competitors will you begin to estimate the additional costs we just outlined. Therefore, if you expect to outsource all of your production, you may need to take your annual sales and multiply it by the increased cost factor of outsourcing production. That increase cost factor would be added in as an additional extra expense.

➢ **(Add) (Line K.2.) Extend Business Income:** you will need some time to reengage with your clients to bring them back or attract new clients to fill the void lost by clients who will no longer do business with you.

▫ After you determine the length of time it may take you to get back to pre-disaster revenue levels, you will need to determine an estimated shortfall of revenue necessary to cover ongoing expenses.

▫ It would help if you started with an assumption as to a percentage of clients that would still be working with you at the time of you reopening your business. Based on interviews, it would be suggested that you assume lower than you initially believe it will be. Many business leaders stated that they could only retain 40% to 50% of their existing clients through outsourcing. However, some said far fewer customers were kept. If you cannot operate it all or choose to remain closed during the restoration and rebuilding process, you would be starting obviously at 0%.

- You would then have to build a model whereby your revenues would increase clientele over a period of time that you expect to regain 100% revenue. Once again, it is recommended that you err on the side of caution and assume that in your later months, as you approach the end of your extended business income period that may be your income level may still be around 80% or 90%.

- Also, remember that business income coverage is the least costly coverage to purchase but ultimately the most important when it comes to surviving after reopening

➢ **(Total) (Line K.3.) Combined Additional Expenses:** Once you have estimated both the extra expense and extend business income, you can add those two values together for the Combined Additional Expenses.

You would then total the values by adding the **Combined K3** value with the **Business Income Exposure For 12 Months J2** value to determine Line L, which represents 100% of your estimated Business Income exposure for 12 Months, and your necessary Additional Expenses. You would adjust the Business Income and Extra Expense limits for your coverage based on the amount of time you believe you will need during your Period of Restoration. You would then adjust your Extended Business Income based on how long you think you will need from the time you reopen until you are operating at 100% of pre-loss activity levels.

Before making the adjustments, it is essential to understand that the Coinsurance calculation within the Business Income coverage form is based on the **Business Income Exposure For 12 Months**

J2. Therefore, as you adjust your values upwards for longer timeframes or downwards for shorter expected timeframes, you will need to change the Coinsurance value on the declaration page accordingly.

BUSINESS INCOME ADJUSTMENT PROCESS

Before explaining Coinsurance's impact on Business Income, it is necessary to understand the Business Income Adjustment Process. Some essential terms and conditions can impact how much an insurance company pays you when your business cannot partially or fully operate following a covered event. For example, once again, Coinsurance is one of the main policy conditions that can significantly impact the amount you receive. As mention before, after a loss, a forensic accountant is going to pour through your financials and contracts to complete a Business Income Report/Worksheet. They will attempt to use your two most recently completed fiscal year-end financials and Year-to-Date to create a trended 12-Month Business Income Exposure. For example, assuming you have a calendar fiscal year. Suppose your disaster occurred on August 3, 2020. In that case, the insurance company will request your Profit & Loss and Balance Sheet Statements for 2018 and 2019 and Year-to-Date Financials, which may be for June or July of 2020 depending on how current your accounting system is up to date.

If your revenues and profits are trending up, the insurance company will attempt to trend your current year accordingly. The insurance company does pay for the upwards trend as the Business Income (and Extra Expense) Coverage Form states *We will pay for the actual loss of Business Income you sustain due to the necessary "suspension" of your "operations" during the "period of restoration."* Because of this, the insurance company must try to calculate the anticipated amount of business income you *would have actually earned* during your Period of Restoration. Therefore, the flip side is also true. If your revenue and profits are trending downwards, they will also trend your 12-Month Business Income Exposure to be lower.

Here is the twist. A vast majority of business leaders inadvertently minimize the value at the end of the Business Income Report/Worksheet, so they will "need to" carry less coverage and pay less premium. But there is one truth you need to hear:

Every business leader interviewed instinctively fought to prove that their Total Business Income Exposure (Loss) was as large as possible so that they could receive as much money from the insurance company as they could!

Business leaders quickly realized that the insurance company was basing their payments to their businesses on the Forensic Accountant's estimate of their 12-Month Business Income Exposure. Therefore, they worked to prove that they required a more significant total to receive larger claims payments. This was the opposite of what they did when completing the Business Income Worksheet.

Therefore, it does not make any sense to shortchange your calculations when it comes to the Business Income Report/Worksheet because one of two things will occur:
- you may not get paid fully for your loss due to the impact of the Coinsurance calculation, or
- you may not have enough coverage to protect your business's cash flow adequately.
  Both of which will increase the likelihood you would not survive the catastrophe.

After reviewing your financials, the insurance company will take your 12-Month Business Income Exposure and turn that into a monthly value that they will use as a comparison basis. Similar to what occurs with your property claim, the insurance company will provide you with some upfront money to start paying bills from that amount. This will be based on the severity of the loss. For a disaster expected to last months, the amount that they initially provide upfront to you may be based on one or two months of expected continuing expenses and profit. If the expected recovery is shorter, it may be as little as a few days to a few weeks.

You will then begin to submit financial information: revenue - in the form of deposits you made; and expenses in the form of receipts. The Business Income Adjuster, or Forensic Accountant, will then compare your actual revenue (if any) to the costs of your actual expenses to determine how much Business Income payment they will have to pay so that at the end of that month. The goal is for you to have netted the same expected profit. They may also question expenses to determine if they are standard operating expenses or necessary extra expense items.

It is easy for the adjuster to see what your actual Extra Expenses are. It is easy to know what you spend on payroll and other continuing, everyday operating expenses. As a business leader, you want your expected profit at the end of the month to be the same after your disaster as it was before the disaster. Therefore, the Business Income Adjuster is trying to figure out the revenue shortage, so the end of the month's profit (or loss) is the same as pre-loss.

If the insurance company calculates the 12-Month Business Income Exposure to be lower than expected, you will receive less money each month than you anticipated. This process tends to lead to "discussions" as to what the values should be. A business leader will want a more significant 12-Month Business Income Exposure figure and the insurance company wanting a smaller number with the expectations. In most of the cases of the ones we reviewed and those of the ones interviewed, the business leaders paid their own accountant to verify the insurance company's values and make an argument that the amount should be higher.

But there are issues as the calculation is not exactly perfect as "trending" will impact it and seasonality. In the case of John, the machine shop owner, the insurance company used the two most recent fiscal years. However, the oldest of the two years was a record year for that business. Therefore, the Forensic Accountant trended the anticipated 12-Month Business Income Exposure downwards in accordance, which the business owner argued was incorrect. Had John provided more years of financials, maybe four or five years, John may have been able to make the case that his revenues and profits were growing over time. The most recent year was more significant than the financials two years ago but lower than his record year. This would have meant that John most likely would have received more money during his Period of Restoration from his 12 Months Actual Loss Sustained Business Income Coverage and may have enabled John to either last a little longer so that he could possibly turn the corner.

It becomes a little more difficult for businesses with seasonal spikes, especially if they are closed for only a short period of time or through their peak season. It will be necessary to provide the Forensic Accountant monthly financials to demonstrate the impact of the seasonality of income.

The Bizarre Retail Store Disaster

This one of the most impressive retail businesses I have met over the past 35-plus years. The owner, Joseph, understands retail sales, catering to customers, and, more importantly, creates a complete customer experience. This has allowed them to build an item of incredibly successful clothing, shoe, and accessory stores, one that sells more at his location than some big box stores or mall department stores. Like many others, I gladly drive 13 miles from my house each time I need to buy something. I know my guy, Mike, who I deal with each time. He even remembers my shoe size, what I like, etc. It is a fantastic business.

This disaster was probably the most bizarre "total loss" of Business Personal Property the insurance company adjuster said she ever saw and was also undoubtedly true from my perspective. If you walked into the store and look around after the disaster, you would see absolutely nothing wrong, nothing out of place, nothing at all. But you would *smell* it.

Shortly after the clothing store opened in early April, the bedding store next door had a devastating fire caused by wiring within a decoration that the bedding store recently bought. The bedding store was in a separate building. However, the clothing and the bedding store each had their own block walls that touched each business. The problem unknowingly started back when the bedding store was renovating to move in. The contractor built a new overhand facade that jutted out from the building about the same distance as the clothing store's overhang facade. What happened was, rather than installing supports for the overhang onto the bedding store's structure, they structurally tied it into the clothing store's overhang support beam. To be able to do that, they cut a hole into the clothing store's overhang's side and bolted onto their beam. Unfortunately, they did not close the hole that they made. While the fire was engulfing the bedding store building, the smoke could enter the clothing store's business through that very hole. As the clothing store's HVAC system used the open space above the drop ceiling for the air return, the smoke was quickly filtered throughout the business. Fortunately, the owner and all the employees were able to get out safely.

The smoke was so thick that the firemen could not find the windows and doors to open them up to let the smoke escape. Being so familiar with every inch of his store, Joseph was able to put on the fire department's air mask and escort the firemen to each door and window even though the firemen could not find them themselves through the thick, black smoke. The loss was bizarre in that, once the smoke cleared, over $2,000,000 of inventory looked 100% OK. However, none of it can be used as leather, and fabrics absorb the smell of smoke that cannot be removed. Therefore, all their inventory was destroyed even it looked alright. All their carpets, ceiling tiles, and everything porous were damaged beyond repair. Chairs and couches needed their padding and fabric replaced, and several wood chairs needed to be sanded and stained again as the smoke damaged their finish.

Joseph and his son and the whole team were incredible. Understanding that reopening to take care of customers was immensely critical, the very next day, they were repacking the displays while helping the insurance adjuster take inventory. The office team worked with their suppliers and manufacturers to order new stock to be shipped as quickly as possible. On the second day after the fire, the team was loading trucks to get all the inventory out. They were filing dumpsters with destroyed items so fast that they would make the home makeover shows on HGTV jealous. A restoration contractor was also working to remove the carpets and ceiling tiles. On the third day, they ran the ozone machines to remove the smell of smoke from the facility. On day four, they wiped everything down to remove any residual soot left from the smoke. On day five, the business had new ceiling tiles installed, and the following day the new carpet was already going down. Within a week, the clothing store team was ready and awaiting the inventory that was starting to arrive just a week from the fire. The Grand Reopening was mid-April, just 12 days from the disaster, which is an absolutely incredible feat to pull off.

Why did Joseph and his team do that? Well, the Easter and Passover season is their second busiest season after the year-end holiday shopping season. That year, both Catholic and Orthodox Easter was in late April, and Passover and Passover overlapped Easter. They wanted to reopen as quickly as possible. That way, their customers did not feel like they needed to go somewhere else to buy their clothing, shoes, and other accessories in preparation for the holiday.

Unfortunately, as most people buy their clothing and shoes weeks in advance of the holidays, they lost most of their seasonal peak from the holidays. When calculating the business income loss, the insurance company attempted to compare the financials of that April to the prior year April when offering to settle the business income claim. Typically, this would make sense, but as Easter and Passover dates move, this creates a problem. Comparing the prior year to the recent year, the insurance company's initial calculation would negatively impact several hundred thousand dollars for this retail business. Why? During the preceding year, Easter was in the first few days of April, and Passover was from late March through early April. That means that 95%+ of the holiday sales would have been in March of the prior year compared to 90% would have been in April this recent year.

Working with Joseph's accountant, he presented the insurance company with a comparison of March and April for the recent year and the two prior years to show the seasonal financial impact of Easter and Passover. However, the insurance company decided to use January through April. In that February, the problem was compounded when the city had an event that they refer to as *Snowmageddon*. It was an event where there were two back-to-back winter storms in which 26 inches fell over two days and then an additional 18 inches fell three days later. What made it worse was that the moisture content of the first snow was equivalent to what usually would have been a 42-inch snowfall. Schools were closed for over a week, there were thousands of roof damage claims around the region, and dozens of buildings collapsed.

The massive amount of snow leads to a massive sale of winter boots, gloves, and other winter clothing and a new record for sales in February. But pulling February into the Business Income Period of Restoration would short the owner tens of thousands of dollars from what the accountant believed the Business Income insurance payment amount should have been.

The other problem was that the adjuster refused to look at the months of May and June as the retail business had reduced sales from people thinking they were still closed due to the incorrect initial news reports the day of the fire, which stated that the store would be closed for months. The adjuster believed that there was no need to look at the Extended Business Income coverage since they quickly reopened.

Unfortunately, this was the "final offer" from the insurance company, and the fact that they did not want to use the business's accountant reports is still a sore subject for the business owner. But

Joseph accepted it to move on and focus on his business as this "final offer" was made in *July*. In reviewing all the business leaders' events who participated in the research for this book, this is one of the very few times the evidence showed that the insurance company did not pay everything that they should have to the business.

The lesson to be learned from this disaster is that even though this retail business had detailed financial records, it highlights detailed records are critical. Especially if your business has seasonal peaks, you must maintain monthly or even weekly records so that you can recover the appropriate business income payment amounts when a disaster affects you during a peak timeframe.

Although this one does not necessarily meet the exact definition of the other businesses that suffered a complete disaster, one that includes the rule that they were closed for an extended period of time of at least 30 days or more, it does meet the definition in that every item of Business Personal Property was damaged to a point it was unusable, so their insurance policy paid policy limits for their Business Personal Property coverage. If it were not for the speed at which Joseph and his team restored the business post-disaster to be able to reopen, they would have been closed for weeks longer, possibly months. They also had some luck in that the structure was minorly damaged beyond the smoke, where repairs could be made in days and not months, and their computers worked for long enough period of time to get prior inventory records and make new orders before the soot inside of them caused them to start to fail.

However, what was not mentioned during the story was that all of this was possible due to the Disaster Recovery Program Joseph had in place *before* the disaster. Even if the computers did not work, their diligence in backing up their computer system would have enabled them to have a new system installed and operating quickly. Having the computers work temporarily saved them only two to three days of downtime. The owner's recovery plan included information on all of their suppliers, including IT, with detailed necessary computer and software records. The plan also included the wholesalers where they had purchased all their furnishings and finishes and the contractors who worked on their facility. Without the Disaster Plan, determining where and what to buy would delay recovery weeks to months.

BUSINESS INCOME COINSURANCE

Now we are starting to discuss **How Long**. Whereas your commercial property policy Coinsurance is based on property *values*, business income Coinsurance is more of a function of *time* in relation to the 12-Month Business Income Exposure calculated on the Business Income Report/Worksheet. If you recall from some of the examples as to how the adjustment process is handled relating to Building and BPP, one of the first things that the adjuster does is determine whether your business's coverage limits satisfy the Coinsurance requirements of the policy. You may recall from several stories how the insurance company had a contractor create an estimate of the building values to determine if the Coinsurance requirements were met or not met. If they were not, the insurance company would not have to pay the complete loss but instead pay a percentage based on a ratio of how much coverage limit you had versus the amount you should have had given the Coinsurance percentage.

Once you have determined or estimated how long you believe it will take you to have your location released to you after investigations, the site prepped, and construction completed, as well as making sure all the furniture, fixtures, inventory, and machinery are received and installed, the next step is to adjust your 12-Month Business Income Exposure to reflect the timeframe you expect it will take to reopen. If you *really* believe it would take six months, you would use half of the 12-Month Business Income Exposure. This is a warning; most of the disasters reviewed the average time to release the site post investigations at more than two months. Therefore, six months to rebuild is likely unrealistic. You may also want to know that many interviewees initially believed they could pull it off in six months and chose to use that for their business income limit. *Every* failure underestimated the amount that they ultimately needed.

If you believe it would take ten months to reconstruct, you will use 83.3% of the 12-Month Business Income Exposure, and if you expected 18 months, you would use 150% of that amount. You would then add into that amount the necessary Extra Expense and Extended Business Income coverage you believe you need.

The final step is to determine the maximum Coinsurance percentage you should use in your policy. ISO publishes a limited number of Coinsurance percentages; 50, 60, 70, 80, 90, and 125%. Now some insurance companies may have filed proprietary Coinsurance percentages. The highest one I have seen so far has been 150%. As Coinsurance with business income is a function of time, each percentage represents a portion of a year. Therefore, if you believe that you should be rebuilt and move into your new facility within nine months, the highest Coinsurance percentage you should use is 70%. At no time should you round up to the next level.

Here is how that was calculated:
- 50% = 6 months (12 months times 50% = 6 months)
- 60% = 7.2 months
- 70% = 8.4 months
- 80% = 9.6 months
- 90% = 10.8 months
- 100% = 12 months
- 125% = 15 months

In the example of nine months, nine divided by 12 equals 0.75 or 75%. As there is no 75% Coinsurance limit available, you go to the first available lower percentage limit, 70%. Once again, do not round up.

You may recall the example of the large printing press company. The owners determined that it would take a minimum of 18 months for them to order, receive, and have installed their largest printing press. Therefore, we would take their Business Income Exposure for 12 Months from line J2 of the worksheet, divide that by 12 months to determine a monthly value, and then multiply that by 18 months for a total value needed for their expected shutdown timeframe.

Continuing with that, if the printing company's Business Income Exposure for 12 Months calculation were $9,000,000, we would divide that $9,000,000 by 12 and arrive at $750,000 for one month, and then multiply that by 18 months to arrive at $13,500,000 of necessary business income coverage for their entire expected Period of Restoration. As the 18 months exceeds the 15 months on the table above, we would use the 125% Coinsurance, which would allow us to buy the business income with the lowest rate possible.

As you increase the Coinsurance percentage that you use from 50% to 125%, your business income coverage rate drops, essentially allowing you to buy more coverage limits for the same premium. But you must be careful about the Coinsurance percentage you use as you do not want to overstate it as you could suffer a penalty if not done correctly. In the initial example, if you felt your facility could be rebuilt within nine months, nine months divided by 12 months is 0.75, and as there is no 75% Coinsurance, you move down to 70% to allow for a margin of error. You would not want to go to 80%, or else you may be penalized.

Once you determine the Business Income limit you need for your period of restoration, however long that might be, you can add what you decide your need for the Extra Expense and Extend Business Income coverage.

After adding all three of those together, that total limit will be far greater than the Business Income Exposure for 12 months in line J2. Here is a trick to help you afford higher limits for your Business Income policy. The coinsurance condition only pertains to the Business Income Exposure for 12 Months in line J2 and not to Extra Expense nor Extended Business Income. Once you have added all three of those coverage limits together, you will have a much higher number for your policy limit. You then may be able to raise the Coinsurance percentage to a higher percentage that still satisfies the calculation for Coinsurance, as well as reduces the rates used in calculating your premium for business income. The amounts you add in for Extra Expense and Extended Business Income provide you a higher total limit on the policy and allow you to move the coinsurance percentage up on your policy, reducing your rates and premium.

The calculation of satisfying the Coinsurance is the same as that of the Building and Business Personal Property Coverage Form. They would calculate your Business Income Exposure for 12 Months and multiply it by your Coinsurance percentage. If the value they determine is less than your policy limit, there would be no Coinsurance penalty. However, if your limit were lower than their calculation, they would take the amount you have as a limit on your policy and divide it by their calculated amount. That percentage would be how much they would pay each month of your business income claim.

It is time to see the impact of an incorrect Coinsurance amount. When the calculation was done to determine the Business Income Exposure for 12 Months, the calculated value was $8,500,000. You believe that you should be able to rebuild and reopen within nine months, which would mean you would use a policy limit of $6,375,000. 70% of $8,500,000 is $5,950,000, and 80% would be $6,800,000, therefore you would normally use 70% Coinsurance. But in the example, instead of 70% Coinsurance, 80% was used, which is only *one* level too high.

Business Income Exposure For 12 Months:	$8,500,000
The Coinsurance percentage used:	80%
Your Limit of Insurance for it is:	$6,375,000
The amount of loss is:	$2,300,000

Step (1): $8,500,000 x 80% = $6,800,000

<blockquote>(the minimum amount of insurance to meet your Coinsurance requirements)</blockquote>

Step **(2):** $6,375,000 ÷ $6,800,000 = 0.9375

Step **(3):** $2,300,000 loss X 0.9375= $2,156,250 loss payment

In this example, the insurance company would not pay $143,750 of the loss. If the Coinsurance percentage were raised to 100% to reduce your premium, then the amount paid by the insurance company would drop to $1,725,000, a shortage of $575000. Therefore, you must pay attention to the Coinsurance percentage that you use. The slight movement from 70% to 80% Coinsurance reduced the rates and, therefore, the premiums by approximately 7%. Going to 100% Coinsurance reduces the premium for your coverage by around 21%. Still, you can also now see the dramatic impact that the Coinsurance movement will have on your Business Interruption payments to you when you become penalized by the Coinsurance provision of the policy.

This is a perfect example again of why focusing solely on the limit of insurance being provided on a proposal, and rationalizing that the coinsurance change would not affect you, can come back to haunt you.

Do not forget to consider the requirements and additional construction time needed to meet current Laws or Ordinances and add the **CP1531 Ordinance or Law – Increased Period of Restoration** endorsement. You must add in time for this, which means you should also use a higher limit on your policy.

Playing it Safe

No one wants to overpay for insurance, and therefore no one wants to overstate how much Business Income coverage limit they will need on their policy. But yet, come disaster time, you will want every dollar that you could possibly receive.

ISO created a way that allows you to only pay for as much coverage as your business would need. It is the **CP1520 Business**

Income Premium Adjustment endorsement. What this does, is turn your Business Income coverage into a reporting basis. That means that *after* the policy year is over, the insurance company will request you to complete the **CP1515 Business Income Report/Worksheet** for the policy year just finished and adjust your premium based on your actual fiscal year results. You may think this is more work, but it is not. You should complete the worksheet for your next policy period anyway.

The policy will only return any premium that is more than the limit that would have been required. It does not need you to pay more if you understate the limit on your policy compared to the final actual results. Therefore, it is not like an audit where you could owe more money. However, when a claim occurs, they will not pay more than the policy limit.

Suppose you understate your policy limit at the beginning of the year. In that case, you will not receive any "additional premium" amount due as if the insurance company calculates that you actually needed more for the Business Income Exposure for the 12 Months calculation.

This form allows you to simply overstate what you believe you may need and then have the premium returned based on what you would have required based on your actual results that year.

You can also choose each year if you want to go through the premium adjustment calculation or not. If you do not wish to submit a worksheet for the recalculation, there is no penalty for not doing so. Ultimately, it is the best way to play it safe by overstating what you may need and receiving a premium return if need be so that you pay for only what you did need.

Optional Coverage Forms

Several specialty Business Income endorsements can be used base upon your specific situation and the type of operations you have.

Although referenced before, the Dependent Properties is the most used Business Income endorsements that have not been spelled out in detailed before. When your operations could be financially impacted when another business has closed due to a covered cause of loss, addressing that potential financial risk is essential. The most common of these would be the economic impact due to the loss of your largest suppliers or your largest customers.

For example, when interviewing a business leader for a Disaster Planning/Business Income Coverage Analysis, he strategically relocated his business to be located at the property adjacent to his leading supplier, who supplied him with 80% of the materials needed and then sells the customers. This gave him a significant competitive advantage over his competitors as there was no cost of having the raw material shipped to his location. The business owner was driving his forklift next door to pick it up from the manufacturer. If that manufacturer were to go out of business due to a covered disaster, the business owner estimated that the additional costs of acquiring materials would go up by almost 30% due to delivery charges. Therefore, his profit margin would go down, and he would have to sell at a higher price to maintain his business.

Because of this, the business owner uses the Business Income from Dependent Properties – Broad Form endorsement on his policy.

Your business may have a situation where your proximity is to a "draw of people," such as a large specialty box store, concert venue, casino, athletic field, or stadium. Should that venue have a covered loss, you would suffer from a significantly reduced flow of patrons visiting your business.

What would be the impact on your business and its bottom line when your largest customer, one that represents 5%, 10%, 25%, or more of your revenue, cannot patronize you when they close due to a disaster?

It is recommended you analyze your situation and determine if any of the following forms would be appropriate to be used on your policy:

- CP1501 Business Income from Dependent Properties Limited International Coverage

- CP1502 Extra Expense from Dependent Properties Limited International Coverage
- CP1508 Business Income from Dependent Properties – Broad Form
- CP1509 Business Income from Dependent Properties – Limited Form
- CP1534 Extra Expense from Dependent Properties

Other forms available:
- **CP1506 Off-Premises Interruption of Business – Vehicles and Mobile Equipment**

    Suppose your operations entail the use of vehicles for deliveries or a Food Truck as an example, or you generate revenue through mobile equipment such as excavators or mobile cranes. In that case, you may want to include this endorsement.

- **CP1550 Radio or Television Antennas – Business Income or Extra Expense**

- **CP1505 Food Contamination (Business Interruption and Extra Expense)**

    If your business is ordered closed by the Board of Health or any other governmental authority as a result of the discovery or suspicion of "food contamination," the insurance company will cover the following costs:
    - Your expense to clean your equipment as required by the Board of Health or any other governmental authority.
    - Your cost to replace the food which is, or is suspected to be, contaminated.
    - Your expense to provide necessary medical tests or vaccinations for your employees (including temporary and leased employees) who are potentially infected by the "food contamination."

- The loss of Business Income you sustain due to the necessary "suspension" of your "operations" as a result of the "food contamination." The coverage for Business Income will begin 24 hours after you receive notice of closing from the Board of Health or any other governmental authority; and
- Additional advertising expenses you incur to restore your reputation.

- **CP0430 Electronic Commerce (E-Commerce)**
  In addition to providing some additional definitions of Covered Property for things such as data, the form adds Business Interruption coverage for standard computer network service or function caused by a Covered Cause of Loss. You can also add Computer Virus as a Covered Cause of Loss. However, if you generate revenue from transacting business over the internet, a full, tailored Cyber Insurance Program may be better suited for such a risk.

- **CP1532 Civil Authority Change(s)**
  There is some Civil Authority included in the Business Income and Extra Expense Coverage Form. Civil Authority is when a Covered Cause of Loss causes damage to property other than property at the described premise. The insurance company will pay for the actual loss of Business Income you sustain and necessary Extra Expense caused by the action of civil authority that prohibits access to the described premises, provided that both of the following apply:

  (1) Access to the area immediately surrounding the damaged property is prohibited by civil authority as a result of the damage, and the described premises are within that area but are not more than one mile from the damaged property; and

(2) The action of civil authority is taken in response to dangerous physical conditions resulting from the damage or continuation of the Covered Cause of Loss that caused the damage. This action is taken to enable a civil authority to have unimpeded access to the damaged property.

The Civil Authority Coverage will begin 72 hours after the first act of civil authority that prohibits access to the described premises and will apply for up to four consecutive weeks from the date on which such coverage began.

Civil Authority Coverage for Extra Expense will begin immediately after the time of the first act of civil authority that prohibits access to the described premises and will end four consecutive weeks after the date of that action, or when the Civil Authority Coverage for Business Income ends; whichever is later.

The CP1532 Civil Authority Change(s) endorsement allows you to increase both the duration of the coverage term to greater than four weeks and the distance that Covered Cause of Loss must occur within one mile or less.

The most common scenario where business leaders think this coverage applies to is for a hurricane evacuation. However, the property damage must occur *before* the governmental order, and access to your property would be prohibited, so this coverage typically does not apply to this scenario. The most common would be from a derailment of training carrying chemicals or a fire at a manufacturer spewing toxic smoke.

Therefore, you must think about your situation. To gain access to your location, you must travel through some industrial areas or across the railroad track. Even if these are miles away, you may need to extend your distance or the time that it applies. I once read an article where a tire fire caused an evacuation of an area, and the fire ended up damaging a bridge to a point where access to an island was no longer possible.

- **CP1556 Business Income Changes – Beginning Period of Restoration**

   This endorsement gives you the ability to shorten the start of your Period of Restoration from the standard 24 hours to as early as 0 hours to as late as 168 hours (1 week). Shortening it increases your rates; lengthening it reduces your rates.

- **CP1524 Mining Properties – Business Income**

- **CP1525 Business Income Changes – Educational Institutions**

   This endorsement changes the Period of Restoration for schools. Business Income is still 72 Hours, but Extra Expense can be used immediately after the Covered Cause of Loss. The Period of Restoration is also extended to the day before opening the next school term following the date when the property at the described premises should be repaired, rebuilt, or replaced; or the date when the school term is resumed at a new permanent location.

TAKEAWAYS/LESSONS LEARNED

As you prepare your Disaster Planning/Business Income Coverage Analysis, you should focus on these items:
- As the Nike advertisements state – *Just Do It!* Fully complete the CP 1515 Business Income Report/Worksheet to calculate your Business Income Exposure for 12 Months
- Honestly, add up all those Extra Expenses that you identified in the Chapter 6 exercise.
- Estimate a duration that you will need to regain as much of your pre-loss revenue.

- Determine if Dependent Properties applies to you. *Hint: It typically does.*
- Determine if any of the other endorsements highlighted apply to you and if need be, figure out what options you may need to have listed on those endorsements.
- Estimate your Business Income Estimated Limit:
  - Take your Business Income Exposure for 12 Months
  - Divide that number by 12
  - Then multiply by the number of months you estimate it will take to rebuild, the length of your Period of Restoration
  - But also allow enough time to have all of your "stuff" delivered and installed.
  - Determine your Maximum Coinsurance Percentage.
- Add together your Business Income Estimated Limit and your Extra Expense and Extended Business Income Coverage amount to determine your final Business Income and Extra Expense Limit for your insurance policy.
- Update your insurance policy's Business Income limit. If for some reason the new value is lower than what you currently are insuring its form, do two things: one, leave the policy alone as you are used to paying a premium for it and may still need it; and two, go back and check your math.
  - Are you worried about paying for too much coverage but still wanting cash flow protection coverage for your operations? You can overstate what you believe you will need as a limit and then use the CP1520 Business Income Premium Adjustment endorsement. This will allow you to receive premium back after the year is over for any excessive coverage you purchased.

Chapter 10

Tenants Beware

If what we have discussed thus far were not enough to make you question what is and what is not covered under insurance, well, we are not done yet. The premise of *Insured to Fail* is to help business owners diagnose, understand, and combat the scary statistic that over 50% of businesses that suffer a disaster either do not reopen or close within three years, **despite being insured**.

There are many more issues that can cause a business to have a severe enough uninsured or underinsured claim to put someone out of business or into bankruptcy. There are enough that would require a second or even a third book. Think that comment was made in jest? Remember, we are only focused on the Commercial Property Coverages. We touched briefly on Cyber issues, but only because computers are integral to a business's recovery.

However, we did not discuss all of the various coverages such as General Liability, Business Auto, Inland Marine, Directors & Officers, Employment Practices, Cyber Liability, Cyber Crime, Crime, and the list goes on for a while.

There are one more property coverage issues necessary to address. What happens when you do not own the facility your business operates from?

Fire Legal versus Legal Liability

We have discussed that the Building and Business Personal Property Coverage form covers a building listed on the policy and

Your Business Personal Property and Personal Property of Others that you also list on the declaration pages of your policy. The problem becomes when you do not own your building, and the landlord does not require you to insure the structure on your policy. As mentioned during Bill Coyne's fire, the landlord was expecting payment for the damage to the building from Bill's operations. In this case, Bill purchased a computer battery backup that exploded.

Bill was not required to insure the building under his lease. Each year, Bill was required to provide a Certificate of Insurance showing General and Auto Liability, but no proof of property coverages was requested. Unfortunately, the landlord assumed that the $300,000 of Damage To Premises Rented To You on Bill's CG0001 Commercial General Liability 9and as shown on the Certificate of Insurance) would pay for *any* damage to the building, which was incorrect. It is a pet peeve of mine that it is called this as it was formerly called Fire Legal Liability coverage. Whereas Damage To Premises Rented To You only pays for fire damage, not any other type of damage.

Karen, the owner of a manufacturing firm, provided the story of her employee driving a tractor-trailer through their rented facility so that production equipment she purchased could be installed. The driver somehow lost control or misjudged a turn and took out the main support post, which caused several other beams and pillars to start to sag to a point where it ripped open a hole in the roof. All told, Karen's driver did almost $875,000 of damage to the building, and Karen thought her $1,000,000 Damage To Premises Rented To You would respond to the damage, but it did not. The landlord's building insurance company paid the claim, but then the insurance company subrogated or sued Karen for the damage. Karen had no insurance coverage, which caused her to file bankruptcy and eventually close her operations.

It is essential to look at possible risk or *what-if* scenarios. For example, we discussed the what-if scenarios with Bill Coyne when doing a Risk and Coverage Analysis. *What-if*:

- One of his mechanics drove through the garage door should while pulling in a customer's car, or *what if* they drove their forklift into the wall,
- The storage rack Bill installed weakened structural supports and caused a collapse. The Damage To Premises Rented To You coverage would not pay for the damage caused by Bill

A General Liability policy excludes property in your Care, Custody, or Control, so Bill purchased different coverage. Under Bill's *property* policy, he bought $500,000 in Legal Liability, which would pay for any damage to the building caused by Bill, and that he would be held *legally liable* for that damage.

Tenant Improvements and Betterments

I could not find an example of businesses that failed to reopen or closed within three years from Tenant Improvements and Betterments issues. However, I found a few examples of uninsured claims exceeding $100,000, which are important enough to be mentioned should a disaster occur.

Your interest in Improvements and Betterments are covered under Your Business Personal Property coverage. However, the valuation that is used is Actual Cash Value, and they will use a proportion of the unused time left on your lease from the time you installed the improvements as pay based on that ratio.

Even if you have Replacement Cost Coverage, the insurance company will only pay the replacement cost basis if the property is damaged and repaired or replaced as soon as reasonably possible after the loss or damage. In other words, you may be able to make prompt repairs to your improvements and betterments, but if the building is not accessible for a prolonged period or it has to be rebuilt, and you move elsewhere, you will be unable to repair the existing damage. Your policy would revert to ACV, and you would be paid in proportion to your lease's remaining length.

The **CP0060 Leasehold Interest Coverage Form** provides several coverages, one of which is for the unamortized portion of your improvements and betterments.

The other coverage that can be provided under the Leasehold Interest Coverage Form is to address items that you would lose money over that is not addressed by your Improvements and Betterments nor your Business Income Policy:

- **Tenants' Lease Interest**: This pays the difference in rent from what you were paying pre-loss to either the rebuilt facility or a permanent new facility that is higher in rent.
- **Bonus Payments**: This means coverage for the unamortized portion of a cash bonus you paid to obtain the lease but does not include prepaid rent or security deposit.
- **Prepaid Rent**: coverage for the unamortized portion of any amount of advanced rent paid that will not be refunded to you.

However, you may also fall into the Ordinance or Law exclusion of the Special Form Cause of Loss as a tenant. Suppose a portion of the building is damaged, but your Improvements and Betterments are not, and the local authorities state that the building shall be torn down. The undamaged portion of your Improvements and Betterments will not be covered unless you purchase the **CP0426 Ordinance or Law Coverage for Tenant's Interest in Improvements and Betterments (Tenant's Policy)**. You can also add coverage for debris removal and bringing your Improvements and Betterments up to the current code.

If you are a tenant, your insurance professional should review your lease and understand your situation should appropriate coverage needs to be added to your policy. It is your responsibility to identify if you have favorable lease terms that will disappear following a disaster that destroys your building. It would be best if you let your agent know of such a situation.

TAKEAWAYS/LESSONS LEARNED

The lessons learned from this chapter are pretty simple:
- If you are a tenant in a building, make sure you read your lease provisions and have a conversation with your insurance agent about your improvements and betterments not to lose the value of them after a loss.

Insured to Fail

Chapter 11

Choose your own chapter title:
If you fail to plan, you are planning to fail!
– Benjamin Franklin

Plans are Nothing: Planning is Everything
– Dwight D Eisenhower

Interviews with business owners have shown that many failed to reopen or failed after reopening because the business leader either **had the wrong insurance program or had the wrong plan**. We have addressed having the wrong insurance program as the reason why so many businesses failed. Now it is now time to discuss the failure of the reopening plan or the *lack* of a plan as the culprit. Yes, you may be lucky and able to rebuild and learn on the fly but preparing a Business Continuity Plan ahead of time will dramatically improve your chances of success.

Do you think a Business Continuity Plan is only needed when a physical disaster occurs? Or that the odds of a disaster happening to you are low? If you still have the *Behavioral Risk Bias* of *Optimism* thinking that a catastrophe will not happen to you, well, then please ponder the following few paragraphs.

This book was finalized, taken from notes, stories, and outlines to final form, during a significant worldwide *disaster:* COVID-19. The pandemic led many business leaders to turn to their Business Continuity Plan to identify alternative equipment and materials suppliers; their primary source was not in operation for many businesses due to governmental lockdowns or outbreaks at vendor facilities.

My organization "dusted off" our Business Continuity Plan previously needed during 2011's *Snowmageddon* in Pittsburgh. In 2011, knowing that there would be a potential for a significant snowfall, employees followed procedures and took their laptops and transferred their phone extensions to their mobile phones the day before so they could be prepared to work from home if needed. What transpired was back-to-back winter storms that caused significant snowfalls such that our staff needed to work remotely for a little over a week for safety reasons as the roads were in poor condition.

We learned from that event and refined our procedures. As technology changed, the plan was updated as well. COVID-19 forced my organization to have 91% of our employees, 98 of 108 employees, work remotely from March 22, 2020, until the summer of 2021. On Wednesday, March 18, 2020, the Governor Wolf of Pennsylvania ordered non-essential businesses to close by Saturday, March 21, 2021. Although parts of our organization were later deemed "essential" by the Governor, other portions were not. Thanks to the Business Continuity Plan, our IT Director, PJ Pizarro, oversees, PJ performed a phenomenal job of staging the transition of 98 employees from the office to being fully functional at home over two days. He did so in a way that none of our clients even knew we made the change. There was only a change to the plan "made on the fly." As part of the Executive Team, PJ suggested that the employees take home all of their equipment during our emergency called meeting. This would include their docking stations along with their keyboard and mouse, monitors, VoIP (Voice over Internet Protocol) phones, and phone headset so they could function identically at home as they would be at the office. We did not know how long we would be working remotely, so it was important for the staff to have the higher functionality they would have with all of their equipment versus just a single screen laptop and a mobile phone. Not to mention they were much more comfortable doing so.

All PJ needed to do was create and provide two one-page documents for each employee: One, a checklist of their equipment to take home; and two, sequenced steps for the employees to follow to install their equipment at home and attach to their internet router. It was necessary to do as there was a sequence that needed to be followed when hooking up their VoIP Phone and docking station so that everything would work. The equipment checklist contained blank fields so that PJ would record and verify the appropriate equipment was taken so he could know what they had when needing to perform remote servicing. Both of these lists took PJ less than an hour to prepare.

Based on prior real-time execution of needing to work remotely, a procedure was established. PJ receives a new employee notice from HR that includes if the employee has internet at home. A question we asked new employees. If an employee does not have internet, PJ will assign or even acquire a cell phone hotspot to take with them when they must work from home. When first implemented years ago, the HR Department surveyed the employees about whether they had internet at their home, and periodically we survey if their situation has changed. That way, PJ always has enough cell phone hotspots for employees who need them and a few spares for emergencies. Since PJ had us prepared for what we expected to be periodic weather-related events causing employees to work remotely, that plan made the process of extended remote work quickly possible.

COVID-19 led to employees working remotely for the first time for many businesses. Many struggled early on as they did not plan for remote beforehand, and several business leaders commented in interviews that they suffered for it.

A significant number of businesses opened their Business Continuity Plans due to the 400%+ surge in cyberattacks, cybercrime, ransomware, and cyber extortion events that occurred during the 2020 Pandemic.[24] The need to have computer systems backed up and running as quickly as possible after a cyber event highlights the need for Business Continuity Plans.

The increase in weather-related events has caused a rise in damaged or closed properties due to the lack of utilities. 2019 represented the fourth-highest total number of events (tied with 2018), following the years 2017 (16), 2011 (16), and 2016 (15). The most recent years of 2019, 2018, and 2017 have produced more than a dozen billion-dollar disasters to impact the United States—totaling

---

[24] https://www.prnewswire.com/news-releases/top-cyber-security-experts-report-4-000-cyber-attacks-a-day-since-covid-19-pandemic-301110157.html

44 events. This makes a three-year average of $14.6 billion-dollar disaster events, well above the inflation-adjusted average of six and a half events per year (1980-2019).[25]

Therefore, your planning process should take an "all-hazards" approach for your Business Continuity Plan. Some many different hazards or threats can impact your business. The insurance actuaries know that there will be a certain number of events that will impact businesses. They know that there will be different types of events that occur. Unfortunately, they just do not know what will happen to which business. The probability that a specific hazard will impact your business is hard to determine. That is why it is essential to consider many different threats and risks and their likelihood.

Strategies for prevention and risk mitigation should be created and assembled as part of the planning process. The focus should be on threats or hazards that are classified as hazards that could cause injury, property damage, business disruption, or environmental impact should be addressed.

A good Risk Management process starts with Risk Identification; the first step in a Business Continuity Planning is the process of identifying the risks and hazards your business faces. It will also help identify parts of your company that are most vulnerable to create a plan to recover them if a business interruption occurs. Your Business Continuity Plan will work in conjunction with your Business Income Insurance, and together they will form your complete Business Continuity Management Program (BCMP).

Businesses with a BCMP will be more resilient and improve the likelihood of survival while reducing the impact of any shutdowns on your business's top and bottom lines. You may be able to survive if you purchase enough Business Income coverage, which is much more than you probably realized before reading this book. You may "survive" without a BCMP, but your odds of survival will decrease, or you will most likely be much further behind as compared to where you could be if you had a BCMP. However, if you do not purchase enough Business Income Coverage, your only hope of survival is a solid BCMP.

Therefore, the best option is to do both; have enough Business

---

[25] https://www.climate.gov/news-features/blogs/beyond-data/2010-2019-landmark-decade-us-billion-dollar-weather-and-climate

Income coverage *and* have a Business Continuity Management Program.

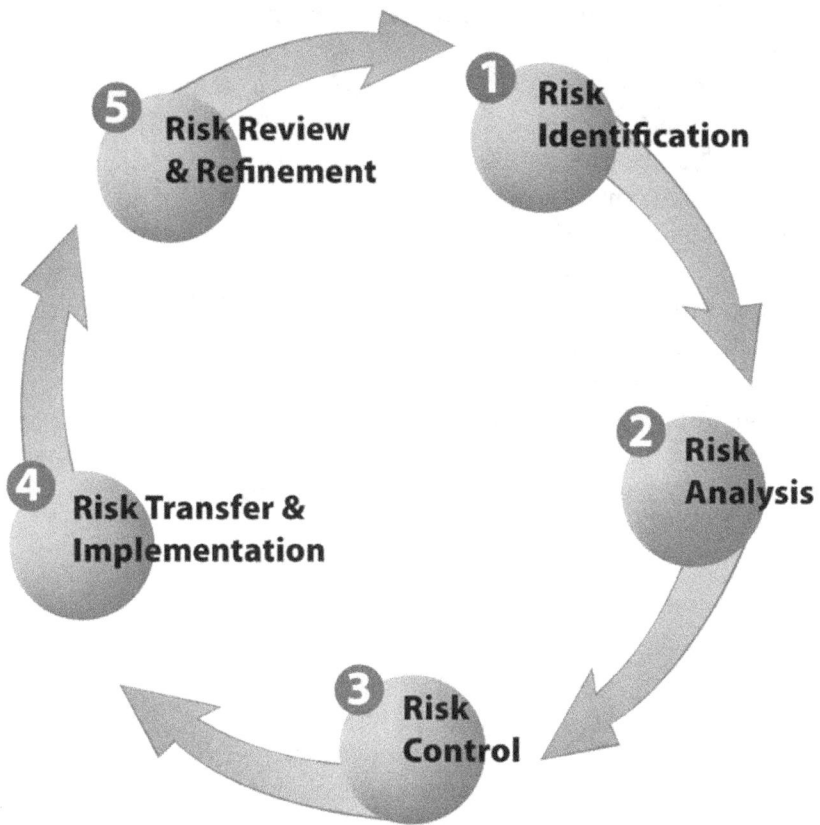

The process of creating and implementing your BCMP should follow the steps of the Risk Management Process, where first is Risk Identification, but we will follow the process of expanding Risk to Risk & Hazard. Therefore, we will focus on **Risk & Hazard Identification** followed by **Risk & Hazard Analysis**, **Risk & Hazard Control**, **Risk & Hazard Finance & Implementation**, and finally, **Risk & Hazard Monitoring & Administration**. All of this aims to identify time-sensitive or critical processes and the financial and operational impacts resulting from disrupting your business. You will need to gather information about resource requirements to support the time-sensitive or critical business processes. This information helps make informed decisions regarding investments to offset risks and avoid business disruptions.

We will discuss the Risk Management Process a little more in

If you fail to plan, you are planning to fail!

the next chapter as well.

WARNING: Business Continuity Plan vs. Your Insurance Program

Associations have referred business leaders that needed assistance (and were also some of those interviewed) relating to disasters that occurred or were facing sizable to financially crushing "uninsured" claims. From these discussions, you need to be aware there is a significant issue. You must make sure that your Business Continuity Plans are not at odds with your contractual responsibilities within your insurance policies. This is particularly important when it comes to IT issues, and in some cases, property claims as well. You should read your ***Duties in the Event of Loss or Damage*** or equivalent section within your policy.

Withing the **CP0010 Building and Personal Property Coverage Form**, the Duties in the Event of Loss or Damage section of the policy form has the following requirements:

> You must see that the following are done in the event of loss or damage to Covered Property:
> (1) Notify the police if a law may have been broken.
> (2) Give us prompt notice of the loss or damage. Include a description of the property involved.
> (3) As soon as possible, give us a description of how, when and where the loss or damage occurred.
> (4) Take all reasonable steps to protect the Covered Property from further damage, and keep a record of your expenses necessary to protect the Covered Property, for consideration in the settlement of the claim. This will not increase the Limit of Insurance. However, we will not pay for any subsequent loss or damage resulting from a cause of loss that is not a Covered Cause of Loss. Also, if feasible, set the damaged property aside and in the best possible order for examination.
> (5) At our request, give us complete inventories of the damaged and undamaged property. Include quantities, costs, values and amount of loss claimed.

> (6) As often as may be reasonably required, permit us to inspect the property proving the loss or damage and examine your books and records.
> (7) Also, permit us to take samples of damaged and undamaged property for inspection, testing and analysis, and permit us to make copies from your books and records.
> (8) Send us a signed, sworn proof of loss containing the information we request to investigate the claim. You must do this within 60 days after our request. We will supply you with the necessary forms.
> (9) Cooperate with us in the investigation or settlement of the claim.

You will see a significant difference when you compare this to the "Duties in the Event of Loss" section of a Cyber Insurance Program. Just so you are aware, Cyber Insurance policies are not uniform, so you should carefully read your cyber policy. For example, the one below reads quite differently:

> All Insureds will cooperate with the Insurer in the handling of the Claim, Enterprise Security Event or Extortion Threat and upon the Insurer's request will:
> 1. furnish the Insurer with copies of demands, reports, investigations, pleadings and all related papers and such other information, assistance and cooperation as the Insurer may reasonably request;
> 2. attend hearings, depositions, conferences, and trials, assist in effecting settlements, assist in securing and giving evidence, obtain the attendance of witnesses; and assist in any other aspect of the investigation and defense.
>
> An Insured will do nothing that in any way increases the Insurer's exposure under this policy or in any way prejudices the Insurer's potential or actual rights of recovery. <u>No Insured will, except at the Insured's own cost, voluntarily make a payment, admit liability, assume any obligation **or incur any expense without the Insurer's prior written consent unless otherwise specifically permitted**</u>. However, the Insured's

> compliance with any Privacy Regulation will not be considered an admission of liability.
>
> Failure to cooperate with the Insurer in the defense of a Claim or in the investigation of a Claim, Enterprise Security Event or Extortion Threat is a breach of this policy and will result in loss of coverage.
>
> With respect to all First Party Coverages, the Insured's duty to cooperate includes, but is not limited to with respect to an Extortion Threat, using best efforts to keep the existence of Computer System Extortion Coverage confidential. The Insured's disclosure of the existence of Computer System Extortion Coverage to the public constitutes a failure of a condition precedent to coverage and will operate to defeat coverage for Extortion Loss under this policy.

There have been many conversations with association members over "uninsured" Cyber Insurance claims, especially when that business purchased Cyber Insurance. We determined that the businesses worked as quickly as possible to restore their IT infrastructure as it is critical to operating their businesses. It did not matter if they had a Business Continuity Plans that stated what they should do or did not have a BCMP, as they followed their instinct reactions. The problem stems from the highlighted bold and underlined sentence above. It basically states that the insurance company wants to be notified BEFORE a business does anything to mitigate the damages or restore operations. Failure to notify may cause the insurance company not to pay your claim. They will state that they may have recommended a different plan of action to address your cyber claim, and therefore will not pay for what you did.

A little over a half dozen interviewed business leaders stated that their insurance company refused to pay for having computers wiped blank and data restored from viable backups from a ransomware attack. Based on the adjuster's experience and the size of the actual ransom demand, their insurance companies believed it would have been less expensive to pay the ransom and have the computers cleaned of the virus. Therefore, the insurance company denied paying invoices they received from the business leader for the third-party IT firm hired to perform the work. Some denied coverage due to violating the insurance company's right to inspect the damage and settle the claim as they see fit to do so. In these cases, as the IT firms did the restoration before the insurance company could investigate, there was nothing left to inspect and nothing to possibly mitigate the claim as the business already completed the restoration. In other words, outside of the IT firm invoice, there was no proof that the event ever occurred.

There were also a few interviewed that attempted to negotiate the ransom themselves before notifying the insurance company. However, the business "negotiated" in such a way that the extortionists increased the ransom demand. Their insurance companies also denied the claims for this reason.

When it comes to Cyber Insurance, the rule of thumb should be to notify your Cyber Insurance Policy insurance company before taking action when you see a ransom demand. Insurance companies have commented that the best practice would be when you receive a ransom demand on your computer, disconnect it from the network and keep the computer on so the screen. It is vital to save the ransom contact information is on the screen and contact the insurance company. However, when a program begins to install that should not be established, shut the computer off and call the insurance company. Either way, your IT department should establish procedures for your organization to follow when certain events occur.

With property claims, you may take photos, and save broken or damaged parts or equipment, that you need to have repaired or replaced to satisfy the insurance company. However, if not handled correctly, there are cases where completely fixing something before the insurance company could thoroughly investigate caused insurance company adjusters not to pay a property claim.

Creating a Business Continuity Plan

A Business Continuity Plan (BCP) compiles all of the details of processes and procedures that will help keep your operations running or restore them as quickly as possible. Whether responding to a major disaster, a physical disaster (i.e., tornado, hurricane), a technological event (i.e., ransomware, cyberattack), or to something like a massive fire or explosion, BCPs are critical to survival.

It does not matter if you are a small business owner or a large enterprise. Business continuity planning will help you respond faster when disruption occurs and help you minimize the significant negative impact on your business.

Without a plan in place, you run the risk of being unable to continue selling and shipping products during unplanned disruptions or even servicing your clients. Without one, your ability to recover from these unexpected disruptions will be much slower and less effective. The consequences can be devastating to both your top and bottom financial lines, as well as your reputation.

There are Four Guiding Principles to building your plan that you should follow:

1. **Comprehensive.**

    It is impossible to plan for every single possible problem that may occur, but it is worth planning for them. Your first plan may not be perfect, and you should make backup plans to your backup plans so that you have ideas as to what to do when the first attempt does not seem to work.

2. **Realistic.**

    Roleplay out disaster scenarios and determine if your plan will work. The last thing you want to do is have a "picture-perfect Business Continuity Plan" and not be functional. By being realistic about your plan, you want to make sure that it can work and have workable contingencies.

3. **Efficient.**

    Your Business Continuity Plan does not need to be simple. But it does need to have the ability to be executed efficiently, and with the resources you have at hand. This will help you avoid massive amounts of stress in a disaster that will make even regular tasks much more challenging to complete or incorrect, and hasty decisions are made.

4. **Adaptable.**

    If the plan doesn't work, change the plan, not the goal. Nothing will prepare you for the curveballs that may be thrown at you. Leave room in your plan to adapt to the moment as circumstances change.

Your Business Continuity Program Team

You have your list in order of workflows. The first is WHO should be on your Business Continuity Planning TEAM. It is much easier, quicker, and less likely to miss something if you build a team that will help construct your plan. It may make sense to break things down into the various departments in your business, as most businesses have departments broken down by how things flow through their company, such as product lines or services offered to customers.

Designating group leaders and the assignment of tasks and deadlines assures that the process of building your BCMP will reach fruition. These same people need to be included in the contacts in your BCMP Manual, and then when you run exercises later to refresh the program, you will need their guidance as they will be the ones most familiar with their portion of the program. In other words, it is better to have a record of who built the portion of a plan when it comes to the time that you have to use it. Thereby, if someone leaves your organization, you will need to find and train the replacement Team member.

Your BCMP Team should be identified and outlined in your manual with complete contact information for internal communication, as well as contacting the team member outside of work when the emergency arises.

Risk & Hazard Identification/Analysis

Now that you have your team, you will begin with Risk & Hazard Identification and focus first on what is at risk when a disaster occurs. Then the Risk & Hazard Analysis will analyze what scenarios are at risk and your options when dealing with them. Identification and Analysis are separate steps, but when explaining why it is necessary to look at what is at risk, it is also easy to explain the analysis you will be going through.

In the previous chapters, you already built lists of all your "Stuff," which are your buildings, equipment, materials, machinery, inventory, and so on, as part of the process of figuring out how best to insure them so that you can have ample insurance to rebuild. So, it is now time to bring those lists out again. Your complete list will go into your BCMP Manual to have a full list of what you need to replace.

Your Workflow/Process Maps are ideal for identifying items you may have missed in your earlier compilation efforts. It is easier to organize your things by order of use in your process, from beginning to end, so that you can complete building your BCMP in a logical order. It also allows you to identify critical places within your workflows where you are most vulnerable if one area of your process cannot operate.

Now that you have your lists and maps in hand, you must start looking at things from the five W's: *Who, What, Where, When, and Why*. Using some poetic license, the *Why* will be why you need to worry about the item, in essence, the possible hazards or scenarios that your stuff will be exposed to that could damage it or render it unusable.

When you do have a disaster, you will need to identify the areas that can be impacted: First Party (You), Second Party (Employees), and Third Parties (Others):

First Party – (You)

When analyzing your own operations, you will need to take a deep look at *Your Stuff,* including your Facilities, Equipment, Materials, and Infrastructure.

It is time to grab your list of Covered Property (as well as possibly your Property Not Covered list) you assembled in the earlier chapters. You will start to build your Business Continuity Plan from that very list. So much time is wasted post-disaster trying to figure out what stuff you had and where you go to get that stuff. It becomes worse when the same item is no longer available where you once purchased it, and that it will cost you significant time researching alternatives. Having the list completed before the disaster will save you vast amounts of time, especially when you do not have post-disaster time to spare. Not to mention, it helps you to avoid the critical mistake of underestimating how long it will take to reacquire each item.

Take the list, and for each of the items you should identify and determine:
- What:
  - What is the item? What is it used for? What are the required functions the item performs?

- o Are there alternatives for that item that you can use? Is the item you have the only option, and therefore you must replace it with the same thing? Or are there better options should you need to replace that item?
  - o What is the current cost to acquire the replacement?
- Who:
  - o Who do you get the item from? This is where you identify the supplier you purchased it from in order to buy or repair the item as quickly as possible.
  - o Are there other suppliers available should your leading supplier not have the item available? List a secondary or even tertiary source.
  - o If you lose that primary supplier, will a secondary supplier be more expensive? If so, you may want to consider adjusting that item's values upwards in your total values for your property insurance coverage.
  - o Suppose the item is the raw material from a key supplier. In that case, you should determine if Dependent Business Income coverage is needed for that supplier should that supplier become unavailable to supply you at some point in the future.
- When:
  - o Determine the length of time it will take to physically acquire the item from ordering to delivery. This is an essential step in determining ***How Much*** and ***How Long*** Business Income Insurance is needed.
- Why:
  - o What hazards or scenarios may occur that will cause the item to be unable to be used and need repairing or replaced?
  - o How critical is the item to your operations? If hyper-critical, what redundancy or backup plans are needed to go into effect until that item is repaired or replaced?

When it comes to production lines or customized equipment/machinery that you made yourself, it is necessary to determine all of the W's for components that make up the overall equipment and the time to source and then fabricate/assemble your line or equipment. When it comes to the costs of the labor to construct the machinery, you may be thinking you will have your employees do it. However, it may be better to outsource its assembly or hire subcontractors to assist in reopening faster. You should also factor the labor costs into your values for the equipment.

When going through this list to update sourcing replacements, you should expend the time to determine the costs of replacing the items to update your values. As mentioned in a previous chapter, business leaders often know what they paid for an item, but they do not know what it costs to purchase that same item today; a significant downfall of many when they tried to reopen successfully after their disaster.

Several of the business leaders interviewed commented that their original source no longer manufactured machinery or equipment. This caused them to spend considerable time researching alternatives that delayed reopening. Some made a rushed decision and effectively did not purchase the best alternative for themselves, which impacted their performance and profitability afterward.

You also need to look beyond your "contents" and also look at specialty items that are built into your facilities that become part of your "building," such as HVAC, filtration, dust collection, paint booths, fire suppression systems, etc. Who you purchased an item from before may or may not be able to supply it to you in the future, especially when you need it the most.

It would help if you also looked at your workflows and processes. You need to determine that if just a portion of your process goes down, Who and Where can you outsource that portion? How long will outsourcing add to your timeframe to make or sell products or deliver services?

One of the business leaders interviewed commented on how they learned the hard way that having a BCMP would have been hugely beneficial. As a sawmill, their raw material, which included massive numbers of logs, starts in the yard and goes through an initial debarking process before entering the mill. Logs are then rough cut to maximize the volume of boards obtained from a single log. From there, they go through the edger to create a straight side that allows them to cut straight boards. The saw operator then cuts the log to yield as much board lumber as they can. From there, a lumber grader determines which wood grade each board is. The boards then go through end trimming, so many will have uniform length, and that is where they are stacked, or "stickered," so that they can be placed into the kiln to be dried. Once dried, the boards are graded again and sorted for sale. This operation had a fire in their initial grading and end trimming building, which is not easily outsourced to others. The process became incredibly slower as they had to do things by hand, board by board. They built a new building next to the old building, which allowed them not to wait for the site to be released to expedite things. The problem then became the amount of time they spent time figuring out what components to purchase and then finding the components needed to construct the new grading and end trimming line and then reconstruct it. However, when about 90% of the way through the assembly, they figured out that they forgot some necessary parts/components and wasted weeks waiting for the missing pieces. Had it been mapped out beforehand, they felt that they could have shaved significant time off the process and not wasted time waiting for missed parts when reopening the middle of their reconstruction.

Having this list compiled for everything in your operation will also help you when just one critical item in your process goes down and needs repairing or replaced. Then, you can cut recovery time by days or weeks by preparing ahead of time.

When it comes to infrastructure, one area that may be important to focus considerable time and effort on will be your Information Technology Infrastructure or your computer/IT. In interviewing business leaders, the number of stories relating to uninsured business losses due to viruses or hacking events has been substantial to catastrophic to employers. This is one area that if you do not plan and have your Disaster Plan ready, it will really come back to haunt you.

Please make sure that you have complete plans that make it possible to purchase and restore your computer servers within a day and have some workstations ready to go in that timeframe. Without access to your systems, or you will be dealing with very distraught customers.

One of the biggest problems many businesses faced post-disaster when the main building was unavailable was that they had to contact the phone company to forward the incoming phone line to a single mobile phone. If you have not already done so, you may want to take the time now to look at a phone system, particularly VoIP phone systems. New systems will allow you to forward each extension to each employee's mobile phone or another temporary telephone with a touch of a few buttons.

Hopefully, you are now starting to see how the *Business Continuity Plan* and your *Insurance Program Design* are contingent upon each other. They are critical in post-disaster response and pre-disaster planning and establishing proper insurance coverage limits.

Second Party – (Your Employees)

During the Risk & Hazard Identification, you will need to pay attention to your employees. At this time, you should grab your Organizational Chart and employee rosters. As you go through your lists, look at each person, position, role, etc., and in doing so, you will need to identify several key things:

- What specific employee or employees can you not do without?
- Are there any that would be difficult or even impossible to replace?
  - You should look at each such employee and think about the impact if that employee could not show up for work, ever again, starting tomorrow.
  - What would be the financial impact of that person not being part of your business moving forward?
  - Work with a Financial Business Continuity/Exit Strategy Specialist to begin a process of several things:
    - Employee Retention – if that employee is that critical, put financial programs in place so that they will not want to leave your business until they retire.
    - Financial-Risk Mitigation – Have a program in place to financially compensate the business should that individual pass away or become permanently disabled.
    - Duplication-Risk Mitigation – start the process of having a younger person begin to learn the job so that they can step into that role in the future. Also, please do not make the mistake of creating a mentoring role without implementing a financial program to retain

the employee. We have seen employers do this, and the senior employee feels like they will be pushed out of a job early, and they leave and later file an age discrimination lawsuit against you.
- Are there categories of employees that need to be available no matter what or others that can be more easily replaced?
  - These will impact your decision on any use of Ordinary Payroll Limitation in your Business Interruption insurance program.
- How much time do you need to train new employees so that they are at least passably proficient?
  - If you do not already have formal Safety & Operations training, including onboarding training for new employees, now would be an excellent time to develop such a program before you are in a time pinch to hire a lot of employees.
  - Therefore, your employee training programs for both Safety & Operations should be included in your BCMP so that they are ready to be implemented when needed.

3rd Party – "Others"

Others are a broad category of organizations that impact your operations, including Your Customers, Your Prospects, Your Vendors/Suppliers, Your Competitors, and Your Bankers/Creditors. Each of these will play a critical role in your ability to reopen and stay open. You are probably thinking already four of the five make sense to include, but as these are each reviewed, why all five are included will become clear.

Your Customers

Your customers are the most required component of your business as, without customers, you have no revenue, no money, and you are broke. Keeping as many of your customers as possible is critical. To keep your customers, you must be able to provide clear, ongoing communications as to your ability to deliver your goods or services, as well as your plans to rebuild and "be better than before."

When interviewing business leaders today, most are confident that they have their list of customers. They state that they are in spreadsheets, their accounting (accounts receivable) software, their operations/production tracking software so that orders can be appropriately identified and shipped to the right customers, or in their email program, such as Microsoft Outlook. But what is surprising in today's technology-driven world is how many do not have them in a web-based Marketing Platform Database. Post-disaster, you may have to wait a significant amount of time to purchase your computer systems, restoring your software platforms, and importing the data backups, all in an effort to finally be able to tell your customer that you have a Business Continuity Management Plan and that you have plans to be able to provide them with their products or services quickly. How much confidence will you instill in your customers when you cannot send that email bragging about your BCMP for several days or maybe a week or more?

Imagine being able to access your cloud-based customer database from your mobile phone while the fire department is still battling to extinguish your fire, or even before the floodwaters start to go down. You would be able to notify all your customers (and prospects) that you are implementing your BCMP and that you will be able to keep them up to date as to fulfilling their orders or services. Being able to communicate that quickly helps instill confidence in your organization.

As part of your BCMP, it is suggested that you pre-craft your email templates. This would include not just the first email but various types of emails. All the emails should contain the ability to insert what occurred and the expected timeframe to provide product or service and several other expected notifications such as how you will fulfill orders and maintain quality controls, new temporary facilities established, reopening, and so forth. It is also recommended that you hire a Public Relations specialty firm to craft such email templates rather than sending out emails internally created that may accidentally send unclear or conflicting information. These types of PR firms specialize in restoring or maintaining a business's image.

Ideally, your cloud-based customer database would also be tied into your production or service platform so that you can determine what orders or services need to be immediately addressed and possibly outsourced for fulfillment.

The ability to quickly communicate with your customers clearly and frequently makes it easier for you to retain or earn back as many customers as possible.

Your Prospects

You probably wonder why prospects are on this list, but it is not one of the five that most business leaders think should be on the list we are reviewing. The reason why they are on it is simple: **People Love Stories**. The story of your disaster, what happened, how you can keep people employed, your ability to operate while rebuilding, your actual reopening, etc., will be an engaging story that people will easily find intriguing. Many prospects will be curious enough to follow. *Why not use it to your advantage?* You may know the expression: *When life gives you lemons, make lemonade.*

Rather than sending the usual product or service-related emails or mailing, use your story. Remember, many of the best movies are actually about comebacks.

Ken Clifton from CCF Industries did just that. Ken used his fire as a story to earn customers back as well as attract new customers. Ken's logo is a dove, as he makes dovetailed drawers and drawer components. Ken played upon his logo and made the dove act like a mythological Phoenix. A Phoenix obtains new life by arising from the ashes of its predecessor. By leveraging his story, Ken's business grew quicker and became larger than before the fire within slightly over a year from the disaster.

The best part is, using the story as marketing is also effective when focused on your customers.

Once again, this is where having your Customer and Prospect database cloud-based makes the process of engagement easier. There are several web-based programs out there that you should look at and determine if they can integrate with your existing systems through the use of API Coding. API is the acronym for Application Programming Interface, a software intermediary that allows two applications to talk to each other. Each time you use an app like Facebook, send an instant message or check the weather on your phone, you are using an API. API allows your web-based marketing and communication platform to speak with your operations software. If your internal software cannot use API, you should build processes where you run a manual data exchange on a daily or weekly basis. Once you map out the data fields, it is a process that can be done with a few minutes each time. This way, you ensure your database is up to date.

Your Vendors/Suppliers

Your Vendors and Suppliers will be critical for you to reacquire your materials, equipment, machinery, parts, etc. While building the list of *What* is at risk, namely *Your Stuff*, you should construct the database of your vendors and suppliers, as well as alternative suppliers. Imagine quickly sending your complete equipment specifications to your list of vendors to purchase exactly what you need. Many failed businesses spent significant time calling around vendors to see what they had on hand that might meet their needs. Having a complete, detailed list will enable you to send out many RFQs and allow you to reopen faster. Seeing a larger order may motivate some vendors or manufacturers to provide discounts or expedited manufacturing times.

By the way, having them in your web-based marketing database may be helpful when you need to contact them. Plus, it is an easy way to keep the list up to date, so if your BCMP contact information is not current, you can quickly find it in your database.

Suppose you identified multiple pieces that you need. In that case, some vendor manufacturers or suppliers will give you prioritization in terms of delivery due to a larger order, so do not forget to take advantage of that ability.

It would be best if you also had conversations with your Vendors and Suppliers before a disaster occurs to explain that you are building a BCMP so you can more efficiently and quickly reopen. They may have suggestions as to options that you may want to think about incorporating into your plan. And if you purchased items from them before, some vendors will be willing to provide you with a list of what you bought before and what it would take to replace it today, and at what cost. Effectively doing some of the groundwork for you.

You will also need to discuss the terms of purchasing the materials or equipment you need. As it will most likely be a large order, they may require a deposit so that they can cover initial production costs, maybe even pay some overtime, to help you get back in business faster. It will be essential to know as part of the claim adjustment process that you may need to receive additional money upfront when the order is made to help maintain your cash flow. Otherwise, you will need to have conversations with your banker about what they can do to help you retain the ability to fund purchases during the claim adjustment process.

Your Competitors

Your Competitors is the one that in this list that most business leaders thought was odd to include on the list of five key relationships to Identify and Analyze. But ultimately, they may be one of the most important relationships you will need to maintain your own customers. You will recall that many of the businesses we discussed thus far went through a catastrophe and needed to reach out to a friendly competitor (or multiple competitors) to provide services or outsource production.

Having spoken at dozens of trade or association conferences over the years, the one thing I know is that everyone has friendly competitors. Those are the ones that business leaders hang out with, go to dinner with, and usually have a few drinks with them. Heck, many spouses attending the events become friends, and they plan extensions to the conferences together.

Come disaster time, you will need to call upon and rely upon those very relationships.

Tony Vecchio needed the services of a friendly competitor to provide state inspections for vehicles. John, the machine shop owner, used four friendly competitors, and Ken Clifton needed to outsource production to almost a dozen different businesses just to maintain 60% of his pre-disaster capacity.

Now, your list of friendly competitors may not be enough. You may also need more materials or production capacity. You will need to have a conversation with your friendly competitors first and determine what they can provide and their capacity. Also, by having the BCMP discussion with them, they will most likely reciprocate with you should something happen to them. Once you know the possible capacity, you will need to research other competitors to use possibly. I would suggest reaching out to or at least identifying your respected competitors first to have a discussion. Once again, they will most likely reciprocate if it happens to them.

In your BCMP documents, you should compile the list of vendors or suppliers you can turn to and their capabilities to know what you can purchase from them. By mapping out their capabilities, you identify if a particular competitor is the only one that can fit a certain void. If that vendor has limited capacity, you do not want to order items from them that other competitors can do. In essence, if ordering other items from that one competitor would chew up their capacity, they could not supply that one item you need that cannot be purchased elsewhere.

Your Bankers/Creditors

Having a conversation with your banker ahead of time is critical. Too many interviewed business leaders were surprised that their banking relationship froze their lines of credit as soon as the disaster struck and then closed them once the bank received payment from the insurance company. Remember, when the bank is listed as Mortgagee or Lender Loss Payee on your insurance policy, any check issued comes to your name AND the bank's name. They must sign off on the check for you to be able to use it, and the bank will not do so. The bank will use the proceeds to pay down the loan, and then they will only sign off to allow you to have access to insurance claim payments AFTER the bank is made whole. In fact, banks will require final payment from you to close the loan as the asset related to it is destroyed should there not be enough coverage to cover the balance of the loan.

After the loans or lines were closed for many business leaders, the banks refused to loan them any money. Some did reopen their account or a new loan after the bank had a chance to review their insurance coverages, particularly relating to the Property and Business Income coverages, to determine if you will have enough coverage to replace items and protect your cashflow. Almost all commented that when they got a loan, they had to agree on drawing upon any line of credit as each amount taken from the line of credit was contingent upon preapproval.

Having a conversation before a disaster, reviewing their policies and procedure, and your program should help make the process go more smoothly after your disaster. After seeing the design of the Business Income programs, particularly the Extended Business Income Coverage timeframes, the banks were willing to provide loans to cover the small insurance shortages and provide some credit lines for working capital purposes.

Possible Event Scenarios to contemplate:
- **Act of terrorism** – assess the impact caused by explosions, bomb threats, hostage-taking, sabotage, and organized violence.
- **Act of Sabotage** – assess the impact caused by the disruption to your organization's operations.
- **Act of war** – assess the impact caused by conflicts between countries which may involve airstrikes, ground strikes, invasion, or blockades.
- **Protests (and Riots)** – assess the impact caused by a planned or impromptu protest due to either civil events or possibly action by you or a neighboring business that could impede access to your business or the area around your business. Also, assess the impact if something causes a peaceful protest to turn into a riot with looting.
- **Theft** – assess the impact caused by the theft of goods, equipment, money, or other valuables.
- **Arson** – assess the impact caused by deliberate attacks on your organization's premises, causing loss of premises, goods, and other assets.
- **Industrial Action** – assess the impact caused by the withdrawal of labor.
- **Pandemic** – assess what would occur to your business due to a shutdown of your operations, outbreak within your facility, disruption to the supply of materials, or shutdown to key customers.
- **Tornado** - assess potential disruption caused by tornadoes. These can cause structural damage to buildings as well as injuries to employees and customers.
- **Hurricane** - assess potential disruption caused by hurricanes. These can cause flooding, structural damage, power failures, as well as injuries to employees and customers.
- **Flood** - assess potential disruption caused by thunderstorms, storms, thaws, and prolonged rainfall. Floods can damage

buildings, equipment, and products, causing power failures and loss of facilities.
- **Snowstorm** - assess potential disruption caused by blizzards, ice, and freezing temperatures. Each of these can impact power, transport, logistics, and communications.
- **Drought** - assess potential disruptions caused by droughts, such as the impact on stored goods, logistics, services, and transport.
- **Earthquake** - assess potential disruptions, such as power, communication, water, and sewerage services. Other issues relate to damages to buildings, bridges, and other infrastructure.
- **Storms** - assess potential disruptions, such as disruption to power, damage to electrical equipment, including computer systems.
- **Fire** - assess potential disruptions, such as damage to facilities, interruption to services, production, staff safety, and associated issues such as theft and looting.
- **Contamination** - assess the impact of polluted water, chemicals, radiation, asbestos, smoke, toxic waste, bacteria, virus, etc., on your company's operations, products, facilities, and employee health.
- **Electrical power failure** – assess the impact caused by interruptions to power, including lights, telephones, faxes, PCs, and other areas such as hardware, networks, servers, and other IT equipment. Such outages could cause customer and/or business data loss, such as online transactions that customers may have partially completed. Consideration should be given to installing Uninterrupted Power Supplies (UPS) systems.
- **Loss of gas supply** – assess the impact caused by the loss of gas supplies and their impact on production.
- **Loss of water supply** – assess the impact caused by the loss of the water, for example, during production, transport, or employee sanitary needs.
- **Oil shortage** – assess the impact caused by oil and petrol shortage, such as impacts on production, transport, maintenance, and other types of operations.

- **Communications services breakdown** – assess the impact caused by interruption to communications as these are required to run most business processes and enable employees to perform
- **Power** – assess the impact caused by interruptions to power services, for example, by internal equipment or cabling failure.
- **Air Conditioning** – assess the impact caused by failures to the air conditioning system, for example, potential damages to products or computer equipment.
- **Production Line** – assess the impact caused by failures to the production line, for example, if vital equipment gets damaged and needs to be replaced. Workers may need to be laid off until the problem is resolved, which may negatively impact sales and erode customer confidence.
- **Cooling plant** – assess the impact caused by damage to cooling equipment, for example, goods or equipment that are dependent on cooling equipment, such as dairy product processing
- **Equipment** – assess the impact caused by damages or unavailability of equipment required to run the business. Explore if it is possible to move to alternative sites to enable the business processes to continue.
- **Information technology** – assess the impact on your computers, networks, websites, customer transactions from shutdowns due to loss of power, computer viruses, hackers, ransomware, or extortion.
- **Cyber Crime** – assess the impact from a breach of employee or client sensitive information, theft of monies from bank accounts, theft or cyber redirection of employee payroll, or phishing or social engineering.
- **Workplace violence** – review the impacts caused by violence, as this may affect morale, absenteeism, and increase the rate of turnover of employees. This may also impact productivity and result in compensation claims.
- **Public transportation disruption** – assess the impact caused by employees' inability to get to their workplace.

This can be caused by accidents, industrial action, equipment failure, or weather conditions.
- **Neighborhood hazard** – assess the impact caused by events that affect your premises and employees, such as hazardous waste from the neighboring factory or toxic gases.
- **Health and Safety Regulations** – assess the impact caused by not complying with Health and Safety Regulations. Inspection can result in facilities being completely or partially closed down, resulting in delays to projects.
- **Employee morale** – assess the impact caused by factors that impact employee morale, such as poor facilities and unpleasant working conditions.
- **Mergers and acquisitions** – assess the impact caused by such arrangements as these may undermine or threaten employees' position in their respective organization. Such scenarios may negatively impact morale and productivity.
- **Negative publicity** – assess the impact caused by negative press coverage as this may lower employee morale and customer confidence.
- **Legal problems** – assess the impact caused by legal issues such as sexual harassment, contract disputes, intellectual property disputes, health and safety regulations, and racial discrimination.

Risk & Hazard Control

After you complete the Risk & Hazard Identification & Analysis, you will then look at the possible event scenarios that could impact your operations. Take your list of event scenarios and score each one using the following for Probability of Occurring and Impact Potential on your Organization:

Probability Occurring Score		Impact Potential Score	
Score	Level	Score	Level
5	Very High	**12**	Terminal
4	High	**9**	Devastating
3	Medium	**6**	Critical
2	Low	**3**	Controllable
1	Very Low	**1**	Minor

First, you would add the **Probably Score** and the **Impact Score** to arrive at the overall **Risk & Hazard Control Score**. You would then work to build a checklist or workflow as to the steps to go through to respond to the scenario starting with the highest combined score to the smallest.

First – For each scenario, you would assign an individual or small team to craft the checklist to follow when a similar event occurs and assign a deadline.

For the small situations where a single machine or piece of equipment is damaged and unusable, it may be as simple as:

Action/Steps	Completed Y/N	Notes
1. contact the appropriate repair contractor;		
2. notify the insurance company as to the event;		
3. work with the contractor to determine if repairable;		
o Order parts if repairable		
4. work with a contractor to determine the root cause of the event;		
5. Capture photos and other documentation of the cause of the problem and		

provide them to the insurance company;		
6. if the cause of the issue was due to a Third Party, capture appropriate documentation so that the third party can be notified that action will be sought and that they need to inspect ASAP (if you "destroy the evidence" when repairing it, you may lose the ability to recover later on);		
7. if the piece of equipment is critical, or the time to repair/replace is too long, contact sources you identified for providing work on a subcontracted basis to you (assuming work cannot be completed elsewhere within the organization);		
8. if the equipment is non-repairable, contact vendors of replacement equipment and supply minimum equipment requirements to obtain pricing;		
9. Make repair or purchase a replacement.		

Your steps may be shorter or longer depending upon the property or equipment damaged and the scenario that occurred. Checklists can be sequenced when a logical order needs to be followed. They can then be laid out in prioritization, or they can be completed as best suited.

When a large event occurs, such as a complete disaster of your facility, the number of areas that need to be addressed will be significant. Therefore, it will be easier to group tasks to achieve a single focus into separate checklists. In essence, it would be best to have multiple checklists by focus area and then a *Master Scenario Checklist* for the Complete Event Scenario so you know which various breakout checklists will need to be followed. Here is a sample of some of the checklists business leaders are using:

- Internal Communications with Employees
- External Communications with Customers/Prospects
- Marketing of Temporary Location/Reopening
- Telecommunications Restoration
- Information Technology Restoration
- Office Environment Restoration
- Production Machinery Replacement
- Warehouse Facility Replacement
- Temporary Relocation Checklist
- Restoration of Property Location
- Reconstruction of Property Location
- Identification of Temporary Location
- Miscellaneous Follow Up Checklists

A Miscellaneous Follow-Up Checklists are needed to make certain that other items that need to be accomplished are taken care of that may not fit one of the other checklists.

A *Master Scenario Checklist* for a flood may need a different collection of checklists focused more on clean-up and restoration of a property location versus a complete fire or tornado that damages a location beyond repair.

One business leader shared their Temporary Relocation Checklist as an example as to what you might want to look at and consider.

If you fail to plan, you are planning to fail!

Action/Steps	Completed Y/N	Notes
Notify insurance companies		
Obtain emergency cash for immediate supplies		
Arrange transportation to and from a backup site		
Arrange living quarters, if necessary		
Arrange eating establishments		
Identify all personnel and their telephone numbers		
Arrange delivery and the receipt of mail		
Arrange office supplies		
Rent or purchase equipment, as needed		
Determine the sequence to startup applications		
Identify the number of workstations needed		
Check all data being taken to backup site before leaving		
Contact vendors for assistance with problems incurred during emergency		
Arrange transportation for additional items needed at a backup site		
Take directions and map to a backup site		
Bring technical documentation and procedural manuals		
Ensure personnel understand their tasks		

Communications

Before a disaster strikes, you may want to think about establishing and preparing the series of communications needed for the various scenarios you come up with and plan for: What information or instructions need to be sent, to Who (Audience), and the Frequency. You should also consider who prepares the communication, the purpose of that communication, the media used to transmit the communication, and who the communication comes from.

Your Internal Messaging to Employees will need to be focused on putting employees at ease so they will feel safe. Explain to the employees what is going to transpire while conveying what they are required to do and actions they should take. Instruct them on what they should not do (such as talk to media) and who will be their point of contact should they have questions or have issues. Remember, an employee of CCF Industries who did not know the rules took it upon himself to speak with the media. By inadvertently exaggerating about "thousands of gallons of chemicals," this leads to an OSHA inspector visiting (still ended with a fine) and panicking neighbors worrying about possible exposure to those chemicals.

Your External Messaging to Clients is to ensure to them that you are working to meet their expectations. Keep them abreast of what is happing with your company to alleviate the situation, how you will fulfill their products or services, the estimated timeframes as to progress updates, and who would be their single point of contact during the restoration period.

Risk & Hazard Implementation/Administration

Implementation and Maintaining/Administration of your BCMP are more of a function of working to ensure that the Plan will meet your goals of restoring operations as quickly as possible and minimizing customer loss.

Table Testing Scenarios

After you built your focused checklists and Master Scenario Checklists, it is time to test the Scenarios.

The first thing you need to do is lay the ground rules and expectations of the tests. The goal of the test is not to criticize anyone but so that everyone knows that the goals of the exercises are meant to ensure that your checklists are as complete as possible. That there is less likely that something is missed. In other words, everyone involved should be told that if there are *no* questions or recommendations when you review the checklists, particularly the first run, that would mean that they collectively are not doing their job properly. One way to coach them to open up is to clearly state that they could be putting the company and everyone's jobs at risk if the company does not survive a disaster.

You should bring together selected members of the team members to form a *Test Team*. The Test Team member should not have been part of the team that created the checklist(s) (*the Checklist Creation Team*) that will be reviewed during that Test Scenario. The Checklist Creation Team will run through the scenario with the Test Team, and the Test Team is required to ask questions, push back, and poke holes. Regarding the checklists so that the checklists will be more complete. If a Test Team does not find any holes, use a second Test Team as that is probably a scenario where people are afraid of hurting someone's feelings, which is not the goal nor acceptable.

It will also be necessary to periodically retest each scenario to make sure that your BCMP stays current with changes within your operations. DO NOT ASSUME that they will not need to be updated or retested.

Additional Business Continuity Management Plan Documents

You will need to fill the BCMP with additional documentation that will be needed to accomplish your goal of restoring your operations as quickly as possible.

- Schedule of Periodic Reviews/Retesting
- Schedule of Audits
- How to Modify and expand the program
- Process improvement guidelines
- Items that may require maintenance include (examples):
    - Equipment List
    - Fax List
    - Inventory List

- Contact List
- Organization Charts
- Standard Operating Procedures
- Business Processes
- Equipment Requirements
- Site Map
- Application Contacts
- Suppliers Contact List
- Telephone Directory
- Technical Documentation

Plan Documentation Access

One of the things you will need to do is make sure that your key BCMP Team Members have access to the complete program, anywhere and at any time. You should look to a shared access cloud-based system to store all the documents that are accessible by the required team members. It could be as simple as posting on your current shared cloud-based intranet system or by using DropBox or Microsoft Teams. Your IT Director should investigate and make the required recommendations of where and how to store your plan documents and organize them so that they can be easily accessed and found.

Business Continuity Management Plan Training and Testing

The last area that needs to be addressed is the training of all personnel. All employees should understand that the organization has a Business Continuity Program, their roles and responsibilities, and the chain of command and contact points. The BCMP Management or Team Leads will need more extensive training, which will be through various tabletop testing exercises.

It would be recommended that periodically the Main BCMP Team Leader, which most likely will be is the President or CEO or possibly COO, should perform an unscheduled, surprise mock event scenario that just occurred and then let the team go into action. The Main BCMP Team Leader will need to act as the observer or have a designated observer that will need to determine if all points of contact and checklists are being followed properly.

The additional training comes through event debriefing meetings where team members offer constructive feedback as well as the main observer compiles a list of positives, failures and lists of things that need to be improved. Any corrective actions and follow-ups must be scheduled in the calendar before the debriefing meeting is completed.

TAKEAWAYS/LESSONS LEARNED

"A journey of a thousand miles begins with a single step." This is a common saying that originated from a famous Chinese proverb. But it is very true here, and if you do not start the process of building your BCMP, you will never complete it.

The Takeaway or Lessons Learned is just one:
- **START THE PROCESS**

But if you need more:
- Start the Process of building your Business Continuity Management Program.
- Establish your team.
- Develop the scenarios that the team is to role play and determine the best recovery steps and plans.
- Establish goals, deadlines, and predetermined checkpoints on progress.
- Start the process again with additional scenarios.
- Set established timeframes to test your plans.
- Set future dates to review if changes need to be made.
- Anytime you must use parts of your plans, review to see if changes need to be made.

Chapter 12

People vs. PDFs

It doesn't make sense to hire smart people and then tell them what to do; we hire smart people so they can tell us what to do.
— Steve Jobs

It plays out in slow motion, like watching two cars heading towards each other and you brace for what will be a loud impact, but also to see if something will cause the cars *not* to crash head-on. You are now staring in disbelief at the spinning coin flipped in the air as gravity takes over, causing the coin to accelerate towards the ground. You instinctively will have to make one of two possible decisions, but you must decide now. One decision is to do nothing and painfully watch the coin's outcome play out before your eyes; will your business survive the disaster? But leaving your business to chance is not something you ever want to do. As the coin that was never in your control is now accelerating towards the ground, the other decision is to act quickly by attempting to reach out and dive like a wide receiver for the game-winning catch. You try to catch the coin and stop it from determining your outcome. But at that point, it is too far out of your reach. You and the coin come crashing to the ground as you pray for a lucky outcome.

The question you need to ask, or better yet, the decision you should have made before the coin even left the hand of fate, was never to let the coin be out of your control. It would be best if you had made plans to keep that ill-fated coin safe in your pocket so you could control the situation and not leave your business to chance.

The analogy here is your insurance program. Do you leave the survivability of your business to chance by continuing to purchase and manage your insurance program the same way you have for years, with the same flawed process that the insurance industry has actually taught you to do? Or do you change your purchasing process and manage your insurance program so that you have a better outcome?

When interviewing business leaders and asking them, "What amount of time over the past year did they spend on the very important function of Risk and Insurance Management?" At best, they answer 10%. They were then asked, "What percentage of that time is spent on just the procurement of your insurance program?" The responses are overwhelmingly 80%-90%. Most of their time spent was providing information, filling out supplemental applications, guiding tours for insurance company personnel supposed to quote their insurance, and reviewing the few quotes they received. Doing the math means that most business leaders only spend 1% to 2% of their available time focused on Risk and Insurance Management.

The lack of significant focus on Risk and Insurance Management is at the heart of many businesses that failed due to a disaster, despite being insured. During the interviews with the business leaders who did not survive, almost all business leaders expressed that they spent less time hiring their agent than they did hiring an employee. They spent more time interviewing, checking references, and performing background checks of the prospective employee than they did look at the quality of the insurance agent. Therefore, when business leaders had to decide which advisor or insurance agent to use, the benchmark they end up using to gauge the agent's quality was the premium they received in the agent's proposal. If there was any uncertainty regarding anything in the proposals, business leaders overwhelmingly defaulted to *Status Quo*. They remained with the "incumbent agent," what the insurance industry calls your current insurance agent. This is the *Behavioral Risk Bias* of *Inertia*.

To further make this point as to why this is a problem, during a Business Continuity Management Plan workshop, when I was asked a question about having a better process for a business leader to use to select an insurance program design advisor or insurance agent, the discussing evolved into several business leaders making their own observation and expressing that they spent more time with their most recent accounting firm selection than they did their insurance agent. As one business leader commented, the reality is possible that an ineffective accountant, at worst, can cause them to pay too much in taxes. In contrast, an ineffective insurance agent can impact you to a point where you cannot survive a disaster.

They then realized that focusing on reducing taxes, something a business must pay every year, was unfortunately made a priority over making sure their BCMP and Insurance Program Design was there to help them survive the actual disaster. Therefore, yes, the *Behavioral Risk Bias* of *Myopia* had set in and affected their decisions to focus more on a new employee or accountant than their insurance design advisor.

Let us explore the typical insurance purchasing process so you may see the problems at hand with the model.

After becoming frustrated with their insurance program, most business leaders feel that they need to shop their insurance program to find relief. However, most business leaders say that their frustration stems from the costs of insurance, which they feel is too high because they pay so much in premiums that far exceeds their "returns" or claim payments received. By the way, there is somewhat a flaw in the logic of looking at insurance based on returns. Business leaders may not fully grasp that $0 in claims is actually a good return. Insurance is based on the law of large numbers, where everyone pays some premium to pay for few businesses that do have losses. We are not saying those with claims do not or should not pay in more, but if businesses that had claims were the only ones to pay premiums, how would those with no claims even have a policy?

Think of it another way. There is no such thing as a zero-premium insurance policy for businesses without any claims in the past. Insurance companies must collect some premium as there is still the *potential risk* of a loss. For most of the failed businesses, their disaster was their first claim ever, or at least their first serious claim. However, businesses with no or few claims are more attractive to insurance companies and earn lower rates. Those with more claims are perceived to be at higher risks to insurance companies, and they pay more in premium. In other words, your *Risk Profile* drives your premium.

Some business leaders stated that they became frustrated following what was viewed as a poorly handled claim or a claim unexpectedly denied. However, other than focusing on that one uncovered claim to see if they could obtain coverage for it, they did not change their insurance shopping process. They did not realize that they left other potential uninsured claims unaddressed.

What even more interesting is that every business leader interviewed seemed frustrated by the actual insurance shopping process.

Face it, somewhere around 90-to-120 days before your renewal, your phone starts to ring off the hook. Every agent is calling to tell you how great the program they have is and how they can save you money. They come in and try to get your policies and your loss runs by saying, "We are going to do a great job for you, we have great insurance company relationships, and we provide great service." In essence, it is challenging for business leaders to determine if they have the right insurance agent.

Adding to the calls, insurance agents also market to you 365 days a year. They send you all kinds of marketing content that shows statistics like the 700% increase in cyber-crime with related marketing materials that cite examples of big-dollar claims. Then they go on to say that they have insurance programs designed to address these for you, "so please buy something from us!" There is nothing wrong with increasing awareness of coverage issues, but these also lead to confusion within business leaders, as discussed shortly. And anytime there is confusion, business leaders will tend to fall back to their *Behavioral Risk Biases* and most likely ignore it or ask their agent, "Do I have Cyber Insurance?" and receive a "YES" response. This response enables a business leader to move on to their "pressing issues" their business has at hand. However, they really should have asked the second question of, "Great, but what cyber insurance *coverages* do I have?"

To make the point clearer, many insurance companies now include $25,000 to $50,000 of Cyber Coverage which typically is just Breach Response Coverage, should you have a release of sensitive Personal Identifiable Information. And when the average cost of notification and providing credit monitoring services is $250 per person, that amount will not go far. Does your Cyber Insurance include coverage for Cyber Forensics costs to figure out the cause and extent of the breach? Does your "cyber insurance program" including anything relating to Ransomware or Extortion Events, or Cyber Crime? One business leader explained how $341,000 of their employees' payroll was stolen when hackers entered the third-party payroll provider's software and changed each employee's paycheck to be redirected to the Cyber Thief's account. And before you ask, the payroll provider did not pay for the stolen funds as the source of the breach was the office manager's business's user ID and password. It was the Office Manager who allowed a Key Logger Virus into their computer system. Once the virus was allowed into the business's system, it records the keyboard strokes of the web address to your payroll company, the email address (User ID), and inevitable what would be the subsequent keyboard clicks: the password and then "enter."

A basic Cyber Insurance program may have two to five different Causes of Loss coverages. Still, a broad Cyber Insurance program will include over 25 categories of Causes of Loss with varying limits of coverage. So, not all cyber insurance programs are the same; *the Devil is in the Details.*

Side note:
The insurance industry has seen a significant increase in lawsuits directed at insurance agents relating to what is and is not covered under a Cyber Insurance Policy. I bring this up at this time as I have heard many business leaders state that they would sue their agent if they had a significant unpaid claim. In fact, most of the failed businesses did sue their agent over their closure, and the vast majority were unsuccessful.

The concern is that the fallback plan to sue your agent for an uncovered claim is not a good Disaster Recovery Plan nor part of a solid Insurance Program Design. Another way to look at it is that if you suffered a significant enough financial uninsured loss that required the effort to suing someone, it should be a significant issue that you should address it ahead of time. Even if you do "win" your case, the financial setback may be unrecoverable. Also, should you win, you would still lose 30-40% to your attorney, and that 30-40% would most likely still be a significant financial impact of which you do not recover.

As alluded to at the beginning of this chapter, the best plan of action is not to allow the hand of fate to toss the coin and determine your outcome.

Strong Marketing vs. Deliverable Results

The Internet also leads us to discuss why it is difficult to choose an agent to work with today. It has to do with marketing, packaging, positioning, and branding that causes further confusion within the insurance industry. Being a degreed and credentialed Risk Manager for over 30 years, it has been fascinating to watch the insurance agency industry's shift over the years to finally focusing on helping employers focus on Risk Management. (Or, at least stating that they are focusing on helping business leaders.)

Risk Management is absolutely something businesses should focus on more. As mentioned before, Risk Management is the necessary ongoing process of identifying risks; analyzing, measuring, and prioritizing them; figuring out how best to control them; and then dealing with the risk transfer and implementation and risk review refinement.

Agencies today are clearly focusing their marketing, packaging, positioning, and branding on Risk Management to help increase sales. It is amazing how many insurance agents place the title Risk Manager, Risk Advisor, or some "Risk" variation as their title on their business card today. I have been an expert witness for many Insurance Agent Errors & Omissions cases. It never ceases to amaze me the number of insurance agencies that hire a new insurance salesperson, send them to an insurance licensing course, and when they pass their insurance licensing exam on Tuesday, the newly minted insurance agent receives their shiny new business card with *Risk Manager* as their title on Thursday.

But yet, newly minted and too many self-appointed risk managers have not gone through any real training to identify risks. They are just handed PDFs of their Risk Management Process brochure, some questionnaires, and checklists and are sent on their way to make sales. Nor do they have the experience to identify risks fully within a business, determine the root cause of an issue, and then advise a business on how to mitigate it.

But as salespeople, they will have their Value Proposition memorized as to how they can help you identify risks, reduce your insurance costs, and better insure your business. *But do they?*

They will have their PDFs as to why you should buy some new coverage but no knowledge about how to help you deal with the risk to help you earn a lower rate for that coverage. And no knowledge on if that coverage is precisely what you need.

But what does this have to do with the point about *The Internet?* These newly appointed, and any self-appointed Risk Managers do have: they are armed with PDFs, lots, and lots of PDFs on all kinds of subjects. Yes, the PDFs being referenced are the Portable Document Format created by Adobe back in 1993. PDFs enable anyone to obtain, read, edit, send and print a document from any computer and printer regardless of its origin and system that is viewing it, such as Microsoft or Apple PC, Tablet, Phone, iPad, etc.

Business leaders do not realize with the multitude of PDFs the agents hand out like they are going out of style that there are dozens upon dozens of Marketing Content Creation businesses out there that provide thousands of marketing documents. While Zywave may be the content king, there are many others: Vertafore, iPipline, Ebix, Setoo, Agency Revolution, Inbound Insurance Marketing, Astonish, Think HR & Think Safety, plus dozens of others. These organizations have hundreds of employees. One has over a thousand employees. The employees do nothing but create insurance marketing pieces and content for insurance agents to provide customers and prospects.

Some marketing content providers even have customer-focused portals that allow a business leader to log into it, search for sample documents or programs, or possibly PowerPoints with talking points to provide employee training or even employee training videos. Of course, as a customer of that agency, you get to use that information. The business leader's question then becomes, what should I focus on and how do I use this information.

But what the interviewed business leaders commented was that all this information, information that can be pulled and provided to them from *The Internet*, made their job of choosing an insurance agent even more difficult. What became difficult is what the Steve Job quote alluded to at the beginning of the chapter; how do you identify the best advisor agent and let them help you achieve a better result?

Now, the information and reports that these services provide are not necessarily bad, but how the information can be *used* is causing a business leaders' task of deciding which insurance agent to work with to become more complex. *Why?* Business leaders struggle to distinguish between an insurance agent that is *simply possessing and dispensing information* **versus** an insurance agent that *embodies the knowledge, experience, and ability to* **use** *the information.* You can look up all kinds of things on the internet today; the verb people use now to look information up on the Internet is *Google*. But having the information does not make one an expert. It makes someone, as the expression goes, *"know enough to be dangerous."* It clouds the situation and makes the business leader's decision much, much more difficult.

Like Neil deGrasse Tyson, world-renowned astrophysicist and Emmy-nominated science show host, stated, *"One of the great challenges in life is knowing enough to think you're right but not enough to know you're wrong."* He went on to clarify that *"Most of us don't spend enough time examining what we know in an effort to understand if it is true. When you get this wrong, you put what you think you do know into the Don't Know category without realizing it."*

It is no wonder why the business leaders openly stated that they struggled to determine the best insurance agent. Is the agent an excellent salesperson with lots of information (PDFs), or do they possess the knowledge or experience to identify issues and resolve them with the appropriate insurance coverages and business recovery plans? However, many business leaders did make a point that most of the "Risk Management" focused insurance agents would gladly drop the "Risk Management" discussion if they were allowed to provide them with a quote. However, the agents would later come back with a proposal that points out a GAP or two for them to consider as either the insurance company included the coverage in their program or some other business that may or may not be similar had the coverage. The agents then also brought up that they offered Risk Management services to help them reduce their premium later on.

The business leaders when on to state that there was no clear, thoughtful process to analyze their company or their needs. For most of the agents who did perform some form of an assessment, their assessment process was not followed by any clear, detailed blueprint on how to address any specific risks or provided clear coverage changes that made sense to the business leaders.

What business leaders continually asked for was a better way to determine if the agent just has information or has the experience and knowledge to use it to help their business achieve a better outcome.

The businesses clearly stated that they are looking for agents that can help them reduce insurance costs, guide them through creating and maintaining their BCMP, and improve their insurance program design. Does their question revolve around if the agent has effective programs that they can help implement or just glossy PDFs to handouts leaving the business to fend for itself? Do they have a sales process where they dangle carrots in front of you by having a "safety professional" stop at a safety committee meeting and make some comments, and is rarely to be seen again? Do they have a "claims person" that is nothing but a liaison versus someone that has clear processes and can add value to the process that can help achieve a better outcome? Or, do they have a "sales process" that may wow you, but a "service process" that leaves you yearning for more?

Some agents convey they have Risk Management approaches but then send the business leaders to a website to use available information and resources. However, this leaves struggling business leaders to figure out what information they should be looking at, when to use it, and *how* to use it. If they did stumble across some resources that they felt they could use, the business leaders then struggled to implement the programs needed.

In other words, did an insurance agent leave you with enough information to make it clear that they can genuinely help you, or did they leave you enough to *"know enough to be dangerous?"*

Why Business Leaders are Frustrated

Why do business leaders feel so frustrated by the insurance process? It is the way the insurance industry has taught employers to buy insurance that has caused the same system to be broken, for two obvious reasons:

Problem One: What *exactly* are you bidding out?

Business leaders were taught to bring in an agent or two, plus your current "incumbent" agent, to get insurance "bids." This process makes sense to a business leader as businesses often compete for their customer through a bid situation—more bids, more likely that you will be able to reduce your insurance costs. However, when a business leader has to bid for their own work (revenue) and supply goods or material, make a part, or construct something, they are doing so by receiving very clear specifications or blueprints as to what you have to deliver should they be the winner. Business leaders will also acknowledge that they know of some of their competitors that will "cut corners" when providing the final product or service and know that the quality will not be the same. But yet, they believe that they will receive an "Apples-to-Apples" insurance bid free of issues. As you have hopefully learned throughout this book, there is no such thing as "Apples-to-Apples" quotes between insurance companies, which leads to uncertainty.

But what business leaders do not seem to realize is that someone vetted the scope of service or the design of the product or structure they are bidding on. An architect worked with the property owner to determine the customer's needs. They designed the complete building with all of the various components, including the placement of outlets, quality of materials. Probably even the color of the carpet or tile. A clear blueprint!

A customer's engineers designed the component that the business needs to make and spelled out the quality of the materials and the exact size, threading, and so forth that the part must conform to be acceptable. Or that some other professional chose the specific product they needed to buy and what deviations may be allowable so that multiple manufacturers' products could work. And then, that professional will vet the specifications provided on the product bids and accept or reject an offer based on the specifications and move on to the next bid if they do not meet them.

So, when you hand out your insurance bid specifications (a.k.a. your policy declarations pages or insurance summary), who is and how are you vetting to determine that everything meets your specifications? Who is deciding what should be the specifications themselves?

Knowing that reviewing an insurance bid is a significant process, specialty firms position themselves as "your insurance shopping expert" when you need to vet insurance quotes. You provide them your complete insurance policies. Taking your current policy declaration pages and enhancement endorsements, they create "bid specifications" from them. Soliciting insurance agents to provide bids, they will also assign which insurance companies an agent can use. Once the quotes are received, they will check the quotes. They may have to ask agents to change coverages if they are short of the current enhancement coverages and note when the agent cannot match a particular coverage. You will receive a compilation of the variations for you to choose an agent or insurance company.

In reality, all the firm did was spit out your current coverage summary and highlight the differences. You are still left to choose who to place your insurance with (with differences known). Then when you read the firms' fine print contract, they are being held harmless of any coverage deficiency as you chose who to go with after they pointed out the differences. Most of the ones I reviewed were an exact list of the current policy's enhancement endorsement "extras."

Many of the documents I reviewed for these failed businesses went through this process, and their "required coverages" were an exact list of the current policy's enhancement "extras." Then if they changed agents or insurance companies during that process, the next time the business went through the insurance shopping firm's process, the firm simply used the new insurance company's specification. After seeing this, it was clear that the firm's focus was on helping a business obtain the lowest quote, or at least make you feel like they did, but not necessarily focus on necessary coverages. In fact, for three of the failed businesses, they would have financially been better off staying with a prior insurance company program than changing. One or two of those probably would have been able to be successful in the end. The business leaders stated that used firms like this indicated that they became overwhelmed by the quotes. That is when *Simplification* set in. In the end, they looked more at the premium and assumed the coverages were close enough to make a change and even felt confident in that switch as the specialty firm compiled the various quotes for them.

However, they may reduce the amount of time you have to spend on the essential process of managing your insurance program. Now, not all services firms like this may be the same. However, based on the conversations with the failed businesses, most of these firms did little to identify risks within their business. They did not help redesign their insurance programs' specifications to meet their needs before the specifications were used to obtain bids from the business leaders interviewed. In other words, if there was a design problem before, there will be a design problem afterward, but the business believed they saved money.

Who is your Architect or Engineer?

Think of it this way: an architect or engineer designs what you are bidding on. You deliver what is requested, and the product does not work; who is responsible for the damages? It would be the architect or engineer as they failed to design it properly. When you provide the insurance specifications, and the insurance you purchase turns out does not meet your needs, who is responsible for any coverage holes or your financial damages? I hope you can see the nuance difference and risk you put upon yourself when assumptions are made that your program is appropriately designed and when you do not have a comparable "expert" guide you with that insurance program design.

When your insurance program is not designed correctly and does not have a clear list of *Minimum Required Coverages*, it makes your agent or program selection even more difficult. This is especially true when you look at various insurance companies. You look at what each coverage should be and then try to figure out all the insurance companies' differences from legal policy language to "Enhancement Endorsements." Your list of Minimum Required Coverages should be a completely separate list that does not mimic your Enhancement Endorsement but is the minimum you must have, or you will decline to accept that particular quote. Otherwise, you lowered your bar to your program's expectations, and you may forget to raise them later on.

So, what type of apple did you ask to be bid, and what time of apple did you receive? Or did you receive a banana?

The real potential for missed coverages is why more business leaders are starting to turn to one insurance agent that has a clear game plan and blueprint of coverages you must have. By allowing them to approach the insurance marketplace, build competition between insurance companies, and bring back proposals that meet your required coverage needs, you will achieve two things. First, You will make sure that the program design meets your *Minimum Required Coverages,* and second, you will build better competition between insurance companies.

Problem Two: Insurance Product vs. Service?

Insurance agents do not supply the insurance product; they are an intermediary between you and the insurance company. Insurance companies provide the coverage, determine the premium they will charge, and even set the insurance agent's commission. Many business leaders commented that they believed that the insurance companies provided their insurance premiums. Then an agent marked it up based on what they would want to make on their policy, much like a wholesaler who buys products from others and then marks it up to resell. Or a retailer that buys from the manufacturers and marks it up. However, in the insurance world, the agent's compensation for servicing your policy is already pre-determined by the insurance company. Every agent will receive the same commission rate from that insurance company. In fact, agents probably make far less than most business leaders realize. Most business leaders thought it was something akin to life insurance where the agent was receiving 40-50% of the premium, when in reality, it may be 5-10%, or maybe a hair more.

One of the main reasons that each and every business is

attractive to insurance agents is that insurance agents receive a commission regardless of how much the insurance company has to pay on your behalf with claims. However, insurance companies look at things entirely differently. They are selective on who will provide insurance to and at what premium they will want for the coverage. If they choose to insure the wrong business with too many and too costly claims, they lose money. Insurance agents do not lose based on the outcome of your claims.

As was mentioned before, interviewed business leaders stated that how they purchased insurance before their disaster was one of the reasons, and if not the main reason, why they failed to survive. Before their disaster, the business leaders viewed insurance as a sunk cost, a cost that must be spent and cannot be recovered. Therefore, they focused on reducing the amount of money they viewed as wasted on insurance by getting more competition and more agents to bid on their insurance. All in an effort to reduce what they feel are sunk insurance costs *(Behavioral Risk Bias of Myopia)*.

Now in reflection, they now realize that by believing their insurance program was adequate *(Inertia)* and that the odds that something catastrophic would happen were highly remote *(Optimism)*, led them to focus more on competition between insurance agents for lower premiums rather than concentrating on what insurance is for: **to pay their claims.** Their *Behavioral Risk Biases* effectively caused them to either not see or overlook the significant weaknesses in their insurance program.

The business leaders who did not survive stated that they essentially confused the importance of an insurance agent by valuing the agent's ability to obtain a lower premium over having a truly experienced and knowledgeable insurance agent who could properly design their insurance program. *(Simplification)* And do so while managing their insurance costs at the same time.

As one business leader put it, "Every few years, I had an agent or two in to quote my insurance. Sure, some agents pointed out what they thought was a gap in my insurance, but the gap they pointed out did not make sense to me, or I figured it would not happen to me. They seemed to focus on adding other policies like D&O (Directors & Officers), Employment Practices, or Cyber. Some pointed out flood or earthquake coverages. However, no one really pointed out the significant gaps that cumulatively caused me not to have enough insurance to rebuild and pay my bills fully. Basically, I focused on getting my insurance costs cheaper but ended up costing me my business by buying cheap insurance."

In other words, you can shop a poorly designed insurance program all you want, and you will still have a poor outcome when you truly need your insurance. In retrospect, these business leaders acknowledged that they should have spent more time identifying and selecting the best insurance agent that would have helped them have a properly designed insurance program. Just like choosing an architect to design your building or an engineer to design you a part, they could have possibly had a better outcome and survived by selecting a coverage expert agent.

One of the advantages of allowing one agent to build competition amongst multiple insurance companies is it can be achieved with a clear blueprint of your insurance program design. Nothing gets missed. That way, a business will have the necessary coverage to survive a disaster while controlling its insurance premium.

From the examples above, in Problem One, it was highlighted that when a business leader bids to obtain work, that some other professional was designing the product and then also vetting the product and bids. When trying to receive Apples-to-Apples quotes, the business leaders interviewed commented that they learned the hard way they "knew enough to be dangerous." They did not realize that their insurance program was improperly designed. Then with Problem Two, it shows how business leaders valued an agent who gets the lower premium over the one that can help them create their insurance program design correctly and leverage the marketplace on their behalf.

Both Problems have foundations found within the issues

outlined in Chapter 1 that kept them from adequately analyzing their Insurance Program Design and implementing a Business Continuity Management Plan. Both stem from *Behavioral Risk Biases*. As you can see, there is much at stake when proper actions are not taken before a disaster strikes. One of which is the selection of your insurance agent.

Traditional Insurance Buying Model

In the traditional model, the agent is in a hurry to sell you a policy. Most insurance companies will not accept an application for a quote until 90 days before your renewal date. They want current information when they determine if they will quote your business and how much of a premium they want to insure you for your risks.

Agents and insurance companies have conveyed the process as "This is how you buy insurance. You go out, get a few agents, and get several quotes." Businesses were taught that they should supply copies of their declaration pages from their insurance policies and three to five years of loss runs. In some cases, the insurance agent will even request a look around their facility, ask a few questions, or hand you some supplements to complete. Either way, it seems the next time they see that agent is a few days before their insurance renewal when presented with a quote.

But there are problems with this process. The fundamental flaw with the 90-day submission and bidding process is that it is solely focused on the sale of an insurance product. It is not a thoughtful, detailed diagnostic system focused on truly identifying and managing your risks. And if your risks are not identified, then how can they be adequately insured?

90 days is not a lot of time:
- Will the agent be able to collect all of the information that they need?
- Will they be able to obtain all the supplemental applications and complete them accurately?

- Will the insurance company accept the application or reject it because another agent applied "first" for a quote from them?
- How well will the agent be able to negotiate with the insurance company?
- Is the insurance company going to be interested in quoting your operations or not?
- Is the insurance company able to provide all the necessary coverages?
- Will the agent prepare a detailed proposal in English as opposed to "insurance-speak"?
- Will you know what the exclusions are?
- Will the agent ultimately even present you with a quote?
- Will the agent provide all of the coverages you requested?
- Will the agent, more importantly, be able to identify and provide the coverages you need?
- Will you have enough time to make a thorough analysis of your options to make sure you make the best decision and determined that nothing is missed?

As mentioned before, many business leaders mistakenly believe their organization is very attractive to insurance companies because they are inundated with calls from agents offering to quote and save them money. They do not realize that they are appealing to *all* agents because agents receive a commission for selling a product; the bigger the premium, the larger their commission. The issue is these agents still have to sell your company to the insurance companies, who may or may not have any interest in quoting your company or offering you better rates.

There are multiple hurdles, barriers, twists, and turns standing in your way. If you are driving down a pothole-filled road, there is a good chance you will hit some of them. Since there is a limited amount of time and effort spent simply trying to get this whole quotation process to work, your critical risk issues and needed coverages may go unaddressed, uncovered, or even worse, unnoticed.

Do you not think the traditional insurance shopping process is broken? Think of it this way, each of us goes through a process when we buy something. It involves identifying, analyzing, controlling, financing or buying, and then using and maintaining the product or service.

Buying a home vs. buying insurance

Suppose you are going to buy a home. Would you ask several real estate agents to show up at your office, show you printouts of several homes in your area that fit your requirements for the number of bedrooms and bathrooms, the overall size of the house and yard? Would you then sit down and look through the listing sheets and determine which one you buy based on the lowest price of the home? So why would you buy insurance this way?

To buy a home, you will go through a thoughtful, diligent process and invest time and effort in selecting the final home of your choice. You will start by identifying the various homes you potentially want to look at and walk through these homes and analyze all of them to determine which one best fits your needs.

But just because you choose a specific home does not mean you are done. You will figure out how to best control or mitigate any problems by hiring a professional to vet the home. In other words, you will have a home inspection completed to reduce the likelihood of buying a problematic home (yes, we should have a conversation on vetting a home inspector, but that is another matter). Once you know the issues, you can deal with them before buying or even choosing to walk away.

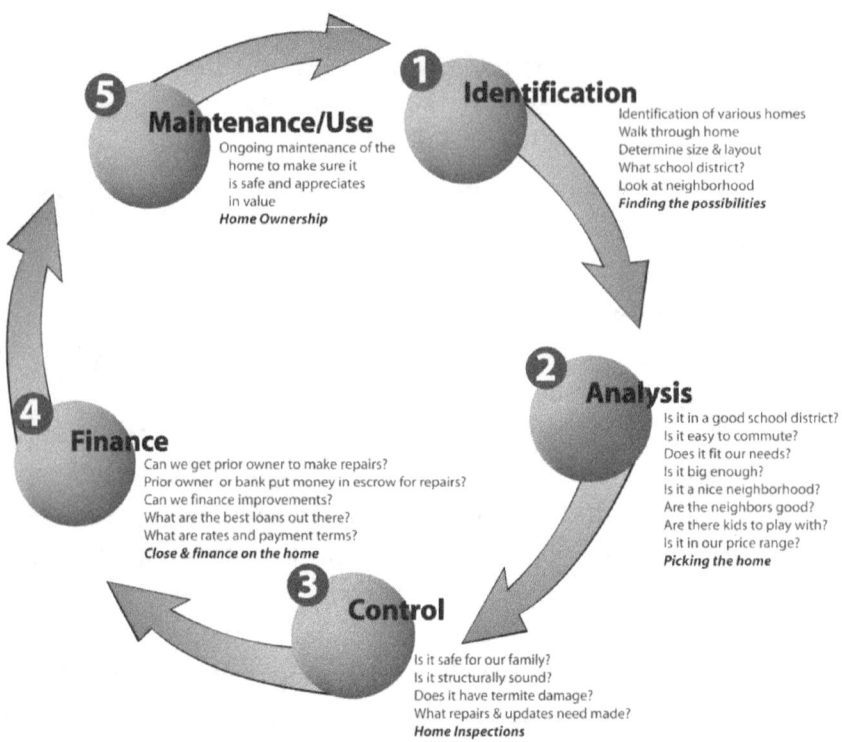

Then you are going to finance the house by searching for the best loan option. You may be prequalified for a total dollar amount you can spend, but you still want to determine which finance program is best for you. Once you decide this, you are going to close and finance the home.

Following closing and moving in, you finally get to enjoy the home and take care of the ongoing maintenance, allowing it to remain safe for your family and maintains its value.

In comparison, the traditional insurance buying cycle lacks that process of identification, analysis, and control. In the identification phase, the agent gathers copies of your policies and maybe conducts a walkthrough, and obtains loss runs. The analysis phase is spent identifying what they believe are "big gaps" in coverage and what other policies they can sell to you. The focus of the traditional process is solely on selling you a product.

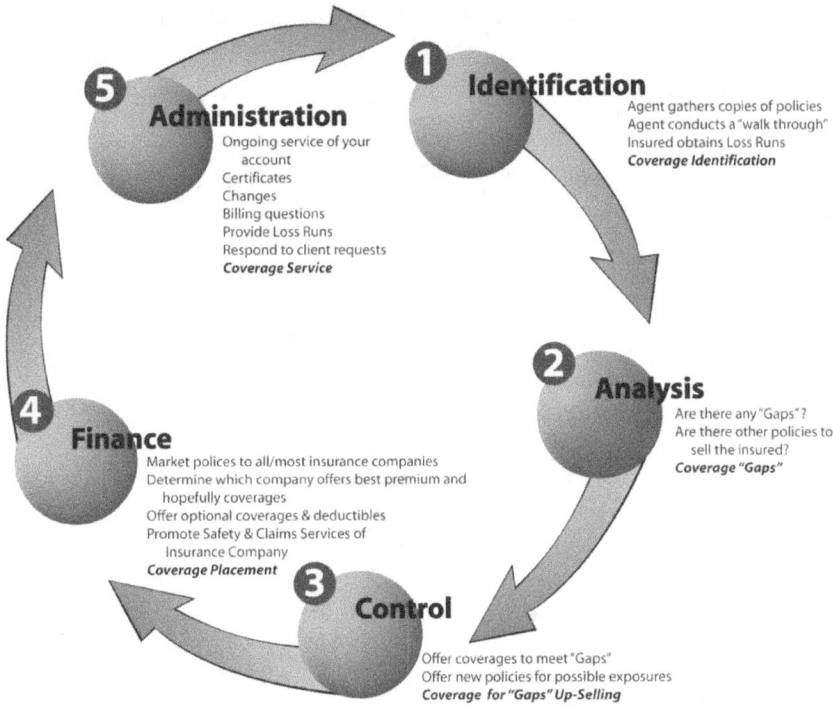

Agents offer coverage to fill those gaps in the control step or offer new policies for possible exposures. In other words, they are looking to up-sell. But, these "new coverages" may or may not make sense for your business.

In the finance step, they market your policies to all or most insurance companies they represent to determine which company hopefully offers the best premium and coverage and offers options and deductibles to fill those gaps. The agents will then promote the safety and claim services of the insurance company, or they may promote somebody that wears a safety and claim service "hat" in their organization.

For the administration phase, they perform the ongoing service of your account, certificates, changes, billings, questions, provide loss runs, and respond to your questions.

As you can see, it is not a deep identification, analysis, or control that you would have when you purchase a home. It is even worse when you want that "Apples–to–Apples quote." Basically, the agent goes from gathering the policies and loss runs to sliding over, skipping analysis and control, to the finance phase where they go to market your policies for quotes, determine which company offers the best premium, and then promises the safety and claim services of the insurance company.

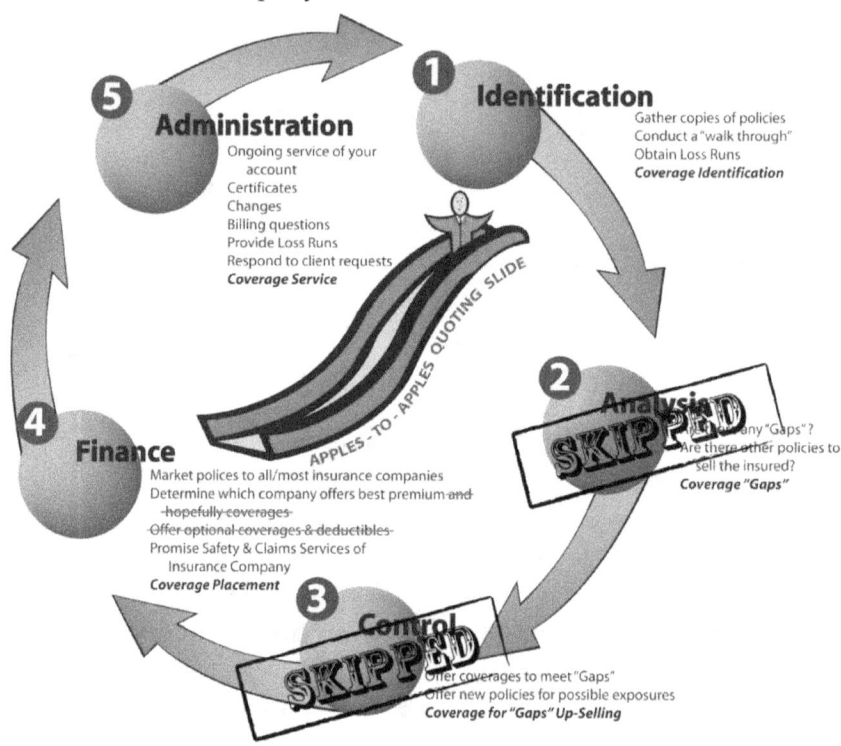

Ultimately, after going through this process, most business leaders interviewed stated that they still felt overcharged. In the back of their mind, they wondered if they even had the proper coverage or protection.

Choosing an Agent

Take a step back. Look at what you really need to do. You must start back at the identification process and change it to identify who the agents are first. Why not interview the agents and determine and understand what their functions and capabilities are?

Ask the agent:
- What is your process of engaging with our company?
- What information do you need?
- How do you gather the information you need to provide a quote?
- What is the process you go through to analyze our coverage needs?
- How do you go about this process?
- What are you and your team's experience and background?

Do not put what you are looking for in the questions you ask. Remember, you are talking to a salesperson who will eagerly tell you what you want to hear. You want to find out why they believe it is best to engage with you.

Many business leaders have told me that they tend to view salespeople as a great source of information because they see what happens inside other organizations: what works and what does not work. However, you must be sure what they do works best for you to understand what expertise the agent brings.

We discussed before how computers and the internet have changed how insurance agents sell policies. Multiple website-based marketing content services focus on providing insurance agents with information and resources to use for marketing purposes to attract prospective businesses. These website services allow agents to offer employers information on safety, fleet safety, experience modifiers and human resources, and different coverages. However, these website services can also put an employer in the precarious position of determining if an agent can provide *information only* or if the agent truly has the *knowledge* and *experience* to know how best to use that information. These services will make it difficult for you to determine if the agent will adequately identify the risks and threats you face and determine the best course of action as a solution. Or decide whether the agent is essentially throwing marketing materials at the wall, hoping that some of it sticks.

Therefore, you should collect resumes or bios of the salesperson and their service team. Determine precisely what risk management background and training they have undertaken and determine their insurance education as they will be providing recommendations to you as to the coverages you need. Being a licensed insurance agent means that you know enough to pass the state's insurance exam. Still, it does not mean you know anything in addition to that or have the experience to use that knowledge to benefit a business.

Therefore, as a business leader, you should drill down into the additional education that they have gone through and what professional designations that they have earned. Some professional designations are better than others:

- Some designations require a half-day or one full day class and a test with no follow up continuing education; these are what can be referred to as a designation used for marketing purposes,
- Some designations may require you to attend five 20 plus-hour courses and pass written short answer exams with ongoing continuing education requirements,
- The best destinations require you to pass multiple college-level courses to earn the designation, with ongoing continuing education requirements.

As you can now see, there is a varying level of designations, and the best ones require multiple courses and continuing education to maintain the designation. Dig into their education and what their designations are, and what they require to maintain those designations.

To make the point a little clearer, here is something you may find as shocking. A CPA must go through 80 hours of specific regimented continuing education courses every two years. An insurance agent may only have to attend 24 hours, and few states monitor what the classes were taken. We already talked about how an ineffective insurance agent can ultimately cost you much more than a poor-quality accountant.

When it comes to insurance agents, they should help employers identify risks and issues being faced and help design their insurance programs. One of the biggest frustrations for business leaders comes from many insurance companies and agents using the term "risk management" to mean "loss control." Loss control is when a person visits you, makes a list of physical hazards they see, and then wants you to fix them, or they will not insure you or will insure you at a higher premium.

Risk Management is much more than loss control. Risk Management is an ongoing process of identifying risks; analyzing, measuring, and prioritizing them; figuring out how best to control them; and then dealing with the risk transfer and implementation and risk review and refinement. Do not confuse loss control with risk management, even if risk management is in someone's title.

You should obtain testimonials and references from multiple satisfied clients. More importantly, call them! Find out precisely what they did for them, versus hearing only "they did a great job for us!" Ask them to explain the agent's process of risk and hazard identification to you and find out how often they experience that process. Ask them how the agent performs for them when it comes to understanding their business and designing their insurance program. Have they gone down the path of scenarios and virtually testing their insurance program designs?

Talk to the agent and determine what processes and programs the agent will implement to help you become a better risk and design your insurance program. What is their mapped-out service schedule?

Yes, you should ask the agent which insurance companies they represent. You may be surprised to learn that 10-15 years ago, most insurance agents represented just 5-10 insurance companies. With consolidation and aggregation in the insurance industries, many agents represent over 50 insurance companies, some even over 100.

First and foremost, never get "happy ears" at the initial answer. Always ask more questions.

For example, I worked with a client looking to identify what agents they may want to use. While interviewing prospective agents, one agent said they had a workers' compensation claims

person on staff. The owner said, "Great, that will help us."
I proceeded to ask some more questions:

Questions I asked:	Agent's Response:
What process does your claims person play in the injury process?	They take the claim and report it to the insurance company. They then follow up to make certain that the insurance company gives a claim number to the customer, and if not, gets the claim number and adjuster's name and provides it to the customer.
What do they do after the insurance company provides us with a claim number?	They constantly follow up with the adjuster as to the status of the claim.
How often do you do that?	They do that very often, probably once or twice a week.
Will you contact the business owner during this process?	Yes, they would call the owner periodically to make sure everything is going well from their perspective.
What if it is not going well?	He said that he "guesses" they would follow up with the adjuster and see if they could get the claim back on track.
Anything else?	Not really.

My question to the business owner was, what was the agent doing to improve the outcome of claims? What were they doing other than basically chewing up the adjuster's time with really no benefit to you as an organization? It was clear. They were not really adding to the process. They were trying to see where everything was, and that was about it.

Another example was that a prospective agent offered a "Coverage Expert" to advise them on their insurance program structure. It sounded intriguing until we received the resume and interviewed the "Expert" to find that he was a British accented person that had a little over a year of experience in insurance. When it comes to the marketing of products, you may notice that marketing firms always use a voiceover with a British accented person to convey luxury and quality... so this agency had the idea of doing the same thing. The employee mentioned that they used to work for Lloyd's of London, but the resume showed that they were there for four months. The individual had no other industry credentials other than having an insurance license. Therefore, just like you would do for a prospective agent, dig in and verify the agent's experience.

Included in the Appendix is a section on *Answers to Get Before You Hire an Agent/Broker*. Remember, you need to interview this prospective agent as if they were going to be your employee. Take your time. Determine who the best agent would be to help you improve your risk and guide you in enhancing your BCMP and Insurance Program Design. You need to find one that provides the services that you ultimately need that will lead you to lower premiums and then allow that one agent you chose to go to market for you. And first and foremost, do not do this during the typical 90-day time frame before the renewal process. Start the process of talking to agents when there is no pressure to make a buying decision.

Business leaders quickly learn that the whole bidding and quoting process with multiple agents going to numerous companies is nothing but a headache. It frustrates employers, frustrates agents, and frustrates insurance companies. In most cases, it can actually make you look less attractive to insurance companies. When you have multiple insurance agents, you increase the likelihood important coverages are missed or the inability to properly maintain your insurance program design.

Many insurance companies may pass on quoting because they believe there is a lack of control by the business in terms of this shopping process. They see so many agents making submissions that they feel they have no real opportunity to succeed.

As many underwriters have commented over the years, what is concerning is that underwriters can become very uncomfortable in quoting a particular business's insurance when they receive information from various agents that differs it was provided, contradicts other submissions, or has glaring differences in coverages requested. Insurance companies typically only recognize the agent who first applies to them. Still, they will look at *all* the information that they receive (as correct or incorrect as that information might be), but they will only quote the coverages that the Agent of Record is requesting. They will not quote something another agent asked for in terms of coverages.

What interviewed business leaders commented on was that they *wished* they did before, and for those still in business are doing now to go down a different path than multiple agent bids. In most cases, the business leaders said that they ultimately achieved a better result by determining *who* would be the best agent/advisor for them in terms of helping their organization achieve their goals and representing their business, and then they let that one agent/advisor go to the entire insurance marketplace on their behalf. That way, they were sure to have the coverages they requested and needed to be quoted and achieved a better, less frustrating outcome.

What is in your agent's submissions to insurance companies?

Suppose you are still in doubt that the insurance purchasing process is broken. In that case, there is a straightforward question to ask, *"Have you ever seen what the agent's submission looks like before it has been submitted to the insurance company?"* So how do you know that the agent is positioning you in the best light to get you the best rates? How do you know that they requested your required coverages? Most business leaders only see the applications *after* deciding which insurance company/agent to go with, and they need to sign the applications to change insurance companies.

You really should see and understand the quality of an agent's submission before it is given to an insurance company, as it will become part of your permanent computer record. Does the agent have a "write-up" or cover letter that conveys a straightforward story of the quality of your operations? Or are they just sending into the insurance companies the industry-standard applications and loss runs? What is necessary to submit to get a quote or "block the market simply" will not convey how good you are to an underwriter. Does the submission contain the details as to what your minimum required coverages are? Or is the agent shopping for price and hoping that the insurance company's Enhancement Endorsement will be good enough for you? Suppose you have not seen an agent take photos, read their submission cover stories of your operations, or see how they convey your required coverages and other things like that. In that case, you will not receive the best rates. What is worse, you do not know how much time and effort they made to make sure that you receive the coverages you need to insure yourself to survive are even requested.

You also want to know which insurance companies they are approaching. Not because you are trying to assign markets and prevent arguing between who gets what insurance company, but because you want to know who they are approaching. No, the goal is to eventually see the matching response or quote from each insurance company. Like Newton's Third Law – *For every action, there is an equal and opposite reaction.* I like to use the rule of – *For every insurance company submission action, there should be an insurance company reaction (good or bad).* You need to see the actual physical quote and its details, not just a premium or description of "declined." If they did not quote, you also want to know *why* they specifically did not quote.

A pat response from an insurance company on why they did not quote is "losses" or "cannot compete." These are usually their first lines of defense that they did not want to take the time and effort to quote your insurance. You need to ask, "Are there certain losses that they are afraid of?" "Are there coverages that you need that they cannot provide? Are there risks within my operations that they are concerned about?" Obtain specifics. If the insurance company said, "they cannot compete," you should ask, "What is it from a risk perspective that is keeping the underwriter from using their best rates? Or what are your needed coverages that are not available from them?" They usually say they cannot compete because the underwriter views you as such a risk that they do not want to price aggressively enough to earn your business. Or, they do not want to expend the time and effort to quote your insurance as they see too many impediments to earning or winning your business.

Suppose the insurance company states that it cannot offer necessary coverage. In that case, you should determine if that coverage can be obtained from another specialty insurance company. Sometimes it takes the combination of two insurance companies or more to meet your coverage needs. Also, sometimes by splitting the coverage between two insurance companies, you can more economically meet your needs.

When having an Underwriting Pre-submission Discussion call with a particular underwriter, it was discovered that they had received and declined to quote this specific business several times in the past. The underwriter commented that they did not want to quote this business, as there was a particular machine that was old and not appropriately guarded. Therefore, they were afraid of another employee becoming injured seriously. They also commented that the electrical wiring was older, and no updates or infrared scans of the system were performed, so they were afraid of a potential fire disaster. During the Risk Analysis, no notes were made relating to such a dangerous machine from my lead safety professional's assessment. After asking, I found out that the business owner replaced the particular machine four years ago after breaking down. We also had noted that some wiring was redone when the old machine was replaced, and several machines were added. When submitting to the underwriter, we documented the improvements and removal of the unsafe machine. We also conveyed that we would have the business perform an infrared scan of their facility and repair any identified issues before the policy's renewal date. Because of this, the insurance company proceeded and actually provided the best program option for the business in the end. This is an example of why allowing a single agent to appropriately make submissions on your behalf versus sending applications quickly to gain access to or "block" markets archives a better outcome.

So that you understand, the report the underwriter was using for their decisions to decline to quote in the past was from an inspection performed eight years earlier. Because of computers, which have lifetime memory, underwriters will assume nothing has changed *unless they have documentation of changes*, and you will not even get to the step where the insurance company might want to quote and would send loss control to verify that something has changed. This also serves as a reminder of why it is good to have old recommendations made by the insurance company analyzed.

Without this conversation and addressing the replaced machine before submitting, the underwriter would have issued a quick declination. Once they issue a declination, it is almost impossible to get an underwriter to reopen a file. Why? You may be surprised to learn that underwriters do not get in trouble for NOT writing an account. They get in trouble for insuring the wrong business. If you happen to have a large claim, the underwriting managers review files to determine if the underwrite should not have written the account and should be reprimanded. And if there was a previous declination, and will ask them why they reversed the declination decision.

Still not convinced the insurance shopping system is broken?

Take the agent for a Test Drive!

We already discussed that you would not buy a home just from an agent bringing you a listing. But, would you buy a car without a test drive? Probably not! (Unless you are into restoring antique cars.) So why do you buy insurance this way?

So how do you take an insurance agent on a "test drive?" The best practice would be to have the perspective agent go through their process to identify risk(s) in your business. You would experience how they could specifically help you improve that particular risk(s), how they would portray you to the insurance company, and what coverage changes would be necessary to meet your insurance needs. This is your test drive; you would not buy a car without taking a test drive, so take any prospective agent for a test drive. If the agent cannot identify your risks and convey a clear plan that you believe will help you, how can they determine what insurance coverages you will need?

As discussed before, do not get "happy ears" when they offer lip services like, "Oh, we've got claims service, or we have loss control and can help you with your safety." It may sound good, but what risks specifically did they identify? What are they going to do to address those risks and insure those risks? This is simple cause and effect. Suppose the agent cannot convey exactly, in detail, what they identified and what they are going to do for you to address this risk. In that case, it clearly means that they do not understand your risks, that they cannot help you improve or insure them, and that they cannot help you leverage the marketplace by showing you are a better risk and help you improve your Business Continuity Management Plan and Insurance Program Design.

TAKEAWAYS/LESSONS LEARNED

Design a job description of your ideal Insurance Purchasing and Coverage Design Specialist position. What would you expect of them? What would be their duties? That will help guide you in terms of selecting an advisor or insurance agent.

If reading this book has led you to question your insurance program design, it is time to take a more active role in helping to achieve a better program. Then determine if the current advisor agent is meeting those needs. Have them go through a Risk and Hazard Identification and come back with clear recommendations about what changes need to be made and why. Determine they would help you implement risk improvement strategies that allow you to earn lower rates from insurance companies, enabling you to afford to purchase any additional coverages or coverage limit that you need.

Make sure you clearly understand what any insurance agent is proposing in terms of coverage. Business leaders have commented that one of their biggest concerns is when they change from insurance company A to insurance company B. Even when not changing agents, it is that many times these business leaders have found out later that some essential coverage they "use to have" was dropped when moving from one company to the other. Have your checklist of required minimum coverages to gauge which insurance company you should use.

Go through scenarios of complete disaster and see how the program will respond.

If an agent cannot help you determine how to address and manage risk, determine what and much coverage you need, it is probably time to begin interviewing for a new advisor. If you do need to do that, take your time and have a thoughtful, diligent process for selecting and screening an agent.

Oh, by the way, do not try to do that interview process during what would be the typical marketing of your insurance timeframe, a.k.a. 90-120 before your renewal. Conduct your advisor search during the off-season, so to speak.

IMPORTANT NOTE:

AOR/BOR – Choosing your agent:
When you decide which agent you want to use, an established process allows you to change the agent representing you for an insurance company.

As insurance companies (with very few exceptions) will only work with ONE agent, you can choose, or change, the agent you want to represent you. The process of designating or changing the agent you want to represent you for a particular company is commonly referred to as an AOR or BOR, which is the use of an Agent of Record (AOR) or Broker of Record (BOR) Letter.

Be careful since many agents will not fully describe what the process means, as they will say, "sign this, and I will get a quote, too," which is incorrect! The AOR or BOR process means you are assigning the agent identified in your letter to be the ONE particular agent to be your representative for that company. The agent who previously submitted or previously was your agent or representative for that insurance company will NO LONGER be your representative. An AOR or BOR is a *transfer of rights to represent you solely*. It is not an "also obtain a quote request."

The letter needs to be on company letterhead, signed by the owner/president/CEO/etc. of your business, and clearly states that you intend to have the agent listed on the letter as the agent to represent you for that particular insurance company or any/all companies. Once that letter is submitted to the company identified in the letter, that insurance company will notify the other agent of your intention. To ensure that you are certain that you intend to transfer the rights to represent you to the new agent, and you were not "duped" into signing a letter, insurance companies have a failsafe. They will give the prior agent typically five or ten days to obtain a rescinding or countermanding letter. A rescinding letter states that the first letter was incorrect and you wish to keep the initial agent representative. Assuming you do not sign and submit a rescinding letter, your new representative will not have access to any information from the insurance company until those ten days pass.

You may want to know that the proper protocol is for you to contact your initial agent and inform them of your intention and why you are changing the representative for that insurance company BEFORE you submit the letter to the insurance company. Doing so will make for a smoother transition and allow you to request that the previous agent WAIVE the five or ten-day period, enabling you to begin to work with your new agent sooner. Only by the previous agent contacting the insurance company and "waiving" their rights of a waiting period will such a period be waived, even if waiving the period was requested in the letter.

Appendix A

ANSWERS TO GET BEFORE YOU HIRE A BROKER

When asking your questions, rule number one is to relax and take your time. Remember, do not offer what answer you are looking for in the questioning. Make sure you watch their body language to see if they are comfortable or struggling to answer. Treat this as an interview, as if you are determining whether or not you will hire this person, just like you would hire an employee.

What would be your process of engaging with our company?

What information do you need, and how would you gather the information you need to provide a proposal?

How would you go about this process?

What is the experience and background of your team, their years of experience, who with, and doing what?

Explain to us your process of determining what coverages our organization should have?

Walk us through how you determine our business income insurance needs.

How do you help clients prepare for a disaster?

How do you evaluate the quotes you receive for our business?

How do you determine which one is best for us?

What specific processes or programs will you implement to help reduce our workers' compensation costs? Insurance Costs?

If they mention Loss Control Services:
1. What services does your prevention person provide?
2. How often will we see your prevention person?
3. What credentials does your loss prevention person have?
4. How long have they been doing this?

5. Are they a dedicated injury prevention person, or do they have other duties?
6. How many clients does your prevention person currently work with?

If they mention Claim Services:
1. What involvement will your claims person have with a claim?
2. What type of questions does your claims person ask to determine the severity or validity of a claim?
3. How many claims is your claims person currently handling?
4. Are they a dedicated claims person, or do they have other duties?

What is the best practice to make sure our audit is accurate?

What is the best practice to make sure our experience modifier is accurate?

What is the best practice to make sure an injury is mitigated?

Does your process return injured workers in three days or less?

Who typically establishes your panel of physicians?

What criteria are used to determine who is on your panel of physicians?

How would you improve the Risk Profile of our business?

What steps or processes do you go through to do this?

Can you show testimonials or allow us to call references that are satisfied with their results? May we see or call them now?

Can you send us a resume or bio for each of your (broker's) team members?

REMEMBER: TAKE A TEST DRIVE! See how well they can identify, analyze and help you improve your Risk profile!

ABOUT THE AUTHOR

David R. Leng, CPCU, CIC, CBWA, CWCA, CRM

David R. Leng is author of the International Best-Selling Books *The 10 Laws of Insurance Attraction* – an employers' guide to understanding Risk Management and how making your business more attractive to insurance companies will increase a business's productivity and profitability – *Premiums Into Profits* – a guide to understanding Insurance Captives – as well as one of the top-selling books for employers on how to manage and reduce workers' compensation costs – *Stop Being Frustrated & Overcharged.*

David R. Leng is Executive Vice President and a Managing Partner of the Duncan Financial Group – he is a 35+ year veteran of the Risk Management and Insurance industry and is regarded as one of the brightest minds in the industry due to his unique *Risk Profile Improvement Process*, which identifies, controls and reduces the risk factors inherent in any business that drive costs to an organization's bottom line and hinders a businesses' culture and employee productivity. Since 2004, David has saved his clients well over **$50,000,000** in premiums and overcharges.

David was awarded the *Advisor of the Year for 2008* by the Institute of WorkComp Professionals and is a frequent contributor to *Environmental Health & Safety, Workers' Compensation, Dynamic Business, Construction Executive, Working PArts*, and *HRM Update* magazines, and has been published in a multitude of other periodicals and association newsletters/magazines.

David, who has served as an expert witness in cases involving insurance coverages, sits on the Independent Agents & Brokers National Technical Affairs Committee. The committee is comprised of six insurance coverage experts who advise ISO – Insurance Services Organization – on creating and altering coverage forms to serve individuals and employers better.

David, who has over 25 years of experience specializing in Workplace Culture and Workers' Compensation, is an alumnus of Penn State, where he received a Bachelor of Science in Insurance and Risk Management. His professional designations include Certified Insurance Counselor (CIC), Certified Risk Manager (CRM) and Charter Property Casualty Underwriter (CPCU), Certified Benefits & Wellness Advisor (CBWA), and he's been designated a Certified WorkComp Advisor (CWCA) by the Institute of WorkComp Professionals.

David is also Co-Founder of Keystone CompControl, the nation's largest single network of Workers' Compensation specialists, and is one of only 14 nationwide *Level-5 Advisors* of the Institute of WorkComp Professionals.

David is a frequent speaker for the Wood Products Manufacturers Association, Hardwood Manufacturers Association, Westmoreland HR Association, the National Workers' Compensation Symposium, SMC Business Councils, as well as other organizations. He has performed over a hundred programs internationally for associations and business groups and was added to the *Institute of WorkComp Professionals* faculty in 2012. He is also a contributing Fellow at the Workers Compensation Institute.

David spends his leisure time boating in the summer and skiing in the winter with his wife, Lynn, and their two children, Alizabeth and Luke. David and Lynn are active members of Emmaus and Autism Speaks, organizations that help support individuals with special needs, including their son Luke, who was diagnosed with Autism at the age of 18 months.

David's hobbies include woodworking and ice hockey and donating considerable time to his local high school by helping to design and build sets for their musical productions.

David can be contacted at (724) 307-5364, or emailed at david@davidleng.com.

WHAT THEY ARE SAYING ABOUT DAVID

I am so glad I met with David Leng and the team of professionals at the Duncan Financial Group.

I used to be the type of person that would get quotes on my insurance every two or three years. Dozens of agents would call me every year, three for four months prior to my renewal, and say they could save me money... get me the same coverage for less, and maybe they would point out holes or gaps in my coverage. When I look back at my old insurance policies, I now realize that if it were up to typical agents and the terrible, traditional quoting process... I would be out of business today.

They came in seven months prior to my renewal and took the time to meet with me and my staff, understand my business, and identify the risks I had in my operation. They put together a Risk Improvement Plan to address our issues. They also overhauled our insurance program to a point where it looked nothing like my old policies, and they reduced my insurance costs as well.

The outcome was beyond belief. Because of Duncan's efforts, which goes well beyond quoting insurance, not one of my employees or myself missed a paycheck. My business, in its beautiful new facility, is thriving, and I am now able to hand this company over to my daughter and eventually my grandson.

Jack Kirsopp - Owner, Kirsopp Auto Body

It was a pleasure to work with David Leng as one of the primary speakers for our recently held Annual Meeting. In addition to being incredibly knowledgeable about what wood products manufacturers require to properly insure their business and manage their risks, David also understands the industry, which is critical to helping companies remain in business should they suffer a major loss.

David was well received and has already helped a number of members.

We would be more than happy to have David address our members at a future meeting.

Philip Bibeau, Executive Director – Wood Products Manufacturers Association

*David Leng's presentation at the Hardwood Manufacturers Association 2016 National Conference and Expo, **Improving Your Risk Profile to Slash Your Rates**, provided immediate take-home value to everyone in attendance. The presentation was insightful, well organized, and very thorough.*

Members surveyed felt the session responded directly to their dilemma of increasing insurance premiums and decreasing coverage. They walked out the door with ideas for manageable solutions to control their rising premiums.

I personally was impressed that David spent time prior to the session acquainting himself with members of our Association, making sure his material was indeed focused on their needs. It was spot-on.

We will continue to collaborate with David regarding our members' concerns with property insurance and Workers' Compensation costs
Linda Jovanovich, Executive Vice President – Hardwood Manufacturers Association

In looking back at what transpired, how I lost my building, tools, equipment, everything, I am still amazed that I was able to rebuild, reopen and continue to have a successful business. If I had not met David Leng and allowed him to overhaul my insurance program, I would not have been able to afford to rebuild. I do not know what I would have done without him!
Tony Vecchio, Owner – Tony's Care Care

David Leng is very knowledgeable about Risk Management, Insurance, and Workers' Compensation and a pleasure to work with. His knowledge allowed our company to reduce its premiums by almost 55%. In addition, he found and addressed significant holes in our insurance program that we now see would enable us to survive a disaster.
Mike Spitznagel, CFO – JetNet Corporation

David was there, almost immediately, to help me walk through what I thought would have been the end of my business. If I had not allowed him to insure my business as he recommended, it would have been over. No one, including me, missed a paycheck. More importantly, he made sure that my cash flow was protected until my business returned to pre-fire income. That took almost a year! If it were not for David, I would have lost my mechanics, lost my business, and lost my family's livelihood.
Bill Coyne, Owner – Coyne's Automotive

An Amazon Leading Selling Book
Stop Being Frustrated & Overcharged
By David R Leng, CPCU, CIC, CBWA, CWCA, CRM

You are not alone in feeling frustrated at the amount of money you have wasted on your workers' compensation program while wishing you could have put that money to better use elsewhere, namely to help grow and run your company.

This book was written to help every business owner, business leader, or executive who has ever been frustrated by the amount of time, energy, and money spent dealing with a workers' compensation program that has never achieved the results they were looking for. *Until now.*

Today's technology has both overshadowed and enhanced much of yesterday's craftsmanship.

Now, most of us would definitely not compare a risk manager or an insurance professional to the craftsman who constructed our home or designed that jaw-dropping structure that makes us say "wow."

However, author David Leng aptly ties together a direct correlation between the risk manager and insurance professional to a craftsman. As a business owner, you will see and understand the uniqueness with which David works with his business clients. You will understand how he "builds a fortress" designed to fend off a multitude of employee injuries, view his varying techniques in which to help you appreciate varying Workers' Compensation insurance plans and how insurance companies think about you, then crush and ultimately control your Workers' Compensation insurance costs.

The Institute of WorkComp Professionals has trained many skilled and passionate insurance professionals. With this book, David Leng shows employers how he combines that skill and passion in creating a textbook approach to creating a Workers' Compensation program that actually benefits your company.

Preston Diamond
Managing Director
Institute of WorkComp Professionals
Asheville, NC

Visit
StopBeingFrustrated.com

The International Best Seller
THE LAWS OF INSURANCE ATTRACTION
BY DAVID R LENG, CPCU, CIC, CBWA, CWCA, CRM

As a successful business owner, why would you keep rolling the dice when it comes to managing your insurance program? Constantly frustrating yourself chasing quotes through the broken insurance industry bidding process? Leaving the determination of your premium up to the insurance industry with their "hard" and "soft" market cycles? Only you can answer these questions. But you can take some comfort in knowing that you are not alone.

Nearly 30 years of experience has shown that *the most successful* business owners do not allow their results to be left to chance. They have found that by *better managing their organizations*, they **become more** *attractive* **to insurance companies and earn significantly lower premiums**. Using these little-known management secrets, they have made their companies more productive, profitable, and enjoyable.

Inside these pages, you will find out how to stop gambling as a way to reduce your insurance premiums and **learn how to put yourself** *in a winning position where you ultimately control the game.*

Like any other business owner, I turned to several friends to find out who they were insured with. I was also receiving quite a few calls from agents offering to save me money. Even my agent at that time, who worked for perhaps the largest insurance agency in the region, was trying to find as many options as he could. With so many agents promising they could save me money and deliver results, I thought we would be seeing a substantial reduction. I was wrong.

I was about to take the "best" quote available when a business associate put in contact with David Leng. Because of David's commitment to resolving our situation, we were able to lower our insurance costs quickly. His approach reduced our premium by 41%, in addition to correcting our premium errors! In two short months, David's program put back over $200,000 in our pocket.

What you will read in this book is a road map to overcoming high insurance rates, a kind of GPS for lowering your premiums while raising both the productivity and profitability of your company. My situation serves as proof that just getting quotes is not enough to manage your insurance program's costs, that you can do better when you use a better way. I can tell you this from first-hand experience; if you are an employer and don't have David Leng's books in your office, you are putting your company at a serious competitive disadvantage.

Mark Duda, President
Duda Cable Construction, Vandergrift, Pennsylvania

LAWSOFINSURANCEATTRACTION.COM

The International Best Seller
Turning Premiums Into Profits
by David R Leng, CPCU, CIC, CBWA, CWCA, CRM

As a business owner or business leader, when you look at the amount of money you have just handed over to the insurance companies and received very little, or nothing in return, and the exhausting amount of time you have spent trying to obtain bids or quotes to reduce the cost of your insurance program, only to fall short of the real results you wanted to occur, how can you not feel frustrated… or like you are going insane? And why do they keep doing the same things year after year when it comes to your insurance programs? After all, isn't that the very definition of insanity; doing the same thing over and over and expecting a different outcome?

But that high-priced insanity stops here.

In his latest book, David Leng shows you how to break this costly insurance cycle and gain more control over your insurance program while simultaneously building equity that will help you and your business, rather than it being pocketed by the insurance company and its shareholders. You will see how businesses that are paying over $100,000 annually in insurance premiums can benefit from *Alternative Risk Financing*, where a business does not purchase traditional guaranteed cost insurance policies but instead purchases insurance where they take on *some* risk to get potential rewards. With a 30-year track record in advising employers on how to save substantial money in their premiums, David spells out clearly and precisely why the use of Captives has become the most popular of the alternative risk financing programs being used today. And why it just might be the solution your company needs to increase both its *profitability* and its *equity*.

> We learned that by utilizing a **Captive Insurance Program** as an alternative to traditional insurance, we can use a type of self-insurance that allows us, in essence, to join with other like-minded, well run and safe companies, to form our own insurance company and, now get this, pretty much insure ourselves. Not only do we gain operational transparency, coverage flexibility, greater control, reduced costs, and increased cash flow, any profits from our insurance program are returned to us and not sent off to the insurance company's shareholders. Plus, our captive premiums are based on the quality of our business and not on the general insurance marketplace rates. For us, it's the definition of a win-win.
>
> For the same reason you probably wouldn't perform surgery on yourself, you need a talented insurance professional to really get into the nuts and bolts of how Captives works and if it is the right path for your company to take. I have known David Leng for years, and during that time, I have trusted him to steer our company in the right direction regarding our risks and insurance. And if David has the knowledge and the resources to put everything you need to know about Captives in the pages of this book, then I would suggest it's a book well worth reading. Don't wait to do so, as waiting for your insurance renewal date will probably cost you more in terms of money and headaches.
>
> **Bob Monpara, President**
> **Aragra Technology**

PremiumsIntoProfits.com

Reader Bonus

A journey starts with one step!

— Lao-tzu, Chinese philosopher 604 B.C.

To help you start your journey to Surviving a Disaster. We would like to provide you with tools and resources you can use to reach your destination.

Visit INSUREDTOFAIL.COM/REGISTER
to receive these *FREE* resources:

ADMISSION – to Workshops and Webinars designed to provide you with more detailed information on the "how-to" of reducing insurance costs, identifying and managing risks, planning for a disaster, and understanding insurance programs.

CONSULTATION – complete our discovery call questionnaire and receive a 30-minute consultation call to help you get further on your *Disaster Planning* or *Insurance Program Design* journey or help in solving a tricky issue.

www.ingramcontent.com/pod-product-compliance
Lightning Source LLC
Chambersburg PA
CBHW072022230526
45466CB00019B/20